Catholics and Protestants
Agricultural Modernization in Two German Villages

STUDIES IN ANTHROPOLOGY

Under the Consulting Editorship of E. A. Hammel,
UNIVERSITY OF CALIFORNIA, BERKELEY

Andrei Simić, THE PEASANT URBANITES: A Study of Rural-Urban Mobility in Serbia

John U. Ogbu, THE NEXT GENERATION: An Ethnography of Education in an Urban Neighborhood

Bennett Dyke and Jean Walters MacCluer (Eds.), COMPUTER SIMULATION IN HUMAN POPULATION STUDIES

Robbins Burling, THE PASSAGE OF POWER: Studies in Political Succession

Piotr Sztompka, SYSTEM AND FUNCTION: Toward a Theory of Society

William G. Lockwood, EUROPEAN MOSLEMS: Economy and Ethnicity in Western Bosnia

Günter Golde, CATHOLICS AND PROTESTANTS: Agricultural Modernization in Two German Villages

in preparation

Peggy Reeves Sanday, ANTHROPOLOGY AND THE PUBLIC INTEREST: Fieldwork and Theory

Catholics and Protestants

Agricultural Modernization in Two German Villages

Günter Golde

Department of Sociology and Anthropology
University of Southern California
Los Angeles, California

ACADEMIC PRESS   New York   San Francisco   London

A Subsidiary of Harcourt Brace Jovanovich, Publishers

ACADEMIC PRESS, INC.
111 Fifth Avenue, New York, New York 10003

United Kingdom Edition published by
ACADEMIC PRESS, INC. (LONDON) LTD.
24/28 Oval Road, London NW1

Library of Congress Cataloging in Publication Data

Golde, Günter.
   Catholics and Protestants.

   (Studies in anthropology)
   Bibliography: p.
   Includes index.
      1.   Württemberg—Rural conditions.   2.   Church and
social problems—Württemberg.   3.   Farm life—Germany
(Federal Republic, 1949-   )—Württemberg.   4.   Villages   5. Germany—
—Württemberg—Case studies.   I.   Title.   Social conditions
HN458.W8G64 1975   301.35'2'094347   75-3967
ISBN 0-12-288250-4

To my companions Esther and Karin

Contents

Acknowledgments   ix
List of Figures   xi
List of Tables   xiii

1 Introduction   1

2 The Regional Setting: Hohenlohe-Franken   5
   Ecological Aspects   5
   A Sketch of the Political History of the Region   9
   Socioeconomic Developments   14

3 The Local Setting: Two Agricultural Communities   21
   Physical Aspects   21
   The *Gemeinde*: A Corporate Territorial Community   26
   The Occupational Structure   36
   The Annual Round of Activities   39

4 Demographic Patterns   51
   Households and Marriage   51
   Fertility Rates   60
   Migration Patterns among the Local Population   68

5 Land Tenure and Inheritance Patterns   73
   Land Tenure   73
   Inheritance Patterns   75

6   The Socioeconomic Structure   87
       Conditions Around the Turn of the Century   92
       The Two Communities Compared   96
       The Structure Today   98

7   The Dynamics of Family Farming: Part 1   101
       Patterns of Land Use and Production   102
       Making Ends Meet   106
       The *Bäuerin*: Cornerstone of the Family Farm   113
       Some Observations on the Plight of the Bachelors   117

8   The Dynamics of Family Farming: Part 2   121
       Tractorization   121
       Mechanization and Co-ownership   126

9   Social Interaction   133
       Dimensions of Face-to-Face Interaction   133
       Intracommunity Patterns of Conflict and Cooperation 143
       Intercommunity Relations   149
       Voting Patterns   152

10   The Place of Religion   160
       Protestants   161
       The Catholics   167
       A Comparative Overview   173

11   Conclusion   177
       The Religious Factor   179

Appendix   185
Bibliography   187
Index   195

Acknowledgments

The field work which forms the basis of this study was supported by the National Institutes of Health (National Institute of General Medical Sciences) Training Grant GM-1224, which is gratefully acknowledged. The research focuses on two rural communities in the northeastern part of Baden-Württemberg, Federal Republic of Germany. These two communities—one inhabited by Catholics, the other by Protestants—had been selected from published statistics prior to going to the field. Field work was carried out from November 1970 through November 1971, with my family (wife and infant daughter) and I residing in the Catholic village from December 1, 1970 through November 20, 1971.

My thanks go to the mayor and all of the local people for their generous cooperation with the nosy anthropologist. Apart from their cooperation with the scholarly ends of this study, they also helped to make our stay a pleasant one in many ways. To preserve anonymity, I cannot here name all the people who were of especial help to us, but they know we have not forgotten.

I also received help and friendly backing from Professors Dr. H. Röhm and Dr. Th. Bergmann of the University of Stuttgart-Hohenheim, as well as from various gentlemen representing the Ministry of Agriculture, and from Mr. Albert Wankmüller, publisher of the *Hohenloher Tagblatt*. I would also like to thank the Deans of the Catholic and Protestant Churches for their kind permission to peruse and photograph various local church records.

In Berkeley my thanks go to Professors May Diaz and Wolfram Eberhard, whose help and guidance are gratefully acknowledged. Dr. Harry Todd gave helpful advice, and I thank him especially for his comments on a first draft of Chapters 2, 3, and 4. I also benefited from the comments of faculty and students in Professor Burton Benedict's seminar (winter/spring 1972) where a tentative version of my findings was discussed. I would also like to thank Professor Jack Potter who first suggested that I return to my native Germany to carry forward a program of anthropological research.

For help at a later stage I would like to express my thanks to Professor Eric Wolf for a critical reading and for his helpful comments.

My special gratitude goes to Eugene Hammel, who has been behind this project from its incipient stages and has greatly helped through his continued interest and support.

My wife, Esther Anschutz Golde, has been a very important part of this venture and has greatly contributed toward its completion; I cannot thank her enough.

List of Figures

1 A map of Hohenlohe-Franken. 6
2 Percentages in total work force of agricultural and industrial jobs, 1882–1970, Hohenlohe-Franken and North Württemberg. 18
3 Population increases and decreases in percentages, 1871–1970, Hohenlohe-Franken. 18
4 "A village beckoned from the other side of the river." 22
5 "A crucifix by the wayside indicated that we were entering Catholic territory." 23
6 Structure of the Protestant commune around 1850. 29
7 But "many a wagon...has to be loaded by hand." 40
8 Loading manure with a frontloader. 41
9 By the side of a house one may be confronted with the halved carcass of a pig. 42
10 Planting potatoes. 45
11 On steep slopes the "scythe is put to good use again" by a widowed mother and her bachelor son. 47
12 A combine harvesting oats under a rain-threatening sky. 48
13 Numerical and spatial distribution of marriage partners who were recruited into households of Catholic village (C) from surrounding communes, for the period 1800–1969. 58
14 Numerical and spatial distribution of marriage partners who were recruited into households of Protestant commune (P) from surrounding communes, for the period 1800–1969. 59
15 Average number of total births per married woman (including premarital births) for 20-year intervals, 1800–1969. 62
16 Families arranged by number of births, and categories of size of family holdings and craftsmen, 1820–1969. 64

17 Population increases and decreases between 1840 and 1970, in
    percentages.   69
18 Population pyramids of resident population, 1971.   70
19 Average (for periods indicated) bi-annual number of sales of
    individual parcels of land, and auctions of holdings, Catholic
    village, 1819-1971.   74
20 Transfers of family farms: civil status of transferor(s) at time of
    transfer, distribution in percentages, 1857-1971.   78
21 Percentage distribution of heirs (*Anerben*) according to kinship
    status vis-à-vis the transferor(s), Catholic village, 1857-1971.   82
22 Percentage distribution of heirs (*Anerben*) according to kinship
    status vis-à-vis the transferor(s), Protestant commune, 1857-1971.   83
23 Percentage distribution of agricultural holdings by area of
    cultivated land, 1907, 1960, 1971.   88
24 Percentage distribution of agricultural holdings by total size (i.e.,
    including forested land), 1933 and 1971.   89
25 Occupations of heads of households, with households arranged
    according to size of agricultural holdings, 1907.   90
26 Occupations of heads of households, with households arranged
    according to size of agricultural holdings, 1971.   91
27 Number of livestock per 10 ha of cultivated land.   103
28 Livestock inventory of four select farms of 8 ha, 15 ha, 25 ha,
    and 35 ha in size (1870, 1954, and 1970).   103
29 Incidence of outside income, farmers with holdings 10-22 ha in
    size (1971).   110
30 Farmers planting trees in communal forest.   110
31 Average age at death, for 10-year intervals, excluding those who
    deceased before reaching the age of 20, and excluding war
    casualties (Catholic commune, 1821-1970).   116
32 Year of acquisition of first tractor by individual farmers, in
    percentages of number of farmers in each community.   123
33 Bonds between individual farms generated by co-ownership of
    machines and implements, Catholic village.   129
34 Bonds between individual farms generated by co-ownership of
    machines and implements, Protestant village.   130
35 Group of men in Catholic village assembled after church.   134
36 Protestants leaving church on Confirmation Day.   135
37 Milk pickup in Protestant village.   136
38 Milk pickup in Catholic village.   137
39 Procession on Ascension Day.   170

List of Tables

1 Population densities: 1970. 7
2 Population, occupations, and commuters in 1961 and 1970. 37
3 Households composition, January–February 1971. 53
4 Origin of spouses marrying into local households, 1800-1969. 56
5 Average age at first marriage, 1820-1971. 62
6 Average number of total years of marriage per woman (including years bearing premarital children): 1820-1959. 63
7 Percentage of parents aged 66 and over at time of transfer. 79
8 Percentage of sons 31 years of age or older at time of inheritance. 80
9 Extent of co-ownership of machines and implements. 128
10 Voter participation and distribution of votes cast for major parties in percentages of eligible voters, and number of valid votes cast, respectively. 153
11 Voter participation in percentages of eligible voters in communes with populations predominantly (i.e., more than 70%) Catholic or Protestant. 156
12 Percentage distribution of valid votes (*Erststimmen*) cast for major parties in communes with populations predominantly (i.e., more than 70%) Catholic or Protestant in the Federal election (*Bundestag*) of September 28, 1969. 156
A-1 Fertility rates per married woman, including premarital births, 1800–1969. 185
A-2 Families ranked by number of births and size of family holding, with a category for craftsmen, 1820-1969. 186

1
Introduction

        This book is about two agrarian communities in southwestern Germany. In following the history of these communities over the last century and a half, it examines a broad range of structrual relations and social processes, and explores the ways in which the local population has been adapting to the pressures of the changing socioeconomic environment of which it is a small part. It deals with the transition of the traditional type of family farm of yesterday to the modernized and highly rationalized family farm of tomorrow—a transition that greatly affects the lives of those who are part of it. In its basic approach, then, this book follows the lines of a community study in analyzing processes of sociocultural change.[1]
The specific focus of this study, however, derives from Max Weber's investigation into possible relationships between religion and economic behavior, and in particular from his hypothesis that "the principal explanation" of certain differences in economic behavior between Catholics and Protestants "must be sought in the permanent intrinsic character of their religious beliefs, and not only in their temporary external historico-political situations [Weber 1958: 40]."
This hypothesis serves as Weber's point of departure into his investigation of affinities between a Puritan ethic and the development of modern capitalism, with which I am not here concerned. Rather, I am concerned with Weber's reference—in support of his hypothesis—to contemporary observations that deal

[1]For some of the methodological considerations, see, for example, Arensberg and Kimball (1965), Bell and Newby (1972), Bennett and Thaiss (1973).

1

with apparent differences between Catholics and Protestants in various behavioral categories. Weber refers in particular to the study of one of his students,
Martin Offenbacher, who utilizes official statistics of the Grand-Duchy of Baden
to demonstrate that there are significant differences between members of the
two denominations in their occupational and educational preferences and in the
ways in which they invest their capital.[2] However, in a fairly recent study,
Offenbacher's findings have been re-examined and found severely wanting; they
turn out to be simply wrong because the data have been analyzed on the basis of
total figures only, without taking the spatial distribution of individuals into
account [Samuelsson 1961:138-14]. When this particular bias is corrected, the
intergroup differences in each of the categories almost completely disappear, and
with them the basis for Offenbacher's findings.

Of course, other empirical studies have shown that differences in certain areas
of social organization may indeed be significantly correlated with the differences
in religious affiliation of the respective groups compared in these investigations.[3]
A study undertaken by Gerhard Lenski may well be the most comprehensive in
this regard. It compares groups of Catholics, Jews, and Protestants in urban
Detroit and is based expressly on two Weberian assumptions, namely, "that
every major religious group develops its own distinctive orientation toward *all*
aspects of life, and that these orientations profoundly influence the daily actions
and hence the institutional structure of society," and "that these orientations
are partially independent of the social situation of the group [Lenski 1963:8;
italics his emphasis] ."

My investigation is based on those same Weberian premises. The setting was
chosen for its promise to yield data that could be subjected to comparative
analyses under closely and systematically controlled conditions (see Eggan 1954
& Diesing 1971). One of the two communities is inhabited by Protestants, the
other by Catholics. The inhabitants of both share the same roots but the Peace
of Augsburg of 1555, with its dictum *cuius regio, eius religio*, occasioned their

[2]See Weber (1958:35-39;188-189). For earlier literature on this subject, which may have
influenced Weber's viewpoint, see Bendix and Roth (1971:Chap. 16); cf. Giddens (1971:
124-125).

[3]See, for example, Glock and Stark (1965), Hardy (1974), Klausen (1968), Lenski
(1963), Vogt and O'Dea (1957), and Willems (1968). I am grateful to Professor Hammel for
having brought Hardy's study, which explores the relationship between religious affiliation
and the production of scholarly doctorates, to my attention.

I am not aware of any German studies expressly designed to explore differences between
Catholics and Protestants on the community level, although there are studies that include
comparative data. For example, Wurzbacher (1954) studied a German rural commune inhabited by both Protestants and Catholics, without exploring differences between these two
groups, however. On the other hand, in a nationwide sampling of German rural population,
aged 17- to 28-years old, Planck (1970) analyzes some of the differences between Catholics
and Protestants.

separation into different denominational camps. The two communities border each other, and they are structurally very much alike. Thus, many of the factors that would otherwise complicate an analysis of possible interrelationships between religious orientation and social organization (such as ethnic, class, and regional differences; differential access to various resources; etc.) can here be held constant, with religious affiliation the one major differentiating factor.

The question thus posed is simply this: Given that we find significant differences in various institutionalized patterns of behavior, will it be possible to determine whether these differences have arisen from, and/or are maintained by, the respective religious orientation, or are we here dealing with phenomena whose interrelations connect with the religious factor in no more than peripheral ways. I have tried to answer this question, however imperfectly, whenever it has presented itself.

At this point, a few remarks on the ways in which the data for this study were gathered might be in order. My family and I resided in the Catholic village during the entire period of fieldwork (December 1, 1970 to November 20, 1971); lack of suitable accomodation prevented us from living in the Protestant village for part of our stay. However, I visited the Protestant community at least every other day (which, at a distance of three miles and access to an automobile, presented no problem) to work in the mayor's office, visit key informants, line up people for interviews, attend church services, or just look around. From May onward, I spent a few hours almost every evening in one of the local inns— though mostly in the Catholic village. I also watched the progress of work in the woods, fields, and barns. I attended most of the public meetings called to deal with a variety of civic matters, and joined the local festivities during carnival and post-harvest times. My wife, committed to the care of our infant daughter, found herself restricted to fewer local contacts than she would have liked to make.

The nature of this study required, of course, that I obtain as much quantifiable data as possible. Hence, I copied or excerpted most of the local commune and church records (family registers; birth, baptismal, marriage, and death registers; land registers; sales and contract books; minutes of the commune council; livestock censuses; etc.); when this proved to be too time-consuming, I photographed many records with the aid of document film. In addition, I made a farm-to-farm survey of agricultural machines and implements owned or co-owned and the year of their acquisition. I also conducted structured interviews with a total of 112 persons; all but the first one were taped. My aim had been to obtain a greater number of structured interviews, but an unusually dry year kept men and women working out in the fields, thus considerably restricting my interview opportunities and gradually creating an anxiety syndrome which other researchers in similar situations seem to have experienced (see Pelto & Pelto 1973:264-268). Although I can not claim the kind of familiarity with the communities of this study which one might develop after repeated visits over a number of years, I feel that I have collected a comprehensive set of reliable data to supply the firm support which the present study demands.

2

The Regional Setting: Hohenlohe-Franken

An ethnography that centers on a relatively small community requires that this community be placed firmly in the context of a larger unit. We are here dealing with two German villages, but to place them in the context of a Germany would lead us too far afield at this point. Even the *Land* of Baden-Württemberg seems too large and diverse to serve as an immediate matrix. Therefore, I have chosen to concentrate on a smaller area, an area which exhibits a considerable degree of sociocultural cohesiveness and one with which their inhabitants strongly identify—the region known as Hohenlohe-Franken.[1]

Ecological Aspects

Location and Population

The region is located in the northeastern part of the *Bundesland* ('federal state') of Baden-Württemberg, Federal Republic of Germany (see Fig. 1). Its

---

[1]Apart from my own observations, this chapter is based on a survey of the following works: Abel (1971), Baden-Württemberg, Statistisches Landesamt (1953), Bosl (1971), Hoyt (1957), Königlich statistisch-topographisches Bureau (1847; 1883), Lütge (1960), Röhm (1957), Schlauch (1964), Schremmer (1963), Saenger (1957), Sprandel (1971), Theiss and Baumhauer (1965), and Zorn (1971). Where not specifically cited, all statistics are taken from official publications of the Bureau of Statistics, Baden-Württemberg, for the year indicated (see Bibliography "Published Statistics").

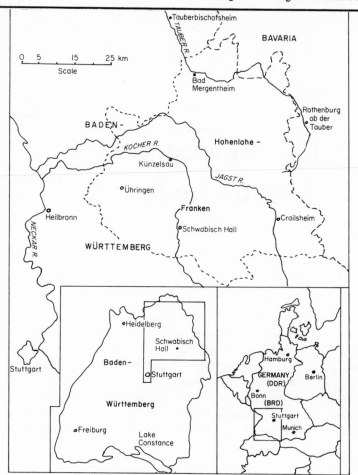

FIGURE 1. A map of Hohenlohe-Franken.

extent is largely contiguous with the area covered by five counties: Crailsheim, Künzelsau, Mergentheim, Öhringen, and Schwäbisch Hall,[2] with a total of 2540 km². Dotted over the countryside are numerous towns, villages, hamlets, and outlying farms and castles, which are organized into 226 *Gemeinden* ('civil parishes', or 'communes').[3] More than half of these communes have populations

[2]This division refers to the ethnographic present of 1971. In accordance with the administrative reforms which have come into force on January 1, 1973, the five counties referred to above have been merged to form two counties, Schwäbisch Hall and Hohenlohe-kreis; a small part has been ceded to a third county, Tauberkreis (see Baden-Württemberg, Statistisches Landesamt 1972a, which already follows the lines of the new divisions).

[3]I am again referring to the ethnographic present of 1971. Since then, there have been a number of consolidations considerably decreasing further the number of communes.

of less than 500, and only 17% have populations in excess of 1000. The five county seats are the largest towns in the region with populations ranging from 8000 (Künzelsau) to 22,000 (Schwäbisch Hall). In 1970, the total population of the 5 counties was 257,000; 65% of the inhabitants were Protestants, and 30%, Roman Catholics.[4] The population density lies below that of Baden-Württemberg as a whole (Table 1).

Table 1

POPULATION DENSITIES: 1970[a]

Hohenlohe-Franken	102 per km^2
Hohenlohe-Franken without county seats	76 per km^2
Baden-Württemberg	249 per km^2
Federal Republic of Germany	244 per km^2

[a]Source: Baden-Württemberg, Statistisches Landesamt (1972c).

Topography, Climate, and Soils

The greater part of the region is dominated by the Hohenlohe Plateau, which ranges in elevation between 240 and 520 m. Rather than a flat expanse, the topography of the plateau is of an undulating nature. It is dissected by the valleys of two rivers (Kocher and Jagst) and numerous tributary creeks. The rivers—which are not navigable—run roughly parallel to each other, first in a northwesterly, then westerly direction toward their confluences with the Neckar River. Their valleys reach a depth of up to 200 m.

The climate is less temperate than in those areas of Württemberg which lie to the southwest, although one has to keep in mind that various topographical features tend to contribute to the formation of micro-climates, especially in the river valleys. Temperatures range from −18° F to 97° F; the yearly mean is 47° F. For the summer month of July the mean is 62° F, and for the winter month of January the mean is 29° F. The average yearly precipitation is 30 in., with July the wettest and January the driest month of the year.

Soils consist mainly of red and clay marls and occupy a medium position on the scale of agricultural fertility.[5] Proper drainage of these soils has been an age-old problem and is usually achieved through a system of drain pipes and

[4]"Protestants" includes the members of all Protestant denominations.
[5]This official scale measures soil fertility (*Ertragsmesszahl*) along a range of 100 points. The western parts of Hohenlohe are generally more fertile and rank between 55 and 65 points, the rest between 45 and 55 points (see Hesse 1965:21; 48a). These are averages only and there are greater variations on more localized scales.

ditches. Underlying the marls are deposits of limestone which tend to crop out along the valley slopes.

The Landscape and Man's Activities

The landscape is largely man-made. The present layout of fields, meadows, and forests is the result of many generations of farming. Today (1970), 24% of the total area of the region is under cover of forest, and 64% is land under cultivation. Almost 90% of this type of land is worked by 11,753 family farms, ranging in size between 5 and 50 ha with the average size of cultivated land per holding around 12 ha. There are only a few estates in excess of 50 ha, and about 10% of the cultivated land is worked in holdings of below 5 ha. The latter are concentrated around larger villages and in the river valleys.

The river valleys were populated earlier than the plateau and here we find most of the towns of the region.[6] Between the settlemens—which are mostly built on the silt deposits of tributary creeks—the rivers are bordered by lines of trees and by meadows. The valley slopes are variously utilized, depending on position, soil conditions, and degree of tilt. Forests covering the steeper slopes consist mainly of beech trees, with firs and pines running second. Where conditions permit, dry cereals and beets are grown, and some of the meadows are used for grazing cattle. In a few locations the slopes are covered by vineyards. Up to around 80 years ago, vineyards were much more widespread, but, after a blight ravaged the vines, locations of peripheral economic value were not brought back into cultivation again.

While the river valleys present some of the more picturesque aspects of the landscape, the elevated areas are better suited for extensive farming. Meadows make up about 40% of the cultivated land area and are indicative of the importance of cattle in the regional economy. Major crops consist of dry cereals, beets, and legumes; most of the crop is used to feed the stabled livestock. Fattened cattle, milk, piglets, and fattened pigs constitute the major sources of farming income.

Villages are rarely more than three miles apart, though often cut off from view because of the undulating terrain, or intervening parcels of forest and rows of fruit trees. Most of the villages and towns in the region have preserved their old settlement patterns reminiscent of their late medieval past. The romantic aura which pervades the region is heightened by the presence of many castles and

---

[6] I am here referring to the period of settlement which began with the incursion of the Alemanni into the river valleys at the beginning of the fifth century. Archaeological finds attest to the existence of earlier (Celtic) settlements along the ridges between the river valleys, but there is no evidence that these settlements continued to exist beyond the first century (Baden-Württemberg, Statistisches Landesamt 1953:32-35 & Saenger 1957:25).

manors that overlook the river valleys from mountain spurs or dominate the center of towns and villages. Some of them lie in ruins, but many are still inhabited by the descendants of those noble families who once were lord and master over the peasants in the surrounding countryside.

A Sketch of the Political History of the Region

The Ethnic Heritage

The region of Hohenlohe-Franken derives its name from an aristocratic family, the House of Hohenlohe, and from an ethnic group, the Germanic Franks. The Princes of Hohenlohe no longer rule the countryside, but they still reside in their castles and some of them participate actively in political and public affairs. As to their ethnic heritage, the inhabitants of the region are quick to point out to the stranger that they are not 'pig-headed Swabians' (*dickköpfige Schwaben*) like their neighbors to the south, but 'amiable Franks' (*liebenswürdige Franken*). In a descriptive publication of the Bureau of Statistics in Stuttgart, we read the following characterization:

> *The strong and tough but at the same time limber people are healthy and resistant to epidemic diseases, especially tuberculosis, in spite of the physical neglect which is frequently found to be the case. . . . In their nature the Franks are more adroit and amiable than the Swabians, but probably do not possess the same depth of feeling.* [7]

The region started to become identified with the Franks when they entered it around A.D. 500, pushing the Alemanni-Suevi toward the south. Frankish rule gradually extended over the Alemanni, although no further movements of large groups of Frankish settlers into Alemanni territory seem to have taken place The southern extent of the region is largely contiguous with a line of bunched linguistic isoglosses (Haag 1929). To the north of this line, people speak a dialect of Frankish (*Hohenlohisch*); to the south lies the speech area of Swabish.

However, the ethnic component alone might not have maintained this particular linguistic "border" had it not also consistently coincided with political divisions. From the late Middle Ages until the demise of the Holy Roman

---

[7]Baden-Württemberg Statistisches Landesamt (1953:91). For a capsule history of the interaction between Alemanni–Suevi and Franks, see Miller (1965:xxii–xxxi). For humorous anecdotes on the contemporary inhabitants of Hohenlohe, with an excellent rendering of the dialect, see Wankmüller (1969; 1970).

Empire in 1806, territorial boundaries within Germany remained relatively stable (linguistic research has shown that today's speech areas still reflect those boundaries [see Haag 1929; cf. Bloomfield 1965:34]).

The Territorial Fragmentation of the Region and its Roots

When we look at the political map of the region around the year 1800, we find no fewer than twenty lords with immediate territorial rights in this comparatively small area (four-fifths the size of Rhode Island).[8] There was a considerable range in size among these territorial possessions. At the one end of the scale were the Barons of Crailsheim at Hornberg with 200 ha of land, 1 castle, 1 hamlet, and 400 subjects. At the other end we find the Princes of Hohenlohe with a total of 167,200 ha of land, 20 castles, 17 towns, 250 villages and hamlets, and 65,000 subjects. Among other territorial lords were the Imperial Free Cities of Hall and Rothenburg, the margraves of Ansbach-Bayreuth, and various imperial knights. Some areas were held by ecclesiastical lords, among them the Bishop of Würzburg, the Elector of Mainz, the Abbot of Schöntal, and the Order of Teutonic Knights. When we descend to the level of the individual village we find a bewildering array of patrimonial relationships between land, lord, and peasant, sometimes with multilayered claims by as many as eight or ten lords to various units of land, labor, and jurisdiction.

At the root of this fragmentation of political and economic power, which is typical of many parts of the Holy Roman Empire, are two interacting factors: the system of vassalage and the lack of a strong central authority. The system of vassalage developed out of the need of the Frankish kings to keep effective control over their newly conquered territories. They delegated their ruling powers to men who initially came from two groups: from the old Frankish "tribal" nobility who held lands in their own rights, and from ranking servants of the royal court whom the kings invested with fiefs and various rights and privileges in return for their past and future services. These two groups were not socially exclusive castes, however, because many of the kings' servants traced their genealogy to the old noble families, and as time went on the distinctions became increasingly blurred. This was mainly the result of systematic efforts by the kings to break the power of the old nobility by forcing them to accept their own lands as royal fiefs. Although this act reduced them to the status of royal vassals, the unanticipated result was an elevation of the institution of vassalage. Fiefs soon became heritable, and high-ranking vassals such as dukes, margraves,

---

[8]That is, they were subject to the emperor only, having received their fiefs directly out of his hands rather than from another vassal. For a political map of Hohenlohe toward the end of the eighteenth century, see Saenger (1957:Map 4).

and counts not only became powerful but often placed their own interests over those of the king.

The central authority of the king (and later, the emperor) was thus backed mainly by the resources that the possessions of his own House could supply. In the power play of shifting alliances, the emperor would also enlist the support of his ecclesiastical vassals, powerful bishops and abbots, against rebellious dukes and margraves.[9] The emperor also tried to check the expansionist policies of high-ranking vassals by investing many of the lower nobility attached to his court with fiefs which he carved out of crown lands. Ultimately, the usefulness of these knights in supporting the power of the emperor remained limited, and with the introduction of modern warfare their services became obsolete. But the knights remained a thorn in the side of the more powerful lords of the realm who wanted to enlarge their own territories, and many of the resulting feuds dragged on for generations. However, by virtue of their imperial status and forming a Federation of Imperial Knights, a considerable number of knights managed to hold on to their possessions until the Empire came to an end in 1806.

The preceding brief outline is merely an attempt to comment on the proliferation of territorial lords. As for the often multilayered array of patrimonial relationships, we have to turn to the nature of the benefits which could be held by a vassal. The three basic rights of feudal institutions—the right to private jurisdiction, the right to land, and the right to personal services—were not always held by the same person. Furthermore, these three basic rights could be subdivided into a multitude of offices, privileges, and benefices. These became negotiable instruments which could be sold, pawned, swapped, bequeathed, given as dowries, as well as divided among several heirs (for a discussion, see Bloch [1970, Part 4, Vol. 1] & Ganshof [1964]). The most skilfull manipulators were those who managed to keep their own territories as free from the rights of other lords as possible. Their skills at this game enabled the Counts of Hohenlohe to obtain political dominance in the region under discussion.

The House of Hohenlohe

The Hohenlohes had started from the small base of a castle and a few offices and benefices which they had received as vassals of the House of Staufen. During the thirteenth and fourteenth centuries, they managed to expand their holdings

---

[9]Ever since the first Frankish king, Clovis, converted to Roman Catholicism, the Church had received control over large tracts of land. For example, the territory invested in the Duke and Bishop of Würzburg in A.D.741, included the region of Hohenlohe. Toward the end of the Middle Ages there were 51 bishoprics and as many monasteries immediately subject to the emperor.

considerably. They also obtained royal prerogatives for the governing of their territories. Because of their adherence to partible inheritance, their holdings became continuously fragmented. The integrity of their combined territories was ultimately ensured, however, through a series of contracts drawn up in the sixteenth century. These contracts stipulated that none of the possessions could be disposed of by any lineage acting on its own. The combined territories were administered as an organic whole along the lines of an entail by the respective senior count. In 1744 and 1764, respectively, the two lineages were elevated from the rank of *Grafen* ('counts') to that of *Reichsfürsten* ('Princes of the Empire'). By the end of the eighteenth century we find the two major lineages subdivided into four minor lineages each.

In contrast to the landholding nobility east of the Elbe River, the Hohenlohes followed the pattern predominant in the western parts of Germany—they preferred the collection of tithes, rents, and taxes to the conduct of farming on large estates of their own. With few exceptions, those estates which they had been operating were subdivided in the eighteenth century and converted into hereditary tenant farms. The Hohenlohes endeavored to be good administrators and kept the burden of their peasants within bounds. In comparison, some of the regional knights would levy a tax burden on their peasants that was often twice as heavy as that borne by peasants in Hohenlohe territories. In general, the cultural orientation of the Hohenlohes was in the direction of the French court. There are several who distinguished themselves as holders of high political, military, and ecclesiastical offices at German, French, and Austrian courts.

For this study, probably the most important aspect of territorial arrangements is the fact that all territorial lords obtained the right at the Peace of Augsburg in 1555 to impose their own choice of religious affiliation upon all of their subjects.[10] When we compare the religious composition of today's population with the political map of the late eighteenth century, it is indeed striking how the resulting pattern of religious affiliation has persevered. The Hohenlohes adopted the new faith in the 1550s, and their villages have remained predominantly Protestant. In 1667, the members of one lineage reverted to Roman Catholicism, but by then the dictum of the Peace of Augsburg no longer applied and their subjects chose to remain Protestant despite pressure from above to revert to the old faith.

[10]The adoption of the new faith by the aristocracy was governed by a variety of considerations and was often preceded by proselytizing efforts of Protestant ministers in the various territories. Where the Reformation was introduced, a period of transition lasting up to 20 years was characterized by both Catholic and Protestant services being performed next to each other, often in the same church. For a discussion of the role of the nobility vis-a-vis the new faith and its introduction among the peasants, see Rössler (1965:64-146) and Riedenauer (1965). See also Franz (1971) for an investigation of the conduct of the Protestant Church in Hohenlohe during the decades following the introduction of the Reformation.

The Napoleonic conquests brought an end to the sovereign status of most lords of the realm and their lands were incorporated into newly created political entities. In 1806, King Frederick I of Württemberg (elevated from duke to elector in 1803, and to king in 1805) signed the *Rheinbundakte* and received the region of Hohenlohe-Franken as partial compensation for territories west of the Rhine he had lost to France. The Hohenlohes became subject to the King of Württemberg and were to be compensated for the loss of their privileges and territories. The "Administrative Laws of Reform" enacted in 1817–18 by King William I (his father Frederick had died in 1816), set the peasants free from all former patrimonial bonds and provided for compensations to be paid both by the kingdom and the peasants to the respective *Standesherren* ('lords of the realm'). The Hohenlohes felt that they were being treated unfairly, however, and brought suit against the king before the Federal Diet of the German Confederation at Frankfurt, thus delaying preliminary steps for the release of their patrimonial rights until 1838, when further laws on the subject were passed. Even then there was very slow progress, and it was not until after the revolution of 1848 that negotiations were pursued more speedily. By 1857, the last contract for compensations was negotiated, and 25 years later all payments were met and the peasants were put in the position of outright ownership of the land that their families had held in patrimonial tenure for so long.

Since 1806, then, Hohenlohe-Franken has been an integral part of Württemberg and as such has shared its political fate. A few highlights ought to suffice to sketch more recent events. During the confrontation between Austria and Prussia in 1866, Württemberg took the side of the Austrians, but her troops were beaten by Prussia. In the same year, the German Confederation was dissolved and Württemberg entered into a treaty with Prussia. In 1870, Württemberg joined the new German Empire of Bismarck and Kaiser Wilhelm I. The demise of this empire with Germany's defeat in 1918 also brought an end to the Kingdom of Württemberg, with the king abdicating in November of that year. The newly designated "*Land* Württemberg" became part of the new German Republic, with a subsequent loss of many of her former sovereign prerogatives. Her autonomy as a separate state was further curtailed after Hitler's rise to power in 1933.

After the end of the Second World War, General Eisenhower decreed the formation of a "*Land* Württemberg-Baden," which was formed out of the northern halves of these two former political entities. The southern parts, which the French were allowed to occupy, became the "*Land* Baden" and the "*Land* Württemberg-Hohenzollern," respectively. A plebiscite held in December 1951, governed by directives of the newly created German Federal Republic (and supported by the Americans, but opposed by the French), in which the inhabitants of the three *Länder* were to vote for or against consolidation into one *Land*, resulted in 69.7% of the electorate opting for consolidation. The resulting "*Land* Baden-Württemberg" was officially launched in April 1952, and came to constitute the third largest state in the Federal Republic, both in terms of size ($135{,}750$ km^2), and population ($6{,}600{,}000$)—for a summary of major political and socioeconomic events since 1806, see Gönner (1971).

Socioeconomic Developments

Medieval Settlement and Agriculture

The regional economy has been dominated by family farming for almost all of its history. Going back 1500 years, we find the region covered by a vast deciduous forest with settlements mainly confined to the river valleys. When the population increased, people moved up onto the plateau and started to cut into the forest. During this period of settlement, which has been placed between the eighth and eleventh centuries, settlements were generally small, ranging in size between one and four households.

Spurred by an apparently substantial population increase, settlement activities accelerated during the years from around A.D. 1000 to around A.D. 1300. The size of the average hamlet grew to around twelve households. By the year 1300, overall settlement density (i.e., the number of inhabited places) had reached a peak which has never been equalled since. But by 1350, only 50 years later, 25% of the settlements lay abandoned. There had been a series of crop failures, but it was especially the plague which ravished Germany from 1347 to 1350 that severely decimated the population. A considerable migration of people ensued, mainly in two directions. The first was from countryside to town; the second from rural settlements with only marginal agricultural possibilities to more favorable areas which now offered many deserted farmsteads. People in the countryside also moved closer together. The crowded, tightly clustered villages that we still find in several regions of west and southwest Germany today had their beginnings in the late Middle Ages. Since that time, the overall settlement pattern of Hohenlohe-Franken has changed in only minor ways.

In the early Middle Ages, agricultural surplus from the average farm of 3-ha tillage seems to have been relatively small. With increasing settlement density and a growing urban population, the three-field system, first introduced during the reign of the Carolingians, became more widespread and led to a general increase in crop yields. Major crops were dry cereals (rye, barley, oats, spelt, wheat); legumes (peas, beans, lentils); and flax. Domesticated animals (cattle, pigs, sheep, goats) were important sources of food. Pigs, which seem to have been especially plentiful, were fattened on the acorns and beechnuts of the forests. During the thirteenth and fourteenth centuries, a number of small towns sprang up throughout the region (only two of the regional towns are older) which offered the peasant an outlet for surplus produce. Trading took place first on a barter, then on a cash basis. The economic importance of this local trade should not be overrated, however, because the towns remained rather small and were also provisioned with produce grown in the fields of some of their own citizens.

By the late Middle Ages, the peasant became increasingly part of a market economy which extended beyond regional and national borders. For example, fluctuations in the price of grain at one of the major seaports affected every peasant to a greater or lesser degree, depending, among other things, on his geographic and market-intensity location. Furthermore, the peasant had to contend with severe inflations, such as the one that followed the Thirty Years War, besides having to bear the devastating effects of war itself.[11] Generally, it was almost impossible for any peasant to keep aloof from the influences of the international market. Although he produced almost all of his own food and he would have been able to get along for a while without items supplied by the town, he still had to pay his patrimonial obligations, which by the late Middle Ages had predominantly assumed the character of cash payments. In order to obtain the necessary cash the peasant was dependent on selling some of his produce. Although conditions were far from uniform, patrimonial obligations generally amounted to around one-third of the average year's crop.

The Agricultural Revolution in Regional Perspective

The eighteenth century brought improvements in agricultural methods which increased the income of both landlord and peasant. A local Protestant minister by the name of Johann Friedrich Mayer became well-known far beyond the region through his publication (in 1769), and personal advocacy of experiments that promised a considerable improvement in the traditional three-field system. He advocated (although he was not the first to do so) utilization of the fallow by sowing it to clover and putting it to potatoes and beets (wide-spread adoption of the potato occurred after the years of great famine, 1771–72). He pointed out that the clover not only helped to enrich the soil, but together with roots and tubers provided feed for more livestock. The livestock could then be stabled on a year-round basis and was no longer dependent on the limited resources of the common pasture. Furthermore, stabled livestock resulted in a concentration of valuable manure which, in turn, helped to boost crop yields.

These improvements were actively supported by the Hohenlohes, but because of a measure of resistance by the peasants against the innovative procedures, and also because of certain practical obstacles (such as the keeping of large flocks of

[11]This is not to say that everyone suffered equally. There were regions, such as that of Schleswig-Holstein, where the peasant managed to prosper while other regions became increasingly impoverished.

sheep), the process of adaptation was still not complete after more than a century had elapsed.[12] However, the extent of initial improvements was sufficient to markedly increase the production of beef for the market. Where a peasant had been limited to grazing two or three steers on the commons before, under favorable circumstances he might now be able to fatten up to ten in his stable. At least half of the regional cattle production was exported to France and in Paris, "boeuf d'Hohenlohe" became synonymous with good quality beef. The 1780s were the peak years of cattle production. Toward the end of the century the French market declined and was by and large lost after the events of 1812. An onslaught of rinderpest had taken its toll, too. Although cattle remained an important item in the regional economy, it has been only in recent years that the number of cattle climbed to the level of 200 years ago.

The Peasant After Liberation

In the previous section, I briefly referred to the process of "liberating" the peasant from patrimonial bonds. Although this process had put the peasant in the position of legal ownership of his land, economically it seems to have brought little change. Before liberation, the average Hohenlohe farmer paid roughly 25% of his gross income to cover a variety of tithes, rents, and taxes. After liberation, the level of communal and state taxes was definitely below that which he had been obliged to pay before, but the new hidden taxes apparently tended to cancel out the ensuing benefits. For the region as a whole, the new political conditions brought certain disadvantages. As part of the new Kingdom of Württemberg, Hohenlohe-Franken found itself in a peripheral position and its leading citizens felt that the government in Stuttgart showed only secondary interest in its development. Industrialization passed it by and agriculture remained the mainstay of the generally stagnating regional economy.

An Industrial Backwater

Apart from the fact that natural resources were mainly restricted to arable land and forests, there were a number of geographic and socioeconomic factors that worked against the establishment of a significant regional industry. First, there was a relative paucity of communications (few all-weather roads and an absence of navigable waterways) coupled with the distance from markets. Second, there was the question of potential manpower with which to meet the needs of industry. In both respects, the Neckar basin with Stuttgart at its center held far greater promise. Not only was there a higher population density because

---

[12]For example, by 1847, the third field in one of the neighboring Protestant villages was still left completely fallow (Königlich statistisch-topographisches Bureau 1847).

of the existence of more numerous and larger cities, but there was also a greater supply of potential manpower in rural areas. This last factor may be explained by a brief look at the prevailing inheritance patterns.

Under a system of partible inheritance as it has been practiced in the Neckar basin, the land is divided among the children in more or less equal portions. Provided these portions are large enough, each of the children is potentially able to remain in the village and found a family of his or her own. The overall effect is an increase in the number of families and individual holdings, but a decrease in the average size of these holdings. With continued division, the time comes when the inherited portions of the parental holding are no longer large enough to support a family, in which case either some of the heirs give up their portion of land to one or more of the others so that economically viable units remain, or they will all have to turn to additional sources of income. On the other hand, under a system of impartible inheritance as it has been practiced in Hohenlohe (except in the river valleys), only one of the children will inherit the land. Thus, the number of families and holdings is held relatively stable over a longer period of time, and the number of smallholders is not bound to increase with each new generation of heirs. When we compare the two types of villages associated with the differential inheritance patterns, we can readily see that the one in the Neckar basin constitutes a greater manpower potential for industrial under-takings, especially in the category of part-time farmers.

Developments during the last 90 years of regional history can most easily be demonstrated by taking the occupational structure as a point of reference (Fig. 2).[13] In 1882, sixty-six percent of the active work force was engaged in agri-culture. This percentage remained basically unchanged until 1933, and by 1939 it had declined by only 4%. Only after World War II did the percentage of persons occupied in agriculture dip below the half-way mark. The 1950 figures reflect mainly the enormous influx of refugees from the east (see Fig. 3, showing population curve), but they also point to the beginnings of a trend which emerges more clearly by 1961. This trend indicates the interaction of two factors: the increasing motorization and mechanization of farming, and the Ger-man industrial and economic boom which started in the 1950s and lasted (with minor fluctuations) into the 1970s.

When we turn our attention to the percentage of industrial jobs, we find a drop from 24% in 1882 to 19% in 1933, with no change until at least 1939. The reasons for this decline become clearer when we look at the composition of the "industrial occupations" category, which was made up mainly of traditional craftsmen working out of small shops. The most prominent ones (in the order of number of persons engaged in particular craft) were shoemakers, tailors, joiners

[13]Because of slightly different methods from census to census, deviations within 2% are possible (see Baden-Württemberg, Statistisches Landesamt 1964a:9).

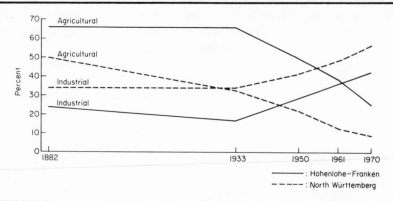

FIGURE 2. Percentages in total work force of agricultural and industrial jobs, 1882-1970, Hohenlohe-Franken and North Württemberg. Data from Deutsches Reich, Kaiserlich Statistisches Amt (1884) & Deutsches Reich, Statistisches Reichsamt (1935; 1942); Baden-Württemberg (1952; 1963; 1972a).

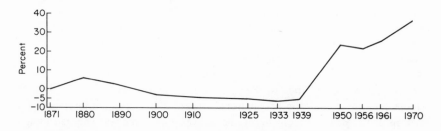

FIGURE 3. Population increases and decreases in percentages, 1871-1970, Hohenlohe-Franken. Data from Baden-Württemberg, Statistisches Landesamt (1965).

and cabinet makers, seamstresses, bricklayers, bakers, blacksmiths, carpenters, and wheelwrights.[14] When factory-produced goods started to compete with their wares, many local craftsmen found this competition severely cutting into their livelihoods. There were many who closed their shops (or lost their employment in such shops) and left the region for more industrialized areas. Most of those who stayed could fall back on their small holdings to supply them with bare essentials. In the towns, shops became generally more modernized and some grew into small factories. A comparison with the relationship of industrial jobs to agricultural jobs for North Württemberg as a whole (see Fig. 2) highlights the industrial "backwardness" of the region.

As late as 1961, the number of persons engaged in the region's agriculture was as high as it had been in 1882. It became clear to everyone concerned that there

[14]See Deutsches Reich (1898:191ff). Also, see Federal Republic of Germany, *Handbook of Statistics* (1967) for current breakdown of the category "Industry and Handicrafts."

was an increasing imbalance in the land–labor ratio. Modernized agriculture simply did not require the same number of workers per given unit of land as in 1882. To halt the potential depopulation of the villages, dispersed secondary industry was badly needed. There are now a number of small plants in various parts of the region (apart from those in the larger towns) tapping the local labor supply; more are expected to come. The government in Stuttgart has acknowledged the weak economic structure of the region, and, between 1957 and 1969, Hohenlohe-Franken has received more than 105 million DM in special subvention funds.

The overall trend in the change of occupational patterns is currently continuing, although its magnitude may be expected to diminish within the next few years. Ecological conditions in the region simply do not favor a large-scale influx of industry, and while farming will continue to dominate the physiognomy of the landscape, the number of agricultural jobs will probably stabilize to around 15% of the total active work force.

3

The Local Setting: Two Agricultural Communities

Physical Aspects

First Impressions

Now that some of the regional background has been sketched in, it is time to approach our two communities. Here I might go back to that first trip which took us (i.e., my wife, our 9-week-old daughter, and myself) to finally view those communities which I had chosen as the setting for my study while still in California.

Starting out by automobile from Stuttgart, a 2-hr drive had brought us close to our destination in the heartland of Hohenlohe-Franken. The traffic had thinned out considerably—a welcome change from the congested conditions we had left behind. The narrow road dipped into the valley of the Jagst and wound along the river, past meadows and sloping fields. Parallel to the road, a two-shared plow pulled by a tractor turned the sod in long furrows, exposing the glistening, black soil. We marvelled at the skill of the driver who somehow managed to prevent the tractor from toppling over and burying him underneath.

An old stone bridge spanning the river led us to a village dominated by the gray slate roof of its church. The narrow slits in the thick walls of the tower spoke of its past function as a last refuge from greedy marauders. A profusion of flowers surrounded many of the half-timbered houses in the village. Above the valley, strongly outlined against the pale blue autumn sky, stood the towers and ramparts of a Hohenlohe castle. The red and white flag of the Hohenlohes with

21

FIGURE 4. "A village beckoned from the other side of the river."

its two black, stalking leopards fluttering from a tower was a sign that the prince
(a first cousin to the children of Queen Elizabeth of England) was in residence.

A few miles down the road a village beckoned from the other side of the river
(Fig. 4), conveying the impression that very little about it had changed since the
Middle Ages. A covered, wooden bridge spanning the river to provide access
heightened the romantic appeal. The houses were huddled around a thirteenth-
century church, the upper portion of its tower half-timbered. This church was
built on the ruins of two previous ones, the oldest going back to the eighth
century.

We proceeded along the river and watched as a huge, gray crane rose from the
meadow near the water's edge and winged its way to the top of a tree in the
nearby forest. At the next village we left the river. The valley of a tributary
creek opened a new vista to our right, and we followed a steep road to regain the
plateau. A forest of beeches and firs formed a canopy over the road, and a
crucifix by the wayside indicated that we were entering Catholic territory
(Fig. 5). Emerging onto undulating terrain, the road was now bordered by apple
and pear trees. Where it reached its highest point we stopped to survey the
landscape.

At right angles and following the crest ran the old "highroad," at this point no
more than a field road. As early as 2500 years ago, this road served as a link in
an important east-west trade route, kept in use for the next 2000 years. It is also

FIGURE 5. "A crucifix by the wayside indicated that we were entering Catholic territory."

along this and similar roads that remnants of Bronze-age settlements have been found.

All around us was the quilted pattern of fields and meadows, interspersed by rows and clumps of fruit trees. The meadows were still green but the fields were either plowed over, torn open from the beet or potato harvest, or still carrying stubble. The individual pieces which made up this patchwork quilt were of all shapes and sizes; some were rectangular, some square, others had zigzagging or curving borders. Here and there a certain regularity appeared, when a row of almost equal-sized strips bordered a row of similar blocks. In the east and south, and the more distant north, the fields and meadows ended at the edge of large parcels of forest. Across the Jagst valley toward the west and northwest shimmered the red roofs of several hamlets.

A scant mile ahead of us and partially concealed lay a half-dozen houses, signaling the immediacy of our first goal: the Catholic village. As soon as we entered the village the road dipped down. The houses were built on an incline which steepened into a ravine, with a small creek hurrying down on its way to the Jagst River. Most of the houses seemed to be clustered around the church, an unpretentious, tall building with a gray slate roof. The usual defense-type tower was missing; a cupola straddled the west end of the roof, its clock striking the quarter hour. Half-timbered walls and red-tiled roofs dominated in the construction of houses and barns and stables, which stood in close proximity to each other in a somewhat unorderly pattern. Some of the houses were four stories high and most looked as if they were built to accommodate large families. In front of one of the houses a farmer stood on a manure pile, using a pitchfork to load a board-lined, old farm wagon hitched to a tractor. Two elderly women with kerchiefs on their heads conversed in front of the general store, between them a fashionable, large-wheeled baby carriage. A man in blue denims drove a huge sow along the village street, and in front of the smithy a piece of farm machinery was being repaired with a small group of men looking on. Everyone cast enquiring glances at the slowly passing automobile.

It did not take long to traverse this village of 50-odd homesteads and soon we were out in the open again. A roadsign told us that the next hamlet (which is part of the Protestant commune) was only 3 km distant. A few tractors could now be seen working in nearby fields. One was pulling a mechanical manure spreader across a meadow, casting a blanket of brown, steaming lumps. The curving road was cresting again, a final effigy of the crucified Christ, and we dipped down toward the Protestant hamlet. Twelve homesteads were strung out in a depression alongside the banks of a creek and a few cows were visible grazing in a meadow. Then up once more, and after a mile or so the view to our right opened to a somewhat larger hamlet than the one we had just passed through. There was some activity in the fields here, too. In a field close to the road a man and a woman were gathering stones which they threw into wire baskets. A little further on to our left, across an intervening valley, another Hohenlohe castle greeted us from the distance. It was located at the end of a spur, with a one-street town leading up to the castle. Ahead of us the tower of the Protestant church peeked from behind a low hill.

The church, which bore a renovated look, turned out to be on the periphery of two major clusters of houses which made up the village. The rectory behind the church was set in a beautiful garden and had the appearance of a stately mansion. To one side of the church was the *Rathaus*, and across the street were two general stores and the post office. The overall topography resembled that of most villages on the plateau in that the houses were built on the slopes of a shallow depression traversed by a creek. As we drove down the curving main street, curious glances followed us here, too. The men were dressed in working clothes of wool or blue denim, their heads covered by peaked caps or narrow-brimmed, soft hats; their legs uniformly encased in rubber boots. Young girls wore their miniskirts as short as we had seen them in the city; women beyond their teens appeared more conservative in their choices of both length and color of dress.

To complete our survey we drove on and headed for the third hamlet which is part of the commune. This hamlet has comprised a total of five homesteads for hundreds of years. As we approached, the first one looked deserted, with the roof of one of the barns caved in, but beyond the other four homesteads we found a cluster of new buildings which had taken the place of the old ones. One thing that struck us about the layout of the fields was that here individual pieces were much larger than we had seen before. This is a typical pattern for hamlets with a relatively large district (*Markung*), where land is divided among only a few holdings.

By now we had reached a major north–south road and with it the limits of the Protestant commune. It was time to turn back to the village, park the car at the *Rathaus*, walk up the steps, knock at the door, extend a cautious greeting, and reveal to the mayor that his village had been discovered by a student of anthropology who was bent on studying it and its people. To my surprise, the mayor did not seem the least bit disturbed by such a fairly unusual revelation and did not ask the expected "Why study *us*?" It turned out quickly that he was the mayor of both the Protestant and the Catholic commune, and he immediately reacted to this novel situation by picking up the phone to try and find accommodations for us.

As it developed that first day, no accommodations could be lined up and even our quest at the nearby castle met with negative results. So we returned to our quarters south of Stuttgart where we were staying with relatives while the mayor promised to keep looking. He did locate a house in the Catholic village which had been newly built by a family that had given up farming several years before. It consisted of two apartments, with the one in the upper story still vacant. We were accepted as prospective tenants and had to wait a few more weeks before work on the apartment was completed. We thus formed our own, separate household, and, although this had the disadvantage of our not being able to get an intimate view of daily interaction in at least one household, it also had the advantage that we were never aligned with one or the other faction in the community.

Some Structural Data

The Protestant *Gemeinde* ("civil parish", or "commune") comprises one village and three hamlets with an area of 1321 ha and a total population of about 400 (in 1971). The Catholic *Gemeinde* comprises only one village with an area of 774 ha, and a total population of 250. In both communes, population density is 31 persons per km.^{2} There are 6 Protestants living in the Catholic village, and 34 Catholics in the Protestant commune (for breakdown, see Chapter 10).

Ecological conditions are very similar. Elevations in the Protestant commune range from 335 m to 486 m, and in the Catholic commune with its proximity to the river valley from 327 to 463 m. The climate falls into the pattern described for the region in Chapter 2. According to the local people, there is only one minor difference in the local weather patterns in that more hail tends to fall on the fields of the Protestant commune. This is explained by the influence of topographical features on the route taken by local thunderstorms—such as the location of the river valley and the patterning of forests on the plateau. There do not seem to be any significant differences in the qualitative distribution of soils;

limestone is prevalent along the slopes and clay marl in most other areas. The same applies to the overall land-use pattern; 25% of the total area of each commune is forested, and 71% is cultivated land (for details see Chapter 7).

Both villages are located on a state road which connects with a federal highway a few miles to the east. There are also some county roads. A network of field roads is maintained by each commune. In this region, state and county roads follow mostly the contours of the old roads which were primarily used by animal-drawn vehicles until after World War II. It was not until the 1960s that they were black-topped. They are curving and narrow, with many stretches bordered by fruit trees. These conditions are not at all favorable for speeding automobiles, but the high rate of fatalities and injuries suffered along these roads bears witness to the fact that too many drivers take their chances.

Four county seats are located in all four major directions of the compass within a radius of between 12 and 20 miles. These towns offer most of the services and shopping opportunities for family and farming needs. There are also a few larger villages closer by, which offer a somewhat more limited range of goods and services. One of these villages is of special importance because of its weekly pig market, reputed to be one of the largest in Germany. Here is also the big auction hall where the region's pride in pure-bred cattle, the "Hohenlohe-Fleckvieh," is auctioned off, sometimes to places as far away as Canada and the United States. This village is only 8 miles distant and also offers the nearest railroad station.

While these distances may seem minute to us now, it might be useful to remember that until the 1950s very few farms had motor vehicles and the roads tended to deteriorate in inclement weather. Then as now, there is only one bus in the morning and one in the evening connecting both communities with the world around them. However, about 80% of the families in either community own an automobile, which is no longer considered a luxury. Some will also ride their tractors to surrounding villages.

The Gemeinde: A Corporate Territorial Community

Administrative Principles

In the administrative hierarchy, each of the two communities of this study constitutes a *Gemeinde*, which is the smallest autonomous unit in German civil government.[1] The *Gemeinde* as a corporate body has the right to enact by-laws,

---

[1] In more precise terms, each constitutes a *Landgemeinde* ('rural commune'), as opposed to a *Stadtgemeinde* ('urban commune'). However, these terms are only used in a more formal context. The word *Gemeinde* translates into such concepts as community, municipality, corporate body, parish, congregation (*Kirchengemeinde*), etc.

to levy property and certain other taxes, to administer its own budget, and, in general, to exercise jurisdiction over all civil matters not claimed by county, state, or federal branches of government (although it is accountable for its actions to higher administrative authority). The *Gemeinde* is governed by the *Gemeinderat* ('commune council') and the *Bürgermeister* ('mayor') who, as the communal executive, takes care of day-to-day business. Both are elected by the permanent residents of the commune through direct and secret ballot—the members of the council for a period of 6 years, and the mayor for a first term of 8 years, and after that for 12-year terms. While the *Gemeinde* has been legally constituted in its present, autonomous form only since the nineteenth century, the history of its function as a corporate, territorial community goes back to the Middle Ages.[2]

The Increasing Need to Regulate Access to Common Resources

In the early Middle Ages, rural settlements were relatively small and generally lacked any form of community-based government. Each individual peasant household had jurisdiction over its own affairs within the framework of rights and obligations that bound it directly to the landlord. From the standpoint of the peasants' projected needs, natural resources were still in abundant supply. Although most of the arable land had to be claimed from the forest, the remaining forested area was more than sufficient to supply lumber and firewood, and feed for the livestock. However, the time came when heretofore unused (albeit not ownerless) land could no longer be taken up without encroaching upon the interests of neighboring settlements. It became necessary to establish fixed boundaries and to formally regulate the usufruct of common resources. The pertinent rights that rested in each individual farmstead were gradually superseded by the rights vested in an association of neighbors, and this basic process culminated with the emergence of the *Gemeinde* as a corporate entity.[3]

Regulations, Restrictions, and Levels of Inclusion

The basic units of the *Gemeinde* have been the *Dorf* ('village'), and the *Weiler* ('hamlet'), with their respective *Markung* (territory marked by boundary

---

[2]In Württemberg, the constitution of the *Gemeinde* was shaped through the reform laws of September 25, 1819, the administrative edict of March 1, 1822, and various pieces of subsequent legislation (cf. Schremmer 1963:170 & Gönner 1971:416, 419).

[3]Bader (1957) examines the legal structure of the medieval village in some detail.

stones).[4] Regulatons were rarely imposed unilaterally by the landlord(s) but were usually worked out between him and the representatives of the *Gemeinde*. The ensuing regulations were laid down in a *Dorfordnung* ('village bylaws'). Such a *Dorfordnung* has been preserved in the archives of the Catholic village. It dates back to 1669 and was (re-)issued by the Bishop of Würzburg "for the advancement of peace and unity." A preamble stating that jurisdiction and land belong to the bishop is followed by a lengthy enumeration of the villagers' rights and obligations, especially in regard to use of the commons. Rights to grazing, lumber, and firewood are spelled out in detail. There are also regulations governing the use and maintenance of wells, roads, and bridges.

The *Gemeinde* assumed corporate responsibility for the collection of tithes and rents for the landlords, and administered its internal affairs through the gradually secured right of jurisdiction over civil matters at the lower level (*niedere Gerichtsbarkeit*; see Lütge (1937:317-318 & 1960:72ff)). The *Gemeinde* also had the right to regulate admission of new citizens and to grant or withhold marriage permits (mostly following guidelines set from above; cf. Neidhardt 1970:39-40). Each person who wanted to settle within its borders had to produce a letter from his or her home parish which gave witness to the moral character and the financial standing of the bearer. Because the community was interested in maintaining a good reputation, and was obliged to take care of its indigent citizens, poor character or insufficient funds were reasons for the refusal of admittance.[5]

However, it is important to point out that not every household in the *Gemeinde* was part of the corporate community. We may best envision this in the form of two concentric circles. In the inner circle were the *Bürger* ('citizens') who were holders of a *Gemeinderecht* ('corporate right'); they constituted the *Realgemeinde*. In the outer circle were the *Beisassen*, who did not hold such

---

[4]Hamlet and village are primarily differentiated on the basis of layout, size, and function. The buildings in a hamlet are further apart from one another than those in a village. In Hohenlohe the size of a hamlet rarely exceeds 30 homesteads; villages usually consist of at least 34 homesteads; and a hamlet rarely has the church, school, and *Rathaus* as well as other service facilities found in most villages (at least until recently). Clusters of homesteads numbering below seven, and those which are very widely spaced, are officially referred to as *Höfe*. For official designations in accordance with structural characteristics of habitation sites, see Baden-Württemberg, Statistisches Landesamt (1953:139-462); cf. Knapp (1964 1:80–87), Jankuhn (1969), & Weinreuter (1969).

[5]For example, in the period from 1847 through 1874, 36 persons asked to be admitted to the Catholic village as citizens, 32 of them for the purpose of marriage. Of the latter, one female and one male were refused admission because neither they nor their prospective spouses in the village had sufficient funds to prove that they would be able to establish an economically viable household. The other four applicants consisted of two married couples, one of whom bought the smithy, and the other one a small holding. (Compiled from minutes of the village council.)

rights. The totality was referred to as the *Personalgemeinde* (Fig. 6).[6] Originally, one *Gemeinderecht* went with each peasant holding and everyone was included in the corporate community. But as time went on, the number of households in the village increased, and, in addition to the original holdings (some of which may have been partitioned), we find small peasant holdings and the households

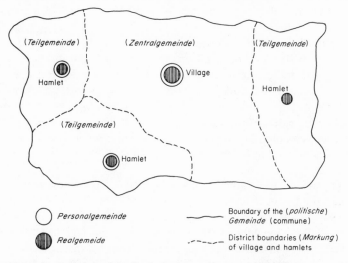

FIGURE 6. Structure of the Protestant commune around 1850.

of day-laborers and craftsmen. Understandably, the body of corporate rights holders was usually intent to restrict the conferral of new rights as much as possible. To obtain such rights, a household had to hold a certain minimum of land. In time, corporate rights ceased to be inalienably linked with one particular holding only; they became negotiable assets that could be split, so that we find some holdings with only one-fourth or one-half of a right, and others with more than one. These rights were of considerable economic importance, entitling the holder to a share in the commons.

Equal Rights for All Citizens

The nineteenth century saw a gradual disappearance of the restrictive *Realgemeinde*.[7] The new legislation of the kingdom, which gave the *Gemeinde* con-

[6]When several hamlets and one or several villages conduct an administrative merger to form one *Gemeinde*, the one which houses the *Rathaus* is referred to as *Zentralgemeinde*, or *Mutterort* (it gives the *Gemeinde* its name), and each of the others is referred to as *Teilgemeinde* (*Teil* = 'part').

[7]It has apparently been preserved, however, in some areas of Switzerland (see Bader 1957:73; cf. Friedl 1974).

stitutional guarantees toward self-government, stressed the equality of all of its residents. However, it was left to the individual *Gemeinde* itself as to when it would decide to dissolve its *Realgemeinde*, and the two communities of this study are a case in point.

In 1861, the citizens of the Protestant village decided to abolish the existing *Gemeinderechte*, which were then held by 57 households; 14 households held none.[8] By that time, not much of the commons was left. The greater part had been distributed between individual rights holders between 1773 and 1816, under the provision that this land was to be held separate from all other land.[9] However, with the compilation of a new land register in 1857, it was found that most of this land had been treated as if it were private property (*walzende Stücke*). It had been sold, swapped, or pawned to such an extent that it was impossible to recreate the former conditions. It was therefore decided to leave the land in possession of whomever it might be at the moment, and to transfer the remaining commons to the *Gemeinde* together with all corporate obligations.

In comparison, the Catholic village had held on to most of its commons, especially the forest, and the *Realgemeinde* was not dissolved until 1902. There were then 55 households with corporate rights, and two without. The *Gemeinde* compensated each holder on the basis of the monetary benefits that would accrue over a period of 100 years for his portion of the rights. Those parcels that had been distributed earlier remained in the possession of their holders, but the bulk of the commons became the property of the *Gemeinde*. The authors of the village *Heimatbuch*[10] praise the wisdom of the then mayor through whose per-

---

[8]*Source*: Local land register of 1857 (1:6-7). Note that I am here referring to the village only, not to the entire (*politische*) *Gemeinde*, which includes the three hamlets as *Teilgemeinden*.

[9]This distribution was apparently triggered by the adoption of the improved three-field system, which made it more advantageous for the farmers to distribute the commons for cultivation as they were no longer needed for grazing. Those who suffered a real economic loss from this distribution were the *Beisassen* who had little land of their own. Although they had held no formal rights to the commons, as a rule they had been allowed to graze a cow or a few goats or sheep. The speed with which the citizens of a commune would push for the dissolution of the *Realgemeinde* no doubt depended on the intersection of a number of variables, such as amount and kind of commons left, the proportion of inhabitants who held corporate rights to those who did not, the frequency of friction over these matters, etc. One of the Protestant hamlets, e.g., did not dissolve its *Realgemeinde* until the turn of the century—at about the same date as the Catholic village. In her investigation of several communes in Hessen, Beimborn (1959:83-85) found that some of them had continued corporate rights to wood and especially grazing until the 1940s, but in the late 1950s had started to offer some of this land for sale for use as industrial or home sites.

[10]This *Heimatbuch* was written by one of the native sons of the village (who had become a school teacher) in collaboration with one of the local priests, and was published in

sistence this conversion was carried out. A considerable amount of friction seems to have evolved around an amendment that was passed by a citizen's council sometime in the nineteenth century, which read that "each citizen is entitled to lumber for construction and repair work *as much as is necessary*." Apparently, this stipulation became "the reason for eternal quarrels between *Gross- und Kleinbauern*" ('large and small farmers'), for there were always some *Neunmalgescheite* ('wise guys') who made sure that they were allotted the best oak trees in the communal forest, which they then sold for a good deal of money. To carry out the repairs on their own buildings, however, they would use inferior lumber from their own piece of forest, which, of course, soon necessitated renewed repairs. An entry in the *Gemeinderatsprotokoll* ('minutes of the commune council') of May 9, 1829, which I have translated in its entirety, sheds some light on the history of problems that center around corporate rights.

9 May 1829. This commune has had its own sheep-holding since January 26, 1700, which is endowed with many privileges, and it also owns more than 300 Morgen (95 ha) of forest and commons. Since time immemorial, the usufruct from this sheep-holding, forest, and commons has been distributed among holders of corporate rights. Originally, there were 26 corporate rights. By and by, these rights have been sold, swapped, pawned, etc. in such a manner that now there are left some full rights, several half, some quarter, and some eighth corporate rights.

Every time these rights were allotted, it appears that everyone was only concerned about the advantages accruing therefrom, and not the obligations which were tied to them. This has caused a feud among the local citizens which has lasted for some 60 to 80 years. The fight has been about the following: whenever the usufruct from the sheep-holding, forest, or other privileges, has been distributed, this has been done in accordance with the holding of corporate rights, so that some who held only a quarter or an eighth of a right enjoyed only small profit; however, when the obligations were distributed, such as statute labor and the construction of roads, these obligations were distributed equally, so that each one had to do what the other one did.

In order to end the complaining and the feuding which has been going on for so long, the commune council has labored hard and has decided today: that those citizens who hold only quarter or eighth rights have to buy, from those who hold full rights, half of their rights, so that everyone will end up holding

Stuttgart in 1941. It presents a history of the village and some of its inhabitants, based on personal recollections as well as extensive documentary research. Because I am trying to preserve anonymity, I regret not being able to cite this work by authors' names and title. A copy of the *Heimatbuch* can be found in every one of the local households.

half of a right (which might now be called full rights). From now on, obligations as well as privileges will be shared in equal parts by the 52 present holders of corporate rights. Five citizens were in the possession of full rights: Joseph Hecht, Anton Jackob, Leonard Knörzer, Georg Kuhn, and Kaspar Goll.

Eight citizens were in the possession of eighth and quarter rights: Joseph Kuhr, Michael Kuhn, Michael Lüllig, Heinrich Dörr, Joseph Gaukler, Franz Knörzer, Georg Ehrler, and Johann Kaiser. Each of the first five citizens divests himself of half of his right and receives 175 florins. The eight latter pay 875 florins to the five former citizens for the five half rights and equalize those among themselves. In order to prevent the same kind of disorder, misuse, and fighting from taking place again, the council has decided as follows:

1. *Only 52 corporate rights are to exist in the future.*
2. *The rights are always to remain tied to the communal obligations (with the exception of the schoolmaster).*
3. *In future, no corporate right is to be divided, sold, or separated from the house in which it has been invested.*
4. *In case a citizen obtains, at some time in the future, two corporate rights, through inheritance or any other means authorized by the commune court, he will also become liable to perform twice the amount of communal services.*
5. *The commune reserves the right to increase the number of corporate rights in case new citizens are accepted, and to sell them a right for 175 florins each.*
6. *Each corporate right encompasses both benefits and obligations. The benefits consist of: eight nights in the sheep pen, as often as it is a citizen's turn, and the fifty-second part of the communal forest, the commons, and the sheep-holding. The obligations consist of: the performance of communal services, hunting fees p. p.*

Although the above decree apparently ended the splitting of rights, the bickering among the rights holders did not cease until the *Realgemeinde* was finally dissolved in 1902.

Some of the Functional Aspects of Today's Commune Government

Let us start with a look at the Catholic *Gemeinde*. First, there is the administration of commune property which includes 108 ha of forest, 5 ha of meadows, 4 ha of roads and wasteland, 8 ha of building sites, 2 school buildings (which are no longer serving their original function), 1 rectory, the former poor-house (which was enlarged and now functions as an apartment house for former refugees), 1 building (which holds fire-fighting equipment and the scales for the weighing of livestock), and a barn and stables for the maintenance of stud bulls and boars.

For the bulk of its income, the *Gemeinde* relies on the proceeds from lumber sales and property taxes. Among minor sources are the leasing of hunting rights, rents from two buildings, fees from weighing livestock and inspecting meat, and subsidies from the state government. Among the expenses are education (primarily payments for the new schoolhouse), administrative costs, and a payroll covering work performed for the *Gemeinde*. Most of this work takes place in the forest and on the field roads. Especially since 1969, the construction and improvement of field and forest roads has constituted the largest single expense for the commune. For example, gross income from lumber in 1970 was 80,000 DM, yet expenses for the construction of roads amounted to 73,000 DM. Except for road construction specialists and certain machines, most of the work is performed on a part-time basis by farmers from the village, who also furnish tractors and wagons.

Among the most important services provided by the commune are the supply of water and the maintenance of bulls and boars. The commune keeps an average of three boars and four bulls. The owner of a sow or cow pays a stipulated fee for each coition. If one of the animals starts to lag in performance, it is sold for its meat and a new one is bought. The animals are cared for by the *Farrenwärter*, a position presently filled by a man who farms one of the smaller holdings in the village.

The village is not connected to the regional water supply and pumps water from several wells in its territory. In dry years, water has become scarce, mostly because the increase in livestock, the installation of bathrooms, and the acquisition of certain farm machinery needing frequent cleaning has led to a rise in the water consumption. To alleviate the periodic shortages, a new well was drilled in 1964, after the exact spot had been determined by a monk who specializes in water-divining (he had also helped one of the Protestant farmers who moved out from the village to find water on his land). However, during my stay in 1971, an exceptionally dry year made water once again a scarce commodity. On most days of the week, pumping was restricted to a limited time during the mornings and evenings, so the livestock would not go thirsty. This situation lasted from July, 1971 to May 1972. The reason why the villagers have consistently voted down proposals to connect their village to the regional water supply is one of immediate savings. The neighboring Protestants are charged more than twice as much per cubic meter of regional water than what the Catholics have to levy on their own supply, and so far a majority of the latter have been of the opinion that their savings outweigh the inconveniences caused by an occasional dry spell. They also hope to tap an additional well.

These are some of the more important items with which the governing body of the Catholic commune has to deal. Conditions in the Protestant commune are not that much different, with the exception that the commune owns only 4 ha of forest (against the 108 ha of the Catholic commune) and therefore lacks this source of income. However, these 4 ha represent only 1% of forested land on commune territory; 58% is owned by individual farmers, and 41% by a city near Stuttgart which bought it not too long ago from its former owner, a prince of Hohenlohe. In comparison, 56% of forested land in the Catholic commune is owned by the commune, and 44% by individual farmers. I might also point out that the tax yield per citizen shows very little difference between the two communities over the last 70 years.

The Mayor

Both the Catholic and the Protestant commune share the same mayor, which is a rather novel situation. Traditionally, mayors have been natives of the communes that elected them; local records show an unbroken line of native mayors over the last 400 years. These mayors were all *Baureschulze*, that is, farmers who would head the commune government on a part-time basis.

The pattern was broken in the Catholic commune in 1938 when the incumbent mayor had to resign from office for his refusal to join the Nazi party; a Protestant mayor from one of the communes in the vicinity was delegated by the county government to take care of commune business. This, of course, went counter to the wishes of most of the villagers.

After the war, the villagers again elected a mayor out of their own ranks, and his successor was also a man born in the village. After this last native mayor died rather young in December 1968, the councilmen decided against electing a new mayor from their midst, but instead opted to bring in a man who had some experience in handling the increasingly complex matters of communal government. They had received favorable reports on the mayor of the neighboring Protestant commune and asked him to take care of administrative matters on an interim basis. A native of one of the nearby Protestant hamlets, he had returned from World War II a disabled veteran and decided to go into communal government. He was elected mayor of the Protestant commune nearest to his birthplace several years before he became mayor of "our" Protestant commune.

In April 1969, he was elected mayor by the Catholic villagers for the customary period of 8 years. He holds stipulated office hours in each of his three communes, and the Catholic villagers have been unanimous in praising the excellent service he renders to their community.

An Epilogue: The Latest Communal Reforms

In his last communication to me (July 1974), the mayor conveyed the news that he will soon join the ranks of the *"Reformgeschädigte Bürgermeister,"* that is, mayors who have been forced to retire in the wake of communal reforms.

As I mentioned in Chapter 2, reforms to enlarge the areas administrated by county and commune had been on the drawing board for some time and were in the final stages of planning during my stay. Hardly a day went by without an article or two on these reforms appearing in the local newspapers. The preservation of one's home county was vigorously defended by many interested persons and groups, even to the point of initiating a state-wide popular vote demanding dissolution of the parliament in Stuttgart; the initiative failed by a wide margin, however. Most local arguments ran: "If our city or town ceases to be the county seat, a lot of revenue will be lost and we will be relegated to a backseat position. Furthermore, many of our people will have to travel uncomfortably long distances if they want to conduct certain county business in the new county seat." Nonetheless, by July 1971, the final borders of the new counties were drawn up, to go into effect on January 1, 1973. The number of *Landkreise* ('rural counties') in Baden-Württemberg had been reduced from 63 to 35.

Parallel to the *Kreisreform*, the government had drawn up master plans to serve as guidelines in carrying out a *Gemeindereform* aimed at consolidation of communes, with a preferred size of between 5000 and 8000 inhabitants. On principle, time and form of consolidation have here been left to the initiative of the communes themselves. They are held to consult with the citizenry, even though the wishes of the citizens are not binding on the commune councils. Ultimate consent to the carrying out of any consolidation plans, however, rests with the respective county planning commissions. The two basic forms of consolidation have been (1) the active cooperation of several communes in communal planning and policymaking—each commune remains otherwise autonomous; and (2) the outright merger of several communes into one. The first form is seen by the government primarily as an interim solution that will eventually lead to the second, more permanent one. A merger is rewarded with up to 20% higher subvention funds than normally provided. Any two communes that merge first are best off in this regard; other communes subsequently joining the first two will get progressively fewer excess funds. Even after the merger, however, each locality is still guaranteed a limited amount of local autonomy in administering certain facilities under the stewardship of an *Ortschaftsrat* ('village council') and *Ortsvorsteher* ('village headman'), but this provision is seen by many as largely a symbolic gesture because the purse strings are controlled by the new commune council, with each locality represented proportionate to the number of its inhabitants.

Understandably, a considerable amount of opposition developed in those communes too small to take over the role of *Zentralgemeinde* after the mergers have taken place. Most of these communes have already lost their schools as a result of the school reform, which was aimed at abolishing all of those schools with too few students to allow the instruction of each grade separately. Now they are faced with losing their *Rathaus*, symbol of autonomous local administration, and the removal of both school and *Rathaus* is seen as leading to the deterioration of community spirit. The complaints, however, have mainly been confined to outspoken criticism at citizens meetings and informal gatherings: "It is generally conceded that ultimately one cannot stand in the way of progress. Today, children have to know so much more than their parents (a remark I heard frequently), and it makes sense that those who have spent their first 4 years of schooling in a one-room school house may find it difficult to catch up with those who have attended larger schools. So, what can one do against administrative reforms to which ultimately all politicians have to feel committed?"

Reactions to the reforms in our two communes were similar to those in most other communes: "It is a great pity that this has to happen, but we will hardly be able to stem the tide." In the Catholic village, the almost unanimous reaction of the citizenry to the prospect of a merger (in which the neighboring Catholic commune in the valley would be the only feasible partner) has been one of "Let's go it on our own as long as possible; we have our profitable forest, relatively few debts, and we should not be in a hurry to merge with our neighbors and help them finance their ambitious' construction projects." In contrast, the question in the Protestant commune from the beginning was not "How long can we hold out on our own?" but rather "Which one of our two bigger neighbors shall we join?" The citizens were almost evenly split on this issue, with a slight majority favoring one over the other. (The favored commune is shown in Figure 6, p. 29, as having the largest number of marriage ties with our Protestant commune; likewise, the commune with the largest number of marriage ties shown in Figure 13, p. 58, is the prospective partner for our Catholic commune.) Negotiations dragged on, but the planning commission did not approve the merger with the commune of the majority's choice because the other commune was slated for this move in the master plan. The merger with this commune took place on January 1, 1975, the same date that the Catholics joined their neighbor on the other side, with satisfactory negotiations now completed. Already having lost the commune in which he was first elected, our mayor lost the other two by the end of 1974, prematurely ending a very successful career.

The Occupational Structure

Changes in the Work Force

Family farming has formed the economic backbone of both communities. Until the Second World War, farming constituted the main occupation for more than 90% of the active work force. All of the work in each community was performed by local residents, including hired-help living in the households of their employers; no one left the community for regular work outside of it. This is now changing, and the figures in Table 2 draw attention to several closely

Table 2

POPULATION, OCCUPATIONS, AND COMMUTERS IN 1961 AND 1970

| | PROTESTANT COMMUNE | | | | | CATHOLIC COMMUNE | | | | |
| | 1961 | | 1970 | | | 1961 | | 1970 | | |
	N	%ᵃ	N	%ᵃ	%ᵇ	N	%ᵃ	N	%ᵃ	%ᵇ
Total population	474		396		-16	281		264		- 6
Persons in work force	258	(54)	207	(52)	-20	183	(65)	132	(50)	-28
(% of total population)					- 2					-15
Distribution of work force:										
Agriculture	198	77	128	62	-15	156	85	87	66	-19
Industry and crafts	38	15	58	28	13	17	9	37	28	19
Trade and communications	5	2	9	4	2	2	1	3	2	1
Services	17	7	12	6	- 1	8	4	5	4	0
Proprietors and helping family members	205	80	133	64	-16	159	87	86	65	-22
'Outcommuters' (Auspendler)	25	10	46	22	12	12	7	35	27	20

Key %ᵃ: Percentage of total number in work force.
    %ᵇ: Percentage change.

Data from: Baden-Württemberg, Statistisches Landesamt (1964a; 1972a).

interrelated points. (They are presented here merely in the form of a survey because they will be discussed in connection with more detailed analyses in later chapters.)

There has been an absolute decrease in the work force between 1961 and 1970, which exceeds the population decline in the Protestant commune by 4%, and in the Catholic commune by 22%. This sharp decline in the Catholic commune is linked directly to the fact that a relatively large number of men and women in the 20–29 age group have left the village for urban jobs (for sex–age distribution, see Figure 18, p. 70). In addition, there are a number of older persons who constituted part of the active work force in 1961, but have since retired. When we look at the work force as a percentage of the total population, we find that there has been little change in the Protestant community, however, the Catholic community shows a decline of 15%.

It is noteworthy that despite the 15 and 19% decreases in the number of agricultural jobs, well over half of the local work force is still engaged in farming. In view of the actual labor requirements, these figures might still be lowered (as will be shown in Chapter 7), but the present age structure of the farming population and the relative scarcity of other jobs tend to maintain the present high rate. It should be pointed out, however, that some farmers earn additional income working for the commune, or on outside construction jobs.

The number of *Auspendler* (people who commute to jobs outside the community) has been on the increase. In the Catholic community, all but two of the commuters also engage in farming their own holdings on a part-time basis. Two-thirds of the commuters hold jobs with road construction companies. This type of job is suited to the needs of the part-time farmer; during periods of peak agricultural activity he is usually allowed time off to attend to his farm, and, in the winter months when bad weather halts construction work, he can catch up on maintenance work at home while receiving compensation of up to two-thirds of his regular pay for work lost. The pattern in the Protestant community is a little different because there are more families without land of their own, and fewer farmers who take on outside jobs.

Local Crafts and Services

The shops of local craftsmen blend into the barns and farmhouses and have long been an integral part of the farming community. In the Catholic village, the only shop left is that of the blacksmith. He and his brother work from seven o'clock in the morning until late in the evening, 6 days a week. Their work is of great importance to the local farmers, especially when a broken-down piece of farm machinery has to be repaired quickly so that the loss in time and money can be held at a minimum. Because the rates charged for repairs tend to be lower than elsewhere, some farmers from the Protestant community are also regular customers. Once in a while the smith will shoe one of the few remaining horses from nearby villages. Attached to the smithy is a small agricultural holding.

There used to be two shoemakers, several wheelwrights and carpenters, a joiner, a cooper, and a bricklayer, but they are no longer in business. Now there is only one wheelwright who holds a full-time job outside the village, but he will work on local orders on his own time.

Of considerable importance in the social life of male villagers are the two inns, which are operated in conjunction with agricultural holdings. They are not prepared to offer overnight accommodations, unless special arrangements have been made (since 1974 this has changed in the case of one of the inns, which is now prepared to take on tourists). Their doors are open seven days a week, however, to accommodate those who seek companionship and a place where they can air their views over a glass of beer or wine. There is also a general store operated by an outside couple from the north. The post office is open during the morning hours and provides communications with the outside world as well as a meeting ground for the dissemination of local news.

The Protestant village has several shops which are doing a fairly good business. There are two joiners and glazers; a small sawmill operated by a carpenter; a small construction company owned by a bricklayer employing about six men; a smithy; and a more modernized machine repair shop. Attached to these shops are agricultural holdings of varying sizes, although the bricklayer and the owner of the repair shop have rented out all of their land. Before the war there were four shoemakers and cobblers, but the introduction of the rubber boot eventually forced them out of business. Much of their business had come from repairing worn-down leather boots and shoes, but when a pair of rubber boots is worn down it is simply replaced with a pair of new ones.

The community is also served by a post office, two general stores, and the branch office of a bank that doubles as the local savings and loan cooperative (the post office has meanwhile been closed). A sister of a Protestant nursing order takes care of the ailing. In contrast to the Catholic community, which lost its resident priest several years ago, there is also a resident minister with his family. Of the five inns that once existed in the community, only two are left. One is located in the village and the other one in the largest of the three hamlets. They are rather less frequented than the inns in the Catholic village.

It should be pointed out that not only the farms and inns but also the shops of local craftsmen in both communities are family-run enterprises, exclusively backed by family capital. When additional operating capital is needed, loans are taken up at the local Savings and Loan Cooperative, or from banks. Borrowing money from neighbors or relatives is not very popular.

The Annual Round of Activities

From the description of the agricultural structure it can easily be inferred that most of the local activities revolve either directly or indirectly around agriculture.

Assuming that we start our observations in December, as I did, we find ourselves in one of the slacker seasons of the agricultural cycle. It has been over a month since the last field crops have been harvested and the sowing of winter grain has also been completed. However, barn and stable doors open in the mornings, and we see farmers or their wives or one of their children placing milk cans on handcarts, which are then pushed to the spot in the village where the milk truck from the dairy coop will stop to syphon the milk into its tank. The milking of cows is a daily chore, and so is the feeding of the livestock which usually takes place in a morning and an evening session. The milking and feeding cannot be observed, of course, unless we enter the stables; the fodder is stored in the attached barn and consists mainly of various kinds of hay (meadow, clover, lucerne) and chopped beets for the cattle, and skim milk, potatoes, or fish meal for the pigs. Grains such as wheat, barley, and oats are also used for fodder.

The stable doors open again when the manure is carted out on wheelbarrows or, in a few cases, on conveyor belts. Thus, next to feeding and milking, the cleaning of the stables is one of the most regularly performed activities all year round. The manure pile is usually located adjacent to the street, in front of the stable or house. Below the recessed cement or board floor on which the manure rests is a chamber that holds the liquid manure seeping down from the stable and from the solid manure that is carried out. Carting both solid and liquid manure to fertilize fields and meadows is an operation carried out during much of the

FIGURE 7. But "many a wagon . . . has to be loaded by hand."

year. Now that a light blanket of snow covers the landscape, we can follow with ease the movements of both the mounted tanks of liquid manure and the mechanical manure spreaders once they have reached their destination and have started to distribute their load. The farmers who do not have a mechanical manure spreader have to do it the old way: unload the manure in piles and then spread it with a fork. Many a wagon load of manure has to be loaded by hand (Fig. 7) too, because not every farmer owns or shares in a tractor-operated frontloader which makes light of the work (Fig. 8).

FIGURE 8. Loading manure with a frontloader.

Here and there by the side of a house one may be confronted with a rack and the halved carcass of a pig hanging from it (Fig. 9). The time around Christmas and the following winter months is the traditional time to slaughter a pig (although this may now be done any time during the year) so the larder will be stocked for the months ahead. Slaughtering takes place early in the morning. The farmer, his wife, and an additional helper or two remove all the necessary implements from their storage place and put them up outside the house or barn. There is the big kettle filled with water and a fire underneath to bring the water to a boil. Then there is a large, open cask that has to be filled with hot water; furthermore, a "table," whose working area consists of five evenly spaced, slightly curved beams fitted into two endpieces supported by sturdy legs; and the rack, which consists of a crossbeam with several pegs held up by four spreading uprights. These items are standard equipment in every farmyard. Then

FIGURE 9.   By the side of a house one may be confronted with the halved carcass of a pig.

the butcher comes and the pig—which may weigh between 200 and 300 lbs— is taken out of the pig sty, usually completely unsuspecting and docile. The butcher—officially designated a "house butcher," who is invariably one of the smaller farmers in the community having learned this trade from one of his local predecessors— dons his rubber apron, checks his knives suspended from his belt in wooden sheaths, and then grabs a cartridge-activated bolt which he triggers off against the pig's forehead. The pig falls down, completely stunned. The butcher pulls it on its side, kneels down, slits its throat, and starts working back and forth on one of the forelegs while a woman catches the blood in an enamel basin. This she empties several times into a larger one (a second helper keeps stirring the blood to keep it from coagulating); this is later used to make blood sausage. After the pig is bled, it is hauled up onto the table, sprinkled with a chemical which will soften its bristles, and short ropes are tied around its fore and hind legs. It is then dunked into the open casket filled with hot water; first one end, then the other. Then it is pulled back onto the table and the removal of the bristles begins, with the aid of cone-shaped aluminum scrapers for the more extensive work and knives for work around the extremities. More dunking and scraping until the pig is completely clean. The hoofs are pulled off, the head is severed from the body, and the hind legs are fastened to the pegs on the rack so the pig hangs free. From the time the butcher has stunned the pig, about 50 min have elapsed. In another 20 min the pig will be completely cleaned out—first comes the removal of the intestines and other internal organs, then that of the layers of fat and of the back-bacon. At this time, one of the local publicans, who is also the official meat inspector, drives up in his Mercedes—sometimes from no further away than across the village square—and after inspecting various organs for signs of disease or parasites puts the official stamp on the carcass. The men have a glass of schnapps and then the next phase of the work begins—the rendering of fat into lard, and especially the making of the sausages which will take the rest of the working day. Most of the inner organs and some of the meat and fat that has been cut off the carcass are being boiled in the big kettle. Besides providing for a hearty lunch, the contents of the kettle find their way into casings or cans where they represent different kinds of sausage meat, depending on their basic ingredients of meat, fat, liver, spleen, lungs, blood, and various seasonings, such as salt, pepper, nutmeg, and pimento. The sausages will be cooked for another 2–3 hr and then hung in the chimney to be slightly smoked until the casing is dry. Hams and bacon are taken to the butcher in the nearest larger village to be smoked in his smokehouse for several days. The carcass, which has hung outside all day, is cut into conventional servings which are wrapped in plastic and put in the freezer. (Before the introduction of the commercial-type freezer, the meat had to be either pickled in brine or preserved in jars.) At the end of the 10-hr day, the butcher partakes in another meal with the farmer's family which usually consists of fried sausages, potato salad, bread, and hard cider. His pay is equivalent to the pay for 8 hr of work in the communal forest, and he also takes home a few cuts of meat and several sausages. In some households there may be two slaughtering days in quick succession—one of them conducted for the relatives in the city, who will have either paid for the pig, or will receive it in compensation for the work which they have contributed during their visits.

Around Christmas time, one may also encounter a group of men dressed in hunter's green as they return from the fields, followed by a farmer on his tractor pulling a wagon with the day's bag of hares. This is the hunting party of the gentleman from Stuttgart who has leased the hunting rights on the territory of the Catholic commune, and he and his hunter friends and the farmers who have helped as beaters will celebrate the day's hunt in one of the inns. In the Protestant commune, hunting rights are usually leased by two or three of the local farmers. There are seven or eight licensed hunters in the two communities. A hunting license can only be obtained by submitting to two days of testing administered by a state board of foresters. The applicants not only have to prove that they are familiar with the dates for various hunting seasons and that they can handle the appropriate weapon for a specific kind of game, but they also have to demonstrate their ability to recognize tracks, sounds, age, and sex of various species of animals. The local season for hares is between October 16 and January 15, that for deer between May 16 and October 15. During the summer months, the local hunters (all of them farmers) spend many a night seated on one of the wooden towers placed strategically along the edge of the forest, waiting for their buck to appear. (The hunters in the Catholic commune get permission from the lessor of the hunt to bag a certain number of bucks out of the season's quota.) Sometimes they even manage to bag one of the elusive wild boars. The game is usually sold to the inns, and word of the occasion will draw many of the locals to partake in a dinner of roast venison. Sometimes sly allusions are made to the effect that some of the villagers may have done a little poaching at one time or another, but nothing of the sort seems to have happened during my stay.

One activity totally confined to the slack winter months is the distilling of fruit mash and hard cider into schnapps. The Protestant commune has only 2 or 3 stills, but the Catholics have 16. The rights for individual households to operate a still go back many years, although this right may lapse if no distilling is undertaken during a period of 5 consecutive years. The owner of each still is allowed to produce a certain annual quota, and those in the community who do not have a still may take their batch to one who does, with the stipulation that only fruit from locally owned fruit trees may be distilled into spirits. A batch of, for example, 350 liters of apple and pear mash, 200 liters of plum mash, and 80 liters of hard cider distills into 65 liters of schnapps, with a pure alcohol content of 50%. The government gets a big bite out of this: 3% of the original measure of apple and pear mash and hard cider, and 4½% of the plum mash, in pure alcohol, amounting to 21.9 liters of alcohol, or 43.8 liters of schnapps. The producer is left with 21.2 liters of schnapps, or 32.6% of the amount distilled. Some of this schnapps is kept for home consumption, but most of it is sold at the going wholesale rate, in some cases amounting to about 10% of a farmer's net income. Later in the year, the state liquor board sends a tank truck to the villages to collect the government's share. Pure plum mash is rarely distilled because then the tax has to be paid in money, not in kind. Stills may only be operated between the hours of sunrise and sunset; anyone caught violating this rule is subject to a heavy fine. Every still is sealed by an inspector after the last batch has been distilled, and, before the first batch can be started in the new season, the authorities have to be notified so that an inspector can come and remove the seal. An ongoing still often attracts neighbors and friends who drop in for a chat and maybe a taste or two. Much of my early information came out of these circles of men and their discussions of local lore, farming, and politics.

There are other local activities that keep people busy during the winter months, such as working in the forest, cutting and splitting firewood at home, tending to the repair of buildings, or checking machines and implements and taking those that need attention up to the smithy or machine shop. Visible activity never ceases, for it rarely snows so heavily that pedestrian or tractor traffic are impeded. Twice a month or so, butchers from larger villages will come to buy some pigs, calves, and a bull or two. This is an occasion for everyone around to come and watch and make some comments as the animals are driven from their stables to be weighed on the public scales before they are loaded onto the butcher's truck. Also, a few farmers can always be seen heading toward the pig market on Wednesday mornings with a box full of piglets attached to their tractors.

February is the month of public festivities, of fairs, markets, and carnival processions in nearby towns and villages which many of the locals attend. But there are also carnival activities at home, 2 days in the Protestant and 4 days in the Catholic village, with singing and dancing, drinking, and general merry-making. The musical background is usually provided with the help of the local choir and other local talent, but small outside bands may also be hired. Men, women, and teenagers sit on benches or chairs at long tables either in one of the inns (in the Protestant community), or in the new schoolhouse (in the Catholic village, with catering done by the innkeepers). The seating arrangements reflect the prevailing pattern of social intercourse; people sit with whom they feel most comfortable, be it relatives with whom they are on good speaking terms, or neighbors or friends. In the Protestant community, families who moved into the village after the war tend to cluster together, but everyone participates in the festivities which tend to take on the air of a family affair.

In March, with the coming of spring, activities in the fields increase; there is the usual carting of manure, but there is also plowing (with tractor wheels slipping here and there on the wet ground), harrowing, and the sowing of sum-

FIGURE 10. Planting potatoes.

mer grain and beets. By the first week in April, the sight of drills driven through the fields becomes rarer; the sowing is almost completed and it is time now to plant potatoes (Fig. 10). Some use a tractor-drawn implement with two seats for attendants who see to it that in the revolving drums there is a constant supply of pieces of potatoes which drop into the freshly opened furrows at regular intervals while two discs close the furrows, covering them with soil. Others use the conventional method of dropping the pieces into the open furrow by hand, and closing it in a second operation. In between these activities one can often see men and women picking up stones and placing them into wire baskets, which are then emptied at the edge of the field or into the wagon. Generation after generation, each plowing seems to produce a new crop of stones. One may also see the members of a household rake up dry leaves in the beech forest for use as bedding in the stables, especially if the preceeding year had been very wet and much of the straw had to be left rotting in the fields. A little further on, a group of men is planting pine trees in the communal forest, while others attend to the weeds which threaten to break up the black-topped field roads. In the village we can watch a team of men helping their neighbor to put a new roof on his house, or lending a hand at building a new barn.

In May the fields are green with sprouting crops. Here and there a kerchiefed woman hoes around the beets, an activity which never really ceases until the beets are harvested in September. Although most of the hoeing is done with tractor-drawn implements, it is generally held that for really good results hoeing ought to be done by hand. The gardens close to the farmyards also require attention, to ensure a steady supply of herbs and green vegetables for the kitchen.

Ascension Day is the first of several processions which the Catholics conduct across the fields to ask for divine blessing of the crops. Now and then the first ominous-looking clouds of the season appear over the horizon, with the distant rumble of thunder coming closer. When the stormclouds blot out the sky and the rain starts to fall, the bells of the Catholic church peal their age-old *Wetterläuten* to keep the worst away.[11] In the history of the two communities, several people have been slain by lightning (not to mention many a fire that was caused by it), and only 2 years before our stay the neighbor's wife escaped with a shock and burns on her back when a bolt of lightning hit the tractor on which she was

---

[11]*Wetterläuten*, the ringing of the bells at the approach of a thunderstorm to drive the storm away, was once practiced by Catholics and Protestants alike. In neighboring Ansbach-Bayreuth, whose possessions reached right up to the two communities of this study, authorities tried to prohibit this custom from the end of the eighteenth century on. However, this move was not very successful, and the bells were then officially allowed to be rung as a call to prayer (see Kramer 1957:125; 1961:185). Several people in the Catholic village whom I asked about this practice claimed not to know why it was done; the man who rang the bells said that it was an old custom and that some people believed the vibrations of the bells would fend off the worst of the storm.

riding home. There is also an annual procession on June 17, which is specifically directed toward asking deliverance from hailstorms.

By June the outside activities are stepped up once more. Cutting green fodder for the cattle is becoming a daily operation which will last through the fall. A few farmers in the Protestant commune drive their cattle out to graze on the meadows, using easy-to-shift, low-voltage electrified fences to keep the cattle penned in. This method can be used more readily by farmers in the hamlets whose farmyards immediately adjoin their fields and meadows. The roads and village streets are now busy with coming and going tractors and wagons starting to bring in the first cut of the hay harvest. People anxiously watch the clouds as they turn the hay with various implements attached to their tractors. With each successive rain prolonging the drying process, the hay will lose in nutritional value. After the hay is dry and pushed together into rows, a tractor-drawn, automated loading-wagon picks up the hay and pushes it into its hold. Some of these wagons are equipped with shears which cut the hay to desired size, otherwise the cutting is done by a combination cutter–blower in the barn, which blows the hay up to its storage space. There are still a few small farmers who perform most of these operations by hand; they turn the hay with rakes, load it onto the standard-type wagon with long-handled pitch forks, and unload it the same way. There is a great sense of urgency during the whole operation—the

FIGURE 11. On steep slopes the "scythe is put to good use again" by a widowed mother and her bachelor son.

work will go on until late at night and even the sanctity of a Sunday may be set aside. Everyone who can, helps; those in the village who hold outside jobs stay home if they can; children pitch in after school; and relatives come from the city to collect their share of aching muscles. The height of the first hay harvest lasts from mid-June into the first week of July. Then, attention is turned to the grass growing on slopes which are too steep to use tractor-driven shears. Here the scythe is put to good use again (Fig. 11), and many a young farmer finds that he can not keep up with some of the older men and women who have retained the skill of cutting the grass in long, even swaths.

Around the middle of July the combines are readied to reap and thresh the first of the oats and the winter barley. This is carried on into August, and every once in a while activities are stepped up to double-quick pace when threatening clouds rear up in the sky (Fig. 12). Many a wife is heard grumbling that her

FIGURE 12. A combine harvesting oats under a rain-threatening sky.

husband is getting more and more *rapplich* (beset by nervous energy). This early phase of the grain harvest has to be synchronized with the second cut of the meadows, which was very meager during the year of our stay due to lack of sufficient rain. When barley and oats are in, it is time to harvest the wheat. The roads to the nearest cooperative warehouses carry some lively traffic, too, and often 10 or more tractors and wagons are lined up at the warehouse awaiting their turn to be unloaded. Depending on the size of the holding and the number of livestock kept, the proportions vary in which the year's harvest of grain is kept as feed or sold. If to be used as feed, wheat may still go to the warehouse to be denatured, and oats and barley are taken there to be cleaned. At home, the grain is blown up three or four stories high to its storage space in the attics of farmhouses, although I saw one of our neighbors still do it the hard way and carry the bags weighing 200 lbs upstairs on his back.

The time of the potato harvest from mid-August until mid-September finds many people stooping in the fields to pick up the potatoes (removed from the soil by a rotating fork attached to a tractor). Only a few farmers share in the use of a fully-automated potato harvester, although one of the smaller Protestant farmers has one all to himself. Those who have grown maize will go out and reap it with a tractor-drawn implement, which cuts up the maize, stems and cobs, and spews it into the wagon hitched behind it. In the farmyard it is placed in silos.

The beet crop is brought in from early September into October, and, while the green fodder is still being cut, manure is carted and the harvested grain and potato fields are getting their first plowing, partly in preparation for sowing to winter grain. Apples and pears need to be picked and taken down to the warehouse to be pressed. Certainly by the middle of October, and often before, work has become more routine and less urgent and the people who have worked so hard can turn to a bit of relaxation. It is the time of fairs and markets again, and of the *Kirchweih* (locally: *Kärwa*), a celebration of long-standing history originally connected with the anniversary of the consecration of the local church in villages and towns all over the country. Now, the period of local celebrations range from the middle of October into November. In the year of our stay, there was a *Kärwa* dance in the Protestant village on Saturday night, October 17, followed by a dinner the next day (i.e., dinner German-style at noon), and an "after-*Kärwa*" dinner served by the inn in one of the hamlets on the following Sunday. The *Kärwa* festivities in the Catholic village lasted from Friday, November 5, through the following Monday. Once again the members of the community have an occasion to interact in a festive, boisterous atmosphere. The *Kärwa* represents the climax of the farmer's work year. By now he knows roughly what that year has brought him in return for the hard work that he and his family have put into the family enterprise. After the *Kärwa*, life in the villages gradually settles into its winter routine.

4

Demographic Patterns

It need hardly be stressed that population dynamics are an integral part of all sociocultural processes. Therefore, knowledge of the demographic make-up of a population greatly facilitates the analysis of a wide range of institutionalized behavior. Among the demographic aspects discussed in this chapter, it is especially the differential patterning of fertility rates that is important to my major theme. But first we shall look at the ways in which people are grouped into households and the extent to which marriage ties create links with the surrounding communities.

Households and Marriage

Households

Both village and hamlet are made up of a number of individual households, whose respective members are linked by bonds of kinship and/or common economic interests. With few exceptions, each house in the villages and hamlets of this study shelters one household. There are no self-contained flats or apartments in these houses, although makeshift arrangements have at times been made so that "feuding" segments of a household could stay out of each other's way as much as possible. The members of a household are recruited into it either by birth or by marriage or, in rare cases, by legal adoption. *Knechte* and *Mägde* (male and female servants), who were usually hired under 1-year contracts, were also considered part of the household; since the 1950s, however, these servants have entirely disappeared from the local scene. The composition of each household varies with the particular point in the developmental cycle it happens to occupy.[1] It is with this consideration in mind that we should look at the results of the household census I took in early 1971.

As might be expected, the demographic core unit of "conjugal pair and resident unmarried offspring" is found in a majority of local households; namely, in 67% of the 63 households in the Catholic village, and 71% of the 109 households in the Protestant commune (for the distribution of households by occupation of head of household and size of agricultural holding, see Figure 26, p. 91. The point in the life cycle of individuals in this core unit may vary considerably from household to household. In some cases, the unmarried children residing with their parents have long passed into adulthood; in others, they are still in their infancy.

As in many other regions where impartible inheritance of holdings is the rule, each household is potentially, if not in fact, a three-generation household. In the region of this study, it is customary for the parents of a son or daughter, to whom the parents transfer possession of the family farm (usually coincidental with marriage), to stay on in the same house and eat at the same table under conditions I will discuss in Chapter 5. Of those local households that contain a conjugal pair and their unmarried offspring, 43% in either commune are three-generation households with one or both parents of one of the spouses present; in two of the cases there is even a fourth generation. As a rule, we never find more than one conjugal pair of child-producing age under one roof. The provisions of impartible inheritance allow only one of the heirs (the "principal" heir to whom the holding is transferred) to bring in a partner and raise a family in the native household; any siblings who decide to stay in the house after the transfer of the holding and the marriage of the principal heir have taken place may do so only as long as they remain single.

These unmarried siblings of the principal heir constitute another category of household members. However, this category is much less represented in today's rural households than it was up to a few decades ago. In the Catholic village there are 10 households (or 27% of households consisting of 3 persons or more) with resident adult, unmarried siblings of the principal heir; in the Protestant commune there are only 3 such households (or 4%). Most of these persons are now in their 60s and represent a holdover from the days when it was quite common for 1 or 2 of the principal heir's siblings to stay on in their native households, obligated to help with the work, and of a status ranging between the servants and the "boss" and his wife. Twenty years ago, when opportunities in

---

[1]On the subject of developmental cycles of domestic groups, see, for example, Berkner (1973), Hackenberg (1973), Hammel (1961; 1972), Hammel and Hutchinson (1974). For a description of this cycle in a setting similar to the one dealt with here, see Cole and Wolf (1974).

industry made a position of this type with its mandatory requirement of celibacy even less attractive, these persons were in their 40s and decided that it was either too late for them to try a different life, or that certain personal handicaps would make it too difficult for them to function in another environment. Often there was also a real need for their services at home, especially when the servants left. One may also find a younger, unmarried person who lives in the native household while pursuing a job in a nearby town or village.

The somewhat higher incidence of unmarried siblings residing in households of the Catholic village is at least in part a reflection of higher Catholic fertility rates, which will be discussed later in this chapter. In line with this factor, we also find the average household slightly larger in the Catholic village: 4.1 persons, versus 3.6 persons (Table 3). One-person households, which were much rarer before the Second World War, are made up mainly of persons who are not connected with any of the old-established households in the community, although there are a few natives in the Protestant commune who either find themselves without relatives with whom they might reside, or who prefer to live alone. Among the two-person households there are several that consist of a widow, or widower, and an unmarried son. One of the Protestant craftsmen is the first one to have broken with the tradition of old and young living under one roof—he and his wife live in the new house they built, and his aged parents live in the old one; both parties represent separate two-person households.

Table 3

HOUSEHOLD COMPOSITION, JANUARY–FEBRUARY 1971[a]

CATHOLIC COMMUNE					PROTESTANT COMMUNE			
A	B	C	D		A	B	C	D
1	8	8	12.7		1	13	13	11.9
2	8	16	12.7		2	22	44	20.2
3	10	30	15.8		3	24	72	22.0
4	11	44	17.5		4	18	72	16.5
5	9	45	14.3		5	14	70	12.8
6	10	60	15.8		6	10	60	9.2
7	3	21	4.8		7	5	35	4.6
8	2	16	3.2		8	0		
9	1	9	1.6		9	2	18	1.8
11	1	11	1.6		11	1	11	0.9
	63	260	100			109	395	99.9

[a]Data from Author's census January–February 1971.

Key A: Number of persons per household.
B: Number of households in category.
C: Total number of persons in category.
D: Percentage of total households.

Most of the old, established households in either community carry specific house names, and in local conversations the members of these households are usually referred to by their house names rather than their proper family names. Thus, even after having taken a census of all of the inhabitants, listing their proper names, I found that I was still unable to identify persons who were referred to in conversation. For example, the information that "Schulzatoni" was planning to build a new house left me at a loss, because I could find no one in my records by the name of Anton Schulz. My next task was, therefore, to find out about and familiarize myself with all of the current house names.[2] Thus, the explanation to "Schulzatoni" could be traced to the year 1757, when a man by the name of Anton Ehrler married the daughter of a *Schulz* ('mayor'). That made him "Mayor's Toni," and the name has stuck with the holding to this day, even though the family names of the respective possessors have since changed.

There are house names derived from proper family names, which in some cases coincide with the family name of the respective inhabitants, especially if the holding has been handed down along a line of male descendants for several generations. Other names may be derived from given names, or combinations of given names and family names, or names that refer to a specific event, a particular location, an occupation, or a combination of some of these. To give some examples: The Drom family has inhabited "Droms" since a Martin Drom married into the holding in 1625. The house name "Kilchs" represents the local version of the given name Kilian and goes back to the marriage into the holding of the great-grandfather of the present occupants in 1868. "Gollakaschber," a combination of the family name Goll and the local version of the given name Kaspar, came into use to differentiate this household from "Golla" when the family branched out some 200 years ago. The house of *"Neubaura"* ('New Farmer') has been so named since the time of its founding in 1758, when a son of one of the local Schmitt families managed to carve out a new holding. *"Seewächner,"* the 'wheelwright,' (*Wagner*) by the 'lake' (*See*), was coined to differentiate that household from the one of another wheelwright, which was simply referred to as "Wächner" (this particular craft has since been given up by both households). *"Kappelhannes"* ('Chapeljohn') is named after a forebearer who showed great diligence in erecting a chapel.

House names may change, however, as the examples imply, either if changed circumstances seem to warrant a new name, or if a particular event in the history of a certain house attains such local significance that it forms the basis of a new name. In local conversations, the head of a respective household is usually referred to by house name only or, if there is an old father or adult son, with the

---

[2]The *Heimatbuch* of the Catholic village was of considerable help in this respect, listing not only the house names of all houses in the village that were current in the 1930s, but also their histories. I have drawn on this source in briefly presenting some examples.

addition of the prefix "young" or "old." Other members of the household are referred to by house name followed by their given names.

Some individuals may also acquire nicknames. There are cases in which the use of house name is quite functional in ruling out possible problems of proper identification—family names such as Schmitt, Hammel, Fuchs, Dietz, and Ehrmann, among others, are shared by a number of separate households.

Marriage

As I indicated, the local custom of impartible inheritance includes the provision that only the principal heir will have the right to raise a family in the native household. This provision has obviously functioned as a mechanism to at least partially restrict the pressure on available resources; the remaining siblings have two choices: move out of the native household if they aspire to found a family of their own, or remain unmarried if they choose to stay. The fact that the number of households has remained fairly stable during the period covered by this investigation bears out that this mechanism has worked.[3]

Of course, even if we assume that the number of households remains fixed over time, that there is a perfect relationship between the number of households and the number of marriages, and that there is no significant incidence of illegitimate births, from a purely demographic point of view the pressure on available resources will still be subject to fluctuations due to the rate of excess of births over deaths and the rate of migration. Also, the number of marriage partners does not necessarily remain stable from one generation to the next; for example, a period of high female mortality rates as the result of complications in childbirth will lead to second and third marriages of males and, consequently, a greater demand on the pool of potential, female marriage partners. I should point out that at least 75% of all marriage partners who have married into local households have been females; as the data discussed in the next chapter will show, of the principal heirs during the last 120 years, 75% in the Protestant commune and 83% in the Catholic village have been males.

The pool of potential marriage partners for recruitment into local households has been restricted de facto to persons sharing the same rural background. Merely in terms of practical consideration, a marriage partner who is unfamiliar with the various tasks required to handle household, livestock, and fields would be a liability rather an immediate asset. The households of craftsmen have been subject to similar considerations because until recently all of them held some land and kept some livestock. Within this pool of persons familiar with agricul-

[3]Obviously, the preservation of this local pattern is largely a consequence of the particular geographic and ecological circumstances; many other villages in Baden-Württemberg, such as the one described in Spindler (1973), have experienced both a heavy influx of outsiders and changes in the local occupational structure, which, in turn, has changed the local demographic structure.

tural tasks, distinctions were drawn (at least up to the Second World War) on the basis of socioeconomic status; for example, well-to-do horse farmers would rarely intermarry with families of small cow farmers or day laborers (a topic I shall return to in a later chapter). Another restriction has been imposed by one's religious affiliation; in only one case in the Catholic village, and three cases in the Protestant commune, were partners brought in who were not of the same denomination.

Table 4

ORIGIN OF SPOUSES MARRYING INTO LOCAL HOUSEHOLDS: 1800–1969[a]

	CATHOLICS		PROTESTANTS	
	n	%	n	%
Total number of marriages	254		425	
Both partners native to the commune	117	46.1	118	27.8
One partner from outside the commune	137	53.9	306	72.2
Of those above, from within a radius of:				
10 km	97	78.8	197	64.4
20 km	128	93.4	279	90.8
30 km	133	97.1	298	97.1
From beyond 30 km	4	2.9	9	2.9
Total number of communes from whom				
partners have been recruited	36		89	

[a]Data from local family registers, *Bürgermeisteramt*; local church records.

When we look at the recruitment of marriage partners in terms of geographical proximity, we find that well over 90% of all partners have been drawn from within a radius of 20 km (12 miles). Table 4 gives an overview of the spatial distribution of marriage partners who have married into local households since 1800.[4] Of course, it is not surprising that so many partners have been recruited from such close quarters, considering the logistics of courtship and the fact that the parties concerned like to be able to fully investigate "what kind of a stable a filly is from" or, conversely, what kinds of conditions the filly will have to put up with in the household of her betrothed. (Because land is never part of a dowry, it does not enter into the proximity factor.) Even among those marriage

[4]The table includes all locally recorded marriages in which at least one partner is a native of one of the two communities (or, in a few cases, has resided there from early childhood), except for a few entries in which the place of birth of the outside partner is not legible. The entries on which the first 40 years of Table 4 are based leave some doubt as to whether the possible outside origin of one of the partners was always properly noted, since these forty years show a significantly higher rate of endogamy in both communities. Without those 40 years, the rate of endogamous marriages for the Catholic village is 36.4%, and for the Protestant commune, 25.4%. For a discussion of the methods used to record vital statistics in Württemberg during the first half of the nineteenth century, see Schaab (1972).

partners who have been natives of communities beyond a radius of 20 km (6.6%
in the Protestant commune and 3.5% in the Catholic village), most had been
working in one of the local households when they met their future spouses.

It is noteworthy, however, that a much larger percentage of Catholic marriages
have been village endogamous compared to the Protestants, despite the fact that
the Catholics have had a smaller resident population. This difference has not
escaped the notice of people living in neighboring Protestant communities who
are apt to remark that "everybody over there is related to everybody else—it
comes close to inbreeding." I put these remarks under the category of "neigh-
borly" comments, but then I heard verbatim statements on this topic by some of
the men in the Catholic village. Actually, marriage proscriptions by the Catholic
Church work to curtail marriages between close relatives. Marriages between first
cousins are prohibited, and second cousins (tracing their relationship through
common great-grandparents) need a special dispensation from the bishop before
they can get married.[5] Among the presently living conjugal pairs in the Catholic
village, there are two such sets of second cousins.

The higher rate of endogamy in the Catholic village is paralleled by the smaller
number of communes from which marriage partners have been drawn: 36 versus
89 (Figs. 13 and 14).[6] Apart from the difference in the number of marriage
partners, this discrepancy may be largely explained in terms of the denominational distribution of the population in the four counties which are here primarily involved. The percentage of Catholics in the counties of Crailsheim,
Künzelsau, Mergentheim, and Schwäbisch Hall was 22.2, 49.7, 46.5, and 23.8,
respectively, in the 1970 census. Thus, within the radius of 20 km around our
two communities there are fewer communes with predominantly Catholic
inhabitants than with predominantly Protestant inhabitants. Another factor that
may have contributed to the wider dispersal of Protestant marriage partners is
the higher percentage of craftsmen in the Protestant commune; in many cases,
craftsmen have spent their apprenticeships and some of their journeyman years
away from home and may thus be credited, as a group, with a more diversified
range of contact with other communes than the farmers.

Besides the discrepancy in the number of communes, it is also noteworthy that
the origin of Catholic marriage partners is more highly concentrated in a very
few communities: 36.5% of the "outside" marriage partners have come from the

[5]This rule does not seem to apply universally, however; for example, see Pitt-Rivers'
(1971:104) remarks on first-cousin marriages in Spain as solutions to inheritance problems.
[6]Each circle represents a commune, i.e., villages and hamlets belonging to one commune
are not shown separately. In looking at these figures, and in following the subsequent
discussions, we should keep in mind that here I am dealing only with the *inward* flow of
marriage partners, not with the *outward* flow to other communes. Thus, if we wanted to
arrive at the total number of kin ties with the "outside world," we would have to add the
outward flow. Parenthetically, there has been no recent trend to extend the average
geographical distance from which partners are recruited.

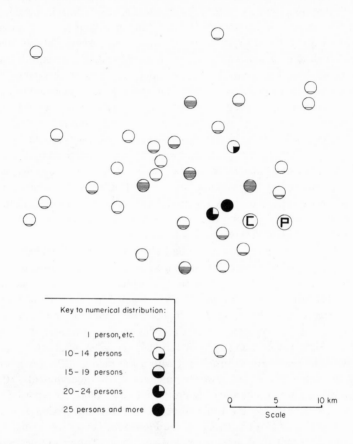

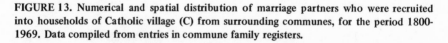

FIGURE 13. Numerical and spatial distribution of marriage partners who were recruited into households of Catholic village (C) from surrounding communes, for the period 1800-1969. Data compiled from entries in commune family registers.

two communes just to the east of our village. When we add those marriage partners who have come from inside the village, we find that 65.7% of the total number of partners have come from only three communes. If we want to apply this to the Protestant commune, we will have to include a total of 17 communes before we reach 66% (communes selected in descending order of number of partners contributed).

It follows that the Protestant commune is part of a more widespread network of kin ties than the Catholic village, and it would therefore appear that the Protestants have been exposed to a more diverse range of information on ways of doing things and looking at the world (at least as generated by such interpersonal ties). We ought to keep in mind, however, that in both communities well over 90% of partners have come from within a radius of 20 km. In other words, the cultural background is highly similar, and the most marked differences between the various communities have arisen as a consequence of adapta-

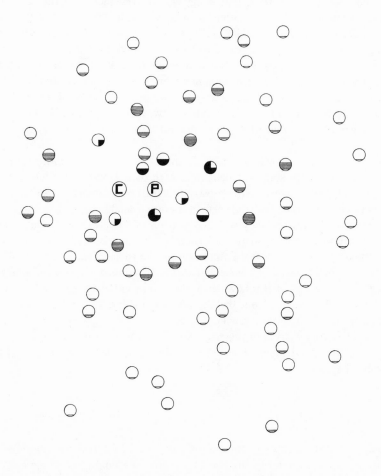

FIGURE 14. Numerical and spatial distribution of marriage partners who were recruited into households of Protestant commune (P) from surrounding communes, for the period 1800-1969. (For Key, see Fig. 13.)

tions to different ecological conditions—primarily differences in topography and amount of precipitation.

According to many of the older people, visiting patterns between members of households related through affinial bonds (except those located in the same community) have changed: "We used to get together more often, but nowadays people have less and less time for each other; everyone has his own business to worry about." Couples who have married fairly recently, however, do not feel the same way, and I noticed that some will get together with the respective families of husband or wife as often as twice a month ("Nowadays it is so easy to get into the car on a Sunday and go for a brief visit between lunch and feeding time"). The emphasis seems to be placed on visiting one's siblings rather than parents, even though the same household is involved, which reflects the preference of social intercourse with members of one's own generation. Thus, visiting patterns may not have changed quite as much as some of the older people claim; it seems, rather, that then as now, visiting is primarily initiated by the younger people, while the older ones get together only on certain festive occasions.

Another category of visitors, which is equally in evidence in both communities, consists of those sons and daughters with their families who had left the village for an urban environment—mostly Stuttgart and surroundings. They can be seen pitching in when the work demands every available hand to be out in the fields or in the barns, but they will also visit on other occasions. In this respect both communities have a comparable number of kin ties extending to urban environments, with quite a few Catholics from the village having married Protestant partners in the city. Of course, before the advent of the private automobile visiting was not as easy as it is now; then, the trip from Stuttgart by train took at least 3 hr and the last leg from the station to the village of 6 miles or so had to be made on foot or by horse-drawn carriage.

There are further aspects of marriage which I have so far neglected to discuss, but some of them will appear in the rest of this chapter, as well as in some of the following chapters.

Fertility Rates

When man started to cultivate the soil, the availability of labor became an important factor in determining the extent and the limitation of agricultural activities. Where a band of hunters and gatherers might be weighed down unduly by a large number of offspring, sedentary peasants have usually welcomed them. A large number of children assured not only the necessary supply of labor despite high infant mortality rates, but also the ongoing existence of the family holding. Although various demographic and socioeconomic factors have greatly modified the need for a large number of children, statistics for Germany show that on the average rural families tend to be larger than urban families, and that rural Catholics tend to have larger families than rural Protestants.[7] I shall now try to show that this difference between Catholics and Protestants can be directly and causally linked to the religious factor.

When we look at Figure 15, we can see that there has been a considerable difference between the local fertility rates of Catholics and Protestants over the last 170 years.[8] Although there is a considerable number of factors that may significantly influence fertility rates,[9] because of the common setting of the two communities we need to consider only a few of those factors—these are the age at first marriage, the length of marriage, socioeconomic status, and personal attitudes or value orientation.

As fecundity tends to decline with increasing age, the age at first marriage may be an important variable if we want to account for differences in fertility rates between two human populations. The figures in Table 5 clearly show that the Catholics have had no advantage over the Protestants in terms of earlier marriages. A noteworthy feature of Table 5 as a whole is the relatively late age at which the men (and to a lesser extent the women) get married, ranging approximately 4 years for men and 2 years for women, above national averages (see Bolte and Kappe 1966:134). This, of course, reflects the practice of the farming community in which marriage traditionally takes place in conjunction with the

[7]See Aschenbrenner and Kappe (1966:225), Mackenroth (1953:268-269), Meerwarth (1932:5-15), Müller (1938:3-12), Müller (1926:174-176), and Neidhardt (1970:48).

[8]These rates represent an almost complete record of fertility of resident females in both communities; women who left either community for permanent residence elsewhere have been, of course, excluded. Premarital children are included, whether subsequently legitimized or not. (In the Catholic community, 0.8% of all births have been illegitimate, as against 4.2% among Protestants; illegitimate children born to women outside of their commune of residence have been recorded in the local registers and are included in the above figures.) Women with illegitimate children who have remained unmarried amount to only 3% of the number of married women, so that their exclusion does not distort the general picture.

In the graph, fertility rates have been grouped into 20-year periods (versus the 10-year periods shown in Table A-1 in the Appendix), thus leveling fluctuations during the last century that seem to be primarily an expression of the uneven distribution of deaths in childbirth early in marriage, and the resulting low fertility rates of the respective females. Married women who remained childless are included; their occurrence amounts to 5.1% of all Catholic and 5.6% of all Protestant women who were married, and are more or less evenly distributed over the entire time period.

[9]For example, as Cox (1970) states:

It has been shown that fertility depends to some extent on personal attitudes and aspirations, which in turn depend on intelligence and education; it may be influenced, directly or indirectly, by government policy of one kind or another and by economic circumstances. It is not surprising, therefore, that it also varies according to race, religion, occupation, social status, urban or rural domicile and geographical region; the manner of variation in these respects itself varies from country to country.

transfer of the family holding from the older to the younger generation. It would also appear from Table 5 that both World Wars I and II have had a greater effect on the postponement of marriages (cf. Planck 1970:26) among the Catholics than it had on the Protestants.

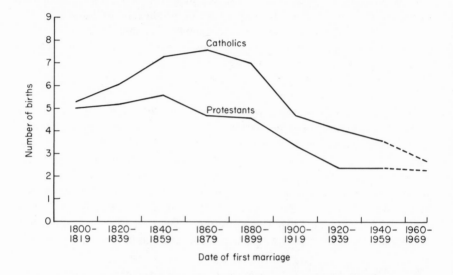

FIGURE 15. Average number of total births per married woman (including premarital births) for 20-year intervals, 1800-1969. Data compiled from local family registers, *Bürgermeisteramt*, and local church records.

Table 5

AVERAGE AGE AT FIRST MARRIAGE: 1820-1971[a]

	CATHOLICS				PROTESTANTS			
	No. of persons		*Aver. age*		*No. of persons*		*Aver. age*	
	M	*F*	*M*	*F*	*M*	*F*	*M*	*F*
1820-1859	45	54	29.9	25.8	81	85	29.1	26.4
1860-1899	61	65	30.0	25.9	123	133	31.1	26.7
1900-1944	59	59	33.4	28.6	121	127	31.3	26.8
1945-1971	33	35	31.8	27.4	60	63	28.5	25.7
Totals	198	213	31.3	26.9	385	408	30.3	26.5

[a]Data compiled from entries in commune family registers.

Table 6

AVERAGE NUMBER OF TOTAL YEARS OF MARRIAGE PER WOMAN
(INCLUDING YEARS BEARING PREMARITAL CHILDREN): 1820-1959[a]

	CATHOLICS		PROTESTANTS	
	No. of women	Aver. years	No. of women	Aver. years
1820–1859	58	17.7	93	21.0
1860–1899	65	19.3	128	20.8
1900–1959	85	18.7	163	20.7
Totals	208	18.6	384	20.8

[a]Data compiled from entries in commune family registers.

The next point which may have an important bearing on fertility rates (especially in populations where more than 90% of all births occur within wedlock) is the length of marriage. Although the age at marriage allows us to determine levels of fecundity, the length of marriage is an indicator of exposure to potential fertility. To get a reliable index for comparative purposes, I counted the number of years of marriage per woman, including the years she bore premarital children, up to the age of 50. The results are summarized in Table 6. Once more the figures demonstrate very clearly that we have not found here a possible explanation for the differences in fertility rates. The marriage patterns are such that Catholic women have not enjoyed a longer period of potential fertility than Protestant women; the general trend is rather in favor of the latter. The shorter, average, marriage durations for Catholic women during the last century may be attributed mainly to the higher percentage among them who died in childbirth or as a result of childbirth-related causes in comparison to the Protestant women (18.7% versus 12.6% of the total of married women), while the same phenomenon in this century seems to reflect the greater effect of both world wars on the marriage patterns of the Catholic community.

Frequently found to correlate with fertility rates are occupation and socioeconomic status (e.g., see Blake 1969:387 & Cox 1970:117). As will be shown in Chapter 6, there are certain differences in the socioeconomic patterning of the two communities for which we might want to establish control. The categories I have established for the purpose of this analysis are not mutually exclusive and should be viewed in the form of a continuum, although each of these categories does represent a cluster of economic activities and levels of social status that render it measurably different from the next category.[10] The results of this

[10]I had separated the Protestant craftsmen according to type of craft practiced and how much land owned, but since there was not a sufficient number of them to render the categories statistically meaningful, I have dealt with them as a single category. Also, remarriages have not been treated as constituting a separate family.

analysis are presented in Figure 16 (see Table A-2 in the Appendix for detailed data). The percentage distributions of fertility within each category show rather conclusively that the slightly different socioeconomic composition can not be held accountable to any significant degree for the intercommunity differences in fertility rates.[11] That is, the relatively larger number of smallholders and crafts-men in the Protestant community does not appreciably influence the overall fertility pattern either way.

As neither marriage patterns nor socioeconomic variables can be held account-able for the differences in fertility rates, we might turn to value orientation as a residual category and examine the attitude of the actors themselves on the question of family size. Within the scope of a series of structured interviews, I asked a total of 73 adults (39 males and 34 females) what they thought the ideal family size should be. The responses generally consisted of the mention of a specific number of children (no numbers were suggested by me), and some additional comments made on a spontaneous basis with which the interviewee justified his or her choice of a particular number. The first part of the responses shows that there is a slight difference in the category of males: Catholic men are more in favor of larger, 4-children families than are Protestant men (6 out of 10

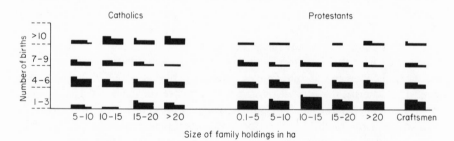
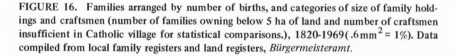

FIGURE 16. Families arranged by number of births, and categories of size of family hold-ings and craftsmen (number of families owning below 5 ha of land and number of craftsmen insufficient in Catholic village for statistical comparisons.), 1820-1969(.6mm^2 = 1%). Data compiled from local family registers and land registers, *Bürgermeisteramt*.

versus 1 out of 10).[12] Both Catholic and Protestant women prefer 2-3 children per family over a larger number at the ratio of 5:1; three women in each community were of the opinion that family size depended entirely on the num-ber of children that happen to come along. When we look at the actual fertility rates, it seems that the Protestants are more or less in tune with their perceived

[11]German pre-war census data have shown that in communities with populations under 2000, fertility rates in families of farmers, agricultural laborers, and craftsmen have tended to be very similar (see Müller 1938:3).

[12]Cf. Planck (1970:207), who finds that persons with stronger ties to their respective churches are less in favor of small families than are those with weaker ties.

ideal; the Catholics seem to be on the way of realizing this "equilibrium" within the current decade.[13]

When we turn to the additional remarks, we can observe to what degree religious considerations enter spontaneously into the thinking of interviewees. Significantly, none of the men in either community thought to mention religious strictures, and neither did any of the Protestant women, yet more than half of the Catholic women did. Some of the latter referred to the teachings and admonitions they had received during their younger years which demanded of them strict noninterference with reproductive processes and promised divine punishment for each possible child they refuse to bear. Others said that having too many children would ruin a woman's health and that God could not possibly want that. One woman told me that the present priest is of the opinion it is better to have only two children than to have more and not be able to take care of them. All of those middle-aged women who themselves have had large families contended that under present conditions they would not have so many children. Today, a mother of six is generally pitied for the burden she has to carry, especially in view of the fact that no servants are available. But I think that despite the expressed preference for small families, neither the Catholics nor the Protestants are using any kind of mechanical or oral contraceptives. Statements from younger men and women such as "Well, when one more comes along there is nothing one can do" led me to believe (as I found this question too delicate to ask of more than a few people) that *coitus interruptus* and voluntary abstinence may still be the most widespread ways in which some measure of birth control is affected. Various remarks from older women to the effect that they were left quite uninformed about processes of procreation by their elders and hardly ever knew when they had conceived or when the baby would be due seem to be sure indications that the rhythm method of birth control has not been practiced in the past. Some men hinted darkly at abortions that they thought had occurred in a few instances, but I have no reliable data on that.

Although references to religious strictures were made by Catholic women only, the one factor most frequently mentioned in both communities was the increasing cost involved in raising children (cf. Neidhardt 1970:48-49). The following comment by a mother of four in the Catholic village indicates the general tenor of similar remarks on this subject.

In the old days everything was very much less complicated. We were 7 siblings and my parents were 10 or 12—well, I find that a little bit too much.

[13]Data from West Germany and from other Western European countries show that this near-equilibrium between ideal and actual family size has generally prevailed among farm families—at most non-farm occupational levels, we find larger discrepancies with couples having fewer children than they think would be ideal (see Blake 1969:387, who also suggests that fertility rates may rise along with improved economic conditions; also Cox 1970:386).

Today, one wants the children to get more education and training; in the old days not everybody learned a trade and many stayed single. All that costs a lot of money; it already starts when they are going to school. There have to be new clothes and shoes, and I know of many examples where each child wears something new, even though the younger sister could very well wear the dresses from the older sister. And then, one wants to keep up a little with the others, too.

Thus, one can perceive a fit between the information on personal attitudes and the long-term trend of local fertility rates. Catholics have been far more conservative, on the average, in their approach to a possible restriction of family size for a longer period of time than the Protestants have been. While the Protestant rate started on a gradual downward trend around the middle of last century, the Catholic rate was still high some 50 years later. Catholic women who married during the period 1900–1909 had 3.5 more children, on the average, than Protestant women married during the same period. Only World War I affected a dramatic decline in the Catholic birth rate.[14]

It is important, however, that we view these local trends against the background of national trends. Accompanied by changing socioeconomic conditions, the second half of the eighteenth century saw the beginnings of a tremendous population increase in Germany and other European countries, which was sustained by an increase in agricultural productivity (the "agricultural revolution"). A gradual decrease in mortality rates, primarily infant mortality, mostly as a result of improvements in hygienic conditions and general health; an increase in the number of marriages occasioned by the lifting of patrimonial marriage restrictions (see Bolte and Kappe 1966:97); and the availability of new economic opportunities resulted in an increase in crude birth rates as well as an increase in fertility rates per married woman. This latter type of increase may be seen as the result of a continuance of the "traditional" reproductive behavior—producing as many offspring as the health of the parents would allow—despite higher survival rates of both children and mothers. The local data certainly indicate that a significant part of the increase in the average fertility per married woman can be attributed—especially in the Catholic population—to a decrease of the number of mothers who died of puerperal fever or other childbirth-related causes. (It was not until the 1920s, however, that this particular mortality rate declined to practically zero, and it has also been since then that the present low level of infant mortality became an established pattern.)

With the gradual introduction of improvements in the three-field system and the corresponding change to more intensive cultivation methods, more people

---

[14] In the Catholic village, about 60% of all adult males were in the wartime Armed Forces; 14% of those men did not return. The corresponding figures for the Protestant commune are about 50% and 11%.

could be absorbed to work the land, and an increasing need for services also offered more job opportunities in town and city, but a sizable portion of the population emigrated to colonizing areas of the world. Only around 1860, with the coming of the industrial revolution to Germany, did a stepped-up migration to the cities begin. Fifteen years later, in 1875, the nation's crude birth rate peaked at 40.6 live births per 1000 of population, and then went on a gradual downward trend.[15] Studies that aim to explain the timing of the fluctuations of birth rates over the last 200 years take into consideration a wide range of empirical observations, especially in the area of socioeconomic change. Although all of these factors are no doubt significantly related to the problem, "Demographers do not know exactly why or how fertility rates have declined."[16]

Although it may not be possible to show conclusively why the Protestant birth rate (in our community) declined when it did, we might at least consider some of the factors that may have exerted some pressure on the demographic structure. Thus, there seems to have been a growing need for cash to buy improved agricultural machines and implements, as well as certain manufactured consumer goods. There was a beginning scarcity of hired help brought about by the lure of higher wages as well as economic and personal independence in the cities (see Weber 1892), which, in turn, tended to increase the workload of farmers' wives. There also was the demand for higher levels of agricultural productivity; emphasizing a more profit-oriented view of family farming. In short, many farmers may have become increasingly aware that a large number of children not only meant an excessive drain on the work potential of their wives, but also a burden on the finances of the family enterprise itself. The Protestants apparently responded to these pressures by reducing their birth rates much sooner than the Catholics did. The peak years of Catholic fertility are associated with marriages formed during the 1870s and 1880s, and it is tempting to see a connection between this phenomenon and the *Kulturkampf* which was waged by Bismarck against (political) Catholicism during this period; historical sources indicate, however, that the population in Württemberg was little affected by this struggle, the king having compromised with the demands of the Catholic Church prior to 1864.[17] It is a fact, however, that the Catholics have always been aware of their minority status within a region or state whose population is made up of more Protestants than

[15]See Bolte and Kappe (1966:131, Table 1). Note also Table 4, which lists the average number of children per completed marriage, 1899–1960, and can therefore be compared with my fertility table: the nationwide rates are slightly below those of the Protestants in this study.

[16]Stycos (1969:421), who is here primarily referring to the predictive value of the European demographic experience as applied to presently developing countries. For a similar view, see Cox (1970:382-385). Also, see a discussion of population waves, natural periodicity, and economic factors in terms of predictive theory by Keyfitz (1972).

[17]See Hermelink (1949:386-391,425) and Gönner (1971:439-440).

Catholics, a situation generally referred to as "we, who live in Diaspora." Thus, it is quite likely that this minority status was stressed from the pulpit, and although the Protestants never waged any campaign aimed at birth control, one might perceive certain parallels between the position of the Catholics at that time and the reactions of some of the less developed nations toward the plans of some of the more developed nations today.

In summary, an explanation for this differential behavior pattern in view of the highly similar setting in which the two populations find themselves is impossible without giving priority to the difference in religious affiliation. The long-enduring normative behavior of the Catholics has mirrored the pervading influence of official church doctrine, which, through the admonitions of the priest, brought home to the villagers that any sexual intercourse was a mortal sin if it wilfully negated the possibility of procreation. These values, which were once accepted as moral guidelines by the villagers, have gradually lost their unchallenged position. This has come about through developments in the larger society and through the shifting, or seemingly equivocal, position of the Church herself. Although procreation is still postulated as the primary goal of married life, unlimited childbirth without regard to human and social consequences is certainly no longer propagated. While Luther's views on this subject were not much different from those of the Catholics, the Protestant Church today no longer places procreation as the primary goal of marriage and has generally left more room for individual decision-making as to the desirability of having children (see Bolte and Kappe 1966:114-117; cf. Mackenroth 1953:349).

Migration Patterns among the Local Population

To round out the demographic picture, we might take a brief look at population movements in the two communities. Figure 17 shows the respective population increases and decreases, taking 1840 as a starting point. As we can see, by 1971 both communities were considerably below their 1840 population levels. The one major break in the generally downward trend was only temporary, occasioned by an influx of refugees in the period following World War II. Today, however, the number of former refugees who have remained in the two communities amounts to only 3–4% of the total population.

As might be inferred from the data on fertility rates, this overall population loss is not due to a deficiency in birth rates, but rather to outmigration. Between 1871 and 1939, the population of the Protestant commune declined by 25%, but with the natural increases (excess of births over deaths, adjusted for war losses) which amounted to 32%, the loss due to outmigration came to 57%. The corresponding figures for the Catholic village are 13%, 55%, and 68% (figures published by the Bureau of Statistics, Stuttgart). These figures point to a factor that the graph does not reveal: While the Catholic population was still increasing

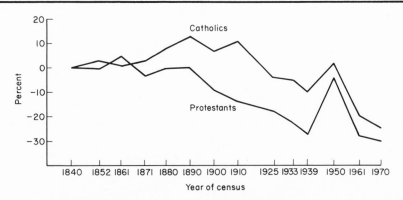

FIGURE 17. Population increases and decreases between 1840 and 1970, in percentages. (Protestants: *n* equals 656 in 1840 and 396 in 1970. Catholics: *n* equals 350 in 1840 and 264 in 1970.) Data from Baden-Württemberg, Statistisches Landesamt 1953, 1965, 1972a.

and the Protestant population had started to decline, outmigration was taking place from both communities at about the same rate.

Throughout the period here under investigation (and no doubt before), there have always been noninheriting sons and daughters who left the village of their birth. Apart from those who married into nearby communities or took up positions as hired help where they could find it, local records show that there had been a steady trickle of emigrants to colonizing countries, especially North America. However, by the turn of the century outmigrations increasingly involved a move from the village to the city. The push for this stepped-up outmigration was partly supplied by the decline, starting in the 1880s, in the prices that the farmer could fetch for his products, and also by the untenable position of many a small craftsman who could no longer compete with manufactured goods that reached the village from the city. The pull was due to rapidly increasing job opportunities in manufacturing and service industries. The records show that those who had learned a trade would mostly gravitate toward jobs in shops and factories; the majority of farmers' sons found employment as streetcar conductors, or with the government-run postal and railroad services. Along with a uniform which conferred a certain aura of authority, the latter positions also brought considerable job security.

During the 1960s, outmigration continued to effect a decline in population levels. A glance at the 1971 population pyramids presented in Figure 18 reveals a substantial underrepresentation of the 20–29 age group, which corresponds with the relative scarcity of jobs outside of family farming.[18] A further underrepresentation exists in the category of females from age 30 to 39 (I shall discuss this

[18]The percentages of women in this age group are 8.3% in the Protestant commune and 5.8% in the Catholic commune, as against 14% for Baden-Württemberg as a whole (for the latter, see Baden-Württemberg, Statistisches Landesamt 1970b:24).

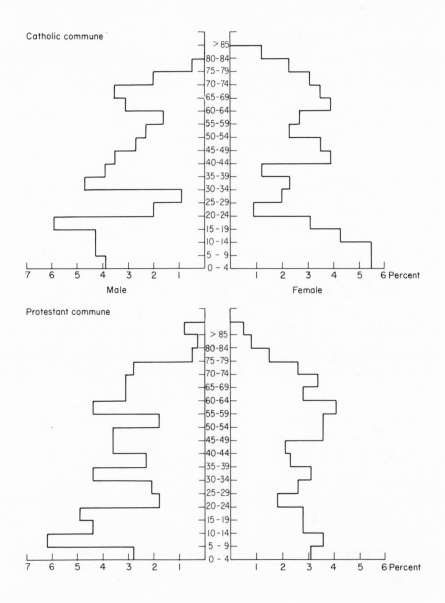

FIGURE 18.   Population pyramids of resident population, 1971. Data from Author's census, January-February 1971.

factor in connection with the plight of the Catholic bachelors in Chapter 7). It seems unlikely, however, that the long-term trend in population decline will continue. When more jobs within commuting distance are made available, more young people will likely decide to stay in the village and possibly build new homes on their families' land, and found families of their own. This has not yet occurred and it will probably never occur to the extent seen in villages closer to large industrial areas. Although some of the local teenagers can not wait to get out of the village with its dearth of youth-oriented entertainment and relative lack of privacy, others profess that they would prefer to stay if they had only a decent job.[19] Their comments made it clear that the attractions of the city with its offerings of anonymity and entertainment are now counterbalanced by the enjoyment of clean country air and the freedom from traffic snarls.

[19] Ulrich Planck conducted a study in 1968 in which he asked a sample of young men and women living in rural communities between the ages of 17 and 28 as to where they would prefer to live, and where they would prefer to work. Here is a summary of the combinations preferred by the interviewees (1970:105):

RESIDENCE	WORK	PERCENTAGE
Rural	Rural	47
Rural	Urban	23
Urban	Urban	13
Suburban	Urban	12
Urban	Rural	5

5

Land Tenure and Inheritance Patterns

Land Tenure

It has only been for the last 120 years that the local farmers have held title of ownership to their land. Before that they were but tenants, although tenants with a contractual right to almost perpetual occupancy. In much of Hohenlohe, peasants held tenure to their holdings in the form of *Erbzinslehen*, or hereditary leaseholds, under a written contract with the landlord. The lease-holder enjoyed the practically irrevocable usufruct of land and accessories and had the right to designate an heir from among his descendants or other relatives to continue that tenure. The holding had to be left undivided to one heir only, and the leaseholder was prohibited from taking up mortgages, from changing the composition of the holding, or from selling it either whole or in part, unless he had express permission from the landlord to circumvent any of the above rules, usually in exchange for payment of an appropriate fee. The only way in which a leaseholder could lose his rights during his tenure was through gross negligence in fulfilling his obligations, namely, if he deliberately and without sufficient cause failed to pay his rent, or if he sold the holding. But even then his rights were safeguarded under statute law, until a court of law had found him guilty of the charges (Schremmer 1963:24). The conditions under which Hohenlohe peasants held their land resembled those of other areas where "the right of inheritance of the tenants was so well established that their title came to resemble full ownership with a perpetual encumbrance [Dovring 1965:159]."

Not all of the land that belonged to a peasant's holding was necessarily part of the leasehold, however; usually, some of it was his own. This land consisted of

73

individual fields (*walzende Stücke*) which either had never been part of the leasehold, or had been released from its confines with the consent of the landlord after payment of a fee. Although these parcels of land were still subject to taxes and tithes levied by landlord and church, the peasant could mortgage or sell them at will. An investigation into conditions of land tenure in 32 *Gemeinden* in the area of this study revealed that in the period from 1699 to 1750 about 20% of the land area per holding (not including small holdings) consisted of these *walzende Stücke* (Schremmer 1963:182-188). Their existence accounted for most of the buying and selling of land that took place before the peasants became "liberated" from patrimonial bonds. With the dissolution of these bonds, title to the leasehold passed from the landlord to the leaseholder. It might be inserted here that the wife of the leaseholder held an active interest in the holding. Since the early Middle Ages, wives of peasants have enjoyed some form or other of joint tenure with their husbands.[1] Locally, about 95% of the marriage contracts written over the last 150 years stipulate either one of two forms of joint ownership of property.

For reasons explained in Chapter 2, the transfer of legal ownership of land in Hohenlohe took place several decades later than in Old-Württemberg, and in contrast to what had happened there, the region of Hohenlohe did not experience a similar increase in the sale of land or of entire holdings, nor did so

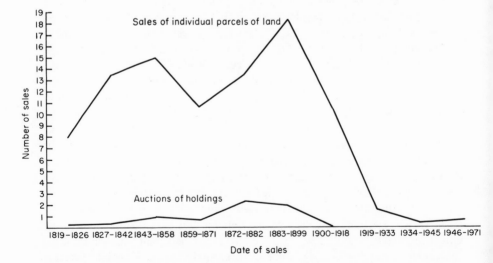

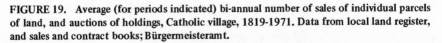

FIGURE 19. Average (for periods indicated) bi-annual number of sales of individual parcels of land, and auctions of holdings, Catholic village, 1819-1971. Data from local land register, and sales and contract books; Bürgermeisteramt.

[1]See Planck (1964:78). The two forms of joint ownership referred to in the next sentence are: *landrechtliche Errungenschaftsgesellschaft* and *allgemeine Gütergemeinschaft*.

many of the farmers get deeply into debt (Schremmer 1963:131-143). Figure 19 is based on the land records of the Catholic village and shows the average number of individual sales of parcels of land as well as the average number of holdings sold piecemeal at public auctions (both computed on a bi-annual basis) from 1819 to 1971. A public auction (*Verkauf im öffentlichen Aufstrich*) was either conducted by the owner himself, or by a land broker. Whether a farmer conducted the auction himself or whether he sold his holding to a broker depended primarily on how urgently he needed the money because payment by other than brokers was usually rendered in several installments. Brokers were mainly Jewish merchants, and occasionally publicans from around the area. Auctions were supervised by the mayor and councilmen. The individual pieces of land thus acquired by local farmers were often the subject of subsequent trading, with the primary aim to align them with the existing holdings as best as was possible.

Most of the holdings put up for auction were small, but occasionally there might be a larger one. Some sales were conducted to pay off debts, although there were only three cases of bankruptcy during the last century and none, so far, in the present one. Other sales were conducted by families who wanted to leave the village. In addition to holdings which were auctioned off piecemeal, there were also some which were sold intact to a new owner. As the graph shows, land sales after World War I fell to an insignificant level and have remained there ever since. The effects of two wars, of inflations, and currency reforms have made the farmers very reluctant to dispose of the family real estate. In the Protestant commune, however, land sales have picked up a little during the last decade, mainly because of the piecemeal sale of three holdings by persons who had just inherited them. Almost all of this land has been bought by local farmers who, in accordance with the law, get preference over non-farmers. A novel situation is the fact that there is an increasing land area that is worked on a relatively short-term lease basis. This land belongs to pensioners or others who have given up working all or part of their holdings and are leasing it to farmers in or around the community.

Inheritance Patterns

The custom of impartible inheritance has not changed with the abrogation of patrimonial bonds. There were only three cases in which holdings were divided between two or three heirs, all of them occurring in the Catholic village around the middle of the last century. The written "sales and transfer contracts," which legally transfer the holding from the older to the younger generation, have changed remarkably little in language or content over the last 150 years. As an illustration to my description of inheritance practices and patterns, I have translated a medium-length transfer contract:

Place: *Catholic Village.* **Date:** *January 27, 1828.*
Known all men by these presents.
*The **Bürger** and **Bauer** Joseph Härtert and his wife Anna Maria, with the
satisfaction of their three children, sell their existing **Bauerngut** the way they
have possessed it, and the way it is marked off, with no exceptions, to their
oldest daughter Katharina Härtertin (husband of Josef Knörzer), for the sum
of 3,000 florins, under the following conditions.*

1. That the purchaser deduct 1,000 fl from the Kaufschilling *of 3,000 fl as
her inheritance portion or dowry. On St. Jacob's Day of 1828, she has to
pay to her sister Anna Maria 1,000 fl in cash, or pay interest at 3 percent
from that date. On St. Jacob's Day of 1829, she has to pay her youngest
sister Barbara 500 fl, and on St. Jacob's Day of 1832, the other 500 fl, in
cash, or pay interest at 3 percent from those dates, wherewith each sister has
received 1,000 fl as dowry, and the purchase price is paid in full.*
*2. With the purchase the purchaser receives all of the existing vessels and
utensils and all movables which are not here withheld; further, one pair of
oxen, two cows, two calves, six sheep, grain as much as is needed for bread
and for seed until August 24; the seller withholds the grain which is still on
hand after August 24, 1828, the wine now on hand, linen, a casket, and a
fattened steer. The purchaser further receives a furnished nuptial bed, 4
cases, 4 sheets, 4 tablecloths, and 4 towels.*
*3. Each of the other two sisters receives an already existing furnished bed,
4 cases, 4 sheets, 4 tablecloths, and 4 towels; further, one piece of cloth, 12
dishes and napkins. When the youngest sister marries, the purchaser has to
furnish her a cloth cap, a black woolen skirt, and a pair of shoes, as her dress
of honor.*
*4. The purchaser is held to order a set of medium-quality household uten-
sils for each of her sisters for 25 fl each and to celebrate their weddings for
one and one-half days, or to pay 30 fl, at the discretion of the sisters.*
5. The seller has to pay all taxes and obligations up to July 1.
*6. As long as the two sisters remain single, they shall retain the right of
entry and exit in the house and the* Dennenkammer *[a room in the upstairs
of the house] for their use, and in days of illness they have to be fed by the
possessor of the holding for four weeks free of charge.*
*7. The purchaser is held to maintain her parents for the rest of their lives
and to let them live in the* Stubenkammer *[room in the downstairs of the
house]: but in case the parents cannot exist under the prevailing conditions,
the possessor of the holding has to furnish the following annuity: 19 simry
[421 liters] of rye; 19 simry of husked spelt; 100 pounds of pork; 6 pounds
of sausages; 1 measure of lard; 150 eggs; 1 measure of barley; 1 stick of flax;
one-third of the fruit and cider; one sheep and one lamb to be kept free; 8 fl.
for a rainy day; one-fourth of the vegetables; the use of one-fourth of the*

summer garden; and wood, fat, salt, and utensils as needed. Should one of the parents die, one-half of the annuity will be canceled, except the lard will remain with 8 small measures, and eggs 100.

8. The parents have to pay for their burial, and, should they be unable to do so, the three sisters will share in the costs.

9. Whatever the parents leave in the way of money, linen, clothing, and bedding will be divided by the three sisters into three equal parts.

10. The purchaser is held to maintain her father's brother Michael Härtert for the rest of his life, to clothe him according to his status, to care for him in days of illness and in days of health, to let him sleep in the Dennenkammer, *and to have him buried after his death according to Christian custom; whereas Michael Härtert is held: to work for the purchaser or the possessor of the holding as long as he can and to the best of his abilities, and to leave them his possessions so that nobody can claim anything from him after his death. For the strict adherence to this maintenance contract signs by his own hands*

MICHAEL HÄRTERT

Everything true without deceit and cunning, the above contract was read clearly and for constant adherence signed by their own hands

Seller	*Purchaser*
JOSEPH HÄRTERT	*KATHARINA HÄRTERTIN*

Authenticated
Mayor Goll

A "sales and transfer contract" such as the one preceding brings out the peculiar legal arrangements surrounding the transmission of family farms under provisions of impartible inheritance of real estate. The holding is "sold" by the parents to one of their children in a legal transaction termed the *Kindskauf.* In the above case, both parents were alive at the time of transfer, but there have also been cases in which one, or both, were deceased. To determine what the prevailing pattern has been, let us have a look at the point in the family cycle at which these transfers have usually taken place.

During patrimonial times it was reportedly "extremely rare" for a transfer to take place *after* the death of the *Altbauer.*[2] The local records indicate, however, that this pattern has undergone some change. Figure 20 shows the breakdown of 281 cases of transfers over the last 115 years, with a division into 3 time periods. When we look at Categories C and D, which represent cases in which the holding

---

[2] According to Schremmer (1963:34). Incidentally, I found in a number of cases that the holding was transferred only a few days, or even hours, before the death of the *Altbauer.* (*Altbauer* translates into 'old farmer', so-called if he has an 'adult son', the *Jungbauer*, who is waiting for his inheritance. The female forms are *Altbäuerin* and *Jungbäuerin.*)

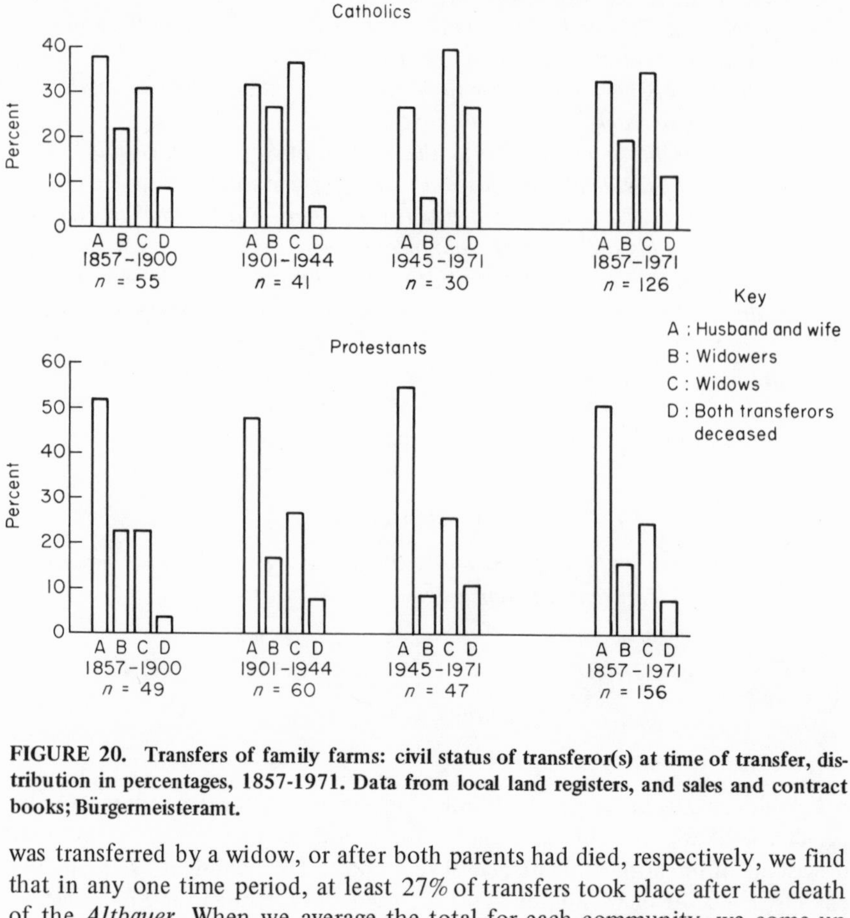

FIGURE 20. Transfers of family farms: civil status of transferor(s) at time of transfer, distribution in percentages, 1857-1971. Data from local land registers, and sales and contract books; Bürgermeisteramt.

was transferred by a widow, or after both parents had died, respectively, we find that in any one time period, at least 27% of transfers took place after the death of the *Altbauer*. When we average the total for each community, we come up with 33% for the Protestants, and 47% for the Catholics—a noteworthy difference of 14%. This pattern is repeated in Category A; in the Protestant community, transfers with both parents still alive show a 19% higher frequency of occurrence than among the Catholics. The differences between Categories B and D are much smaller and amount to only four percentage points in both.

What are the implications of these differences? Are the Catholics more "stubborn," do they like to hang on to their holdings longer and transfer ownership to the younger generation later than the Protestants? A look at a set of interrelated factors indicates that although there is a pattern among Catholics to transfer ownership of the family farm at a later date in life than the Protestants, they do not necessarily enjoy a longer period of individual tenure. The first set of data which we need to demonstrate this case gives us some information on the age of parents at the time of transfer. The figures in Table 7 show that between 1857

Table 7

PERCENTAGE OF PARENTS AGED 66 AND OVER AT TIME OF TRANSFER[a]

	CATHOLICS				PROTESTANTS			
	1857–1900	*1901–1944*	*1945–1971*	*1857–1971*	*1857–1900*	*1901–1944*	*1945–1971*	*1857–1971*
Altbauer (married or widowed)	48	67	60	57	42	46	53	47
Altbäuerin (widowed)	18	33	50	32	18	31	67	38
Totals	38	54	55	47	37	42	57	45

[a] Data compiled from entries in local sales and contract books (*Verkaufs- und Kontraktbücher*), and in family registers; *Bürgermeisteramt*.

and 1971, the proportion of *Altbauern* who were 66 years of age or older at the time of transfer is 10% larger among the Catholics than it is among the Protestants. Adding to this the widows to form a grand total narrows the gap, however, especially because of a reverse situation in the 1945 to 1971 period.[3]

The second set of data relates to the age of the heir at the time of transfer, as well as to his or her age at marriage—marriage and inheritance are closely interrelated factors as they have occurred simultaneously in over 90% of the cases. When we check the demographic data contained in Table 5, we find that, on the average, Catholic men are 1-year older at the time of their first marriage than the Protestant men. This is paralleled by the information we get from Table 8, in which we find an overall difference of 8% between the percentage of men in each community who were 31 years of age or older at the time they inherited the holding. However, the average length of tenure per farmer (not including those who died before the holding was transferred) is fairly close: 35.2 years in the Protestant community, and 35.7 years in the Catholic community. In sum, the average starting and finishing points along the age scale are different, but the average length of individual tenure is not. This difference in the time schedules is apparently maintained by a self-perpetuating process: Most men do not want to give up their tenure until they have at least reached the age (other things being equal) at which their fathers transferred ownership to them. It is difficult to speculate, however, how this intercommunity difference in time schedules originally came about.

Table 8

PERCENTAGE OF SONS 31 YEARS OF AGE OR OLDER
AT TIME OF INHERITANCE[a]

	CATHOLICS	PROTESTANTS
1857–1900	56	51
1901–1944	81	67
1945–1971	63	56
1857–1971	67	59

[a]Data compiled from entries in local sales and contract books, and in family registers; *Bürgermeisteramt*.

[3]There are two factors which may at least partially account for this phenomenon. First, some of the late transfers have occurred when widows waited for their sons to come home from a prisoner-of-war camp (half of the transfers by widows in the Protestant community fall into this category). Second, more women are now surviving their husbands than was the case 100 years ago (see Figure 31).

In terms of long-range trends, there has been a gradual increase in the age of the *Altbauer* at which he transfers the family holding. To a certain extent, this may be seen as a reflection of the gradual increase in longevity (see Figure 31, p. 117). Since the 1950s, another factor is entering into the picture: the length of time between the transfer of control of the family farm, and the transfer of ownership rights. In the past, these two events have ordinarily occurred simultaneously with the signing of the sales and transfer contract, although in some cases the heir may have enjoyed prior usufruct of certain parcels of land in recognition of his long service and to make the waiting period a little easier. Since the 1950s, however, leasing the farm to the prospective heir has become increasingly popular, and about 15% of the local farmers have entered into such contracts. (This fact does not bias the above figures, however, because transfers of titles in cases in which leasing arrangements had been operative have not yet taken place.) There are certain advantages to this arrangement over the standard practice: the heir does not have to work on the farm as a dependent until it is deeded to him, and he is free to channel his energies into managerial tasks as well. The *Altbauer*, on the other hand, retains the title of ownership and the sense of security and satisfaction that is inherent in such a position. In addition, he gets some income from the lease (usually a nominal amount below the going rate). He continues to contribute his labor, but the *Jungbauer* is now in charge of planning and budget. (Ordinarily, a *Jungbauer* does not get much money from his elders, and several of the younger farmers told me stories of how they spirited away bags of wheat which they then sold at the warehouse to have a little extra pocket money.) As far as I could determine, parties to such a lease seemed to be generally satisfied with the arrangements.[4]

The holding is transferred to one (principal) heir, the *Anerbe*; the claims of the co-heirs, or *Miterben* (in most cases the siblings of the principal heir), are usually settled in the form of cash payments. But, before we turn to a discussion of the financial arrangements, let us look at who is usually chosen as the principal heir. All informants are agreed that the local custom has been to give preference to first-born sons, but this has never been handled as an inflexible rule. In the sample contract above, the holding went to the oldest daughter because there were no surviving sons.[5] Only in a comparatively few cases did the holding go to a daughter even though there were sons. Figures 21 and 22 provide a breakdown of the relationships of 291 heirs to their predecessors over the last 115 years. We

---

[4]See Planck's (1964:136-140) figures on nationwide frequencies of leasing contracts and his discussion of general conditions.

[5]The French Civil Code introduced after 1803 did not recognize the customary law of limited inheritance. However, it did not prohibit undivided transfer of holdings, although it made it contingent on the compensation of co-heirs. Not until 1930 did Württemberg make provisions for impartible inheritance in its statutory laws, when it created the *Gesetz über das Anerbenrecht* of February 14, 1930. The provisions for the order of eligibility of heirs were as follows: (1) All of the children resulting from a marriage, with legitimized and

can readily see that first-born sons, together with only sons, have formed the largest single category of principal heirs during any of the periods shown in these graphs. Next in line are brothers of the first-born, who have inherited in 13 and 15% of the total number of cases, respectively. This has occurred when the first-born was either physically or mentally handicapped, or when there was a relatively young father and the first-born decided to seek his fortune elsewhere rather than wait for the holding until he was in his late 30s (first-born in this context means "surviving" first-born). Overall, 78% of principal heirs in the Catholic community, and 74% in the Protestant community, have been sons. (If we disregard the cases in which relatives other than children were the principal heirs—7% among Catholics, and 2% among Protestants—the percentage of sons amounts to 83, and 75, respectively.) The frequency with which daughters were chosen over sons amounts to 13 and 12%, respectively. According to various entries in the local records, some of these choices were made when the holding was in debt and an infusion of capital was badly needed. Ordinarily, a son-in-law could be expected to bring in a larger sum of money than a daughter-in-law. Categories A_3 and B_3 in the graphs reflect the intercommunity differences in

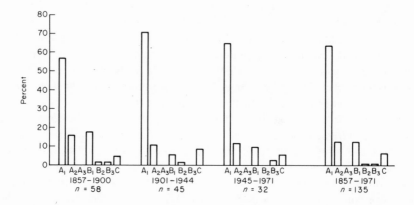

FIGURE 21. Percentage distribution of heirs (*Anerben*) according to kinship status vis-à-vis the transferor(s), Catholic village, 1857-1971. (A_1: oldest and only sons; A_2: second through youngest son; A_3: sons as only child; B_1: daughters with brothers alive; B_2: Daughters without brothers; B_3: daughters as only child; C: relatives other than sons and daughters.) Data from local land register, and sales and contract books: Bürgermeisteramt.

adopted children enjoying equal rights, but with the oldest son enjoying preference to become the principal heir, followed by subsequent sons, and then by daughters; (2) the spouse of the deceased; (3) the father; (4) the mother; (5) siblings and their children; (6) half-siblings and their children [Adapted from Röhm 1957:App. 6].

These provisons for eligibility were only insignificantly changed (at least as far as order of succession was concerned, not in regard to the "racial" and other qualities of a successor to a family farm) in the *Reichserbhofgesetz* of September 29, 1933 (see Dölle 1939:382-406).

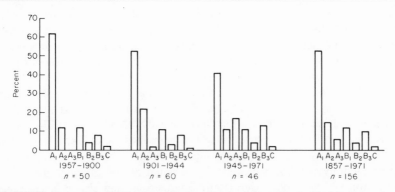

FIGURE 22. Percentage distribution of heirs (*Anerben*) according to kinship status vis-a-vis the transferor(s), Protestant commune, 1857-1971. (Key and sources: see Figure 21.)

family size: in the Catholic village, only in 1% of the total cases was the heir an only child, as against 16% in the Protestant community.

The last category in the graphs, Category C, is made up of cases in which the holding was transferred to relatives other than sons or daughters. This has happened when a marriage has remained childless, when the principal heir never married, or when the children had died—either before or after having had children of their own—in the latter case, illegitimate children. Following is a breakdown of the heirs in this category and their relationship to the transferor(s); i.e., in the case of transferring couples, to either the male or female spouse (numerals in brackets refer to the number of cases): Sister, of unmarried brother (2); brother, of male (1); brother, of female (1); sister's son, of female (2); sister's son, of male (1); brother's son, of male (1); son's son (1); daughter's son (1). In some of the above cases, the transfer price that had to be paid by the heir was higher than what was usually asked of sons and daughters. There were also a few instances in which a holding was sold to a person without kin ties to the transferor(s), but with provisions for the maintenance of the latter on their former holding.

For obvious reasons, the "sales" or "transfer price" of the holding has always been set below the actual market value. In the eighteenth century, this transfer price reportedly averaged between one-fourth and one-third below the recorded estimated value of the holding, although the generally out-of-date nature of those official estimates would indicate a somewhat lower price ratio (see Schremmer 1963:35). In checking prices obtained at land sales around the middle of the last century and comparing these with contemporary transfer prices, I found that the latter then ranged between 20 and 30% of the market value of the holding. In subsequent transfers, these prices usually did not rise in proportion to the increased land values. Today, the average transfer price ranges from 5% to around 25% of the current market value of the holding. Invariably, prices in the upper ranges have been set up to cover existing debts.

However, without adjustments these prices are not strictly comparable, as the conditions attached to them vary from case to case. The price itself is usually reduced by the amount that the heir may deduct as his or her inheritance portion, or dowry. This amount varies from 10% to 90% of the transfer price, depending, in part, on how many co-heirs have to be satisfied. Of course, the more siblings there are, the smaller those individual dowry shares will be. These shares may be apportioned equally, but they may also take into account individual needs and certain benefits that have already been received. The parents usually claim part of the transfer price for themselves. Since World War I, it has become customary that the parents require the principal heir to pay them a modest monthly pension, which usually does not exceed the price that can be fetched for an 8-week-old piglet. (Retired farmers are now also receiving a small old-age pension from the state.) The money which the principal heir owes to parents and siblings is usually paid off in several installments and is subject to interest rates which may range from 2% to 5%, unless no interest is requested. Parents and siblings also have the right to safeguard their money by requiring the principal heir to take up a mortgage, which in fact has often been done. Sometimes there are additional safeguards, such as the inclusion of a provision in the contract that requires the principal heir to pay substantial sums of money to his siblings in case he sells the holding within 10 years after inheritance. One somewhat unusual provision of recent date required the heir to pay a large sum of money to his father in case he had no offspring within 5 years after inheritance (I am happy to report that this provision did not go into effect). When we now look at the net transfer price to be paid by the principal heir in terms of average annual profits from farming, we find a range from as little as 6 months' profit to as much as 4 years' profit. The latter occurs mainly in cases in which the holding is heavily mortgaged.

The parents and single siblings retain the right to live in the house in designated rooms (there never have been separate houses for retired parents in this area), the siblings until they get married and the parents for the rest of their lives. The parents also have to be maintained by the heir (siblings only as long as they work on the holding) and "in case the parents cannot exist under the prevailing conditions," or, as put in another contract, "if the sellers do not wish to dine at the table of the buyer anymore," the contract stipulates in detail the amount of produce that has to be furnished instead. As a rule, these lists are still as detailed today as they were 100 years ago, down to the daily quart of milk for the dog. These obligations are usually summarized in terms of their monetary values, that is, so much for the right to live in the house and so much for the produce and other items that have to be furnished. This constitutes a lien on the holding which has to be taken into account if the holding is sold at a later date. At such time, the extent of the lien is then determined by multiplying the value of the annuity times the number of years of life expectancy of the particular beneficiary.

Contracts may also contain provisions that regulate a variety of daily activities and minor obligations. For example, they may stipulate who is allowed to bathe or to wash clothes when and where and in whose bathtub or kettle, where certain items may be stored, what the cooking arrangements should be in case the parents decide to cook their own food, how often and how far the principal heir has to take his parents for a ride (this provision was usually confined to holdings that owned a chaise; in one case the heir was under obligation to "furnish whatever vehicle would be requested, including the driver, at any time, without fail, and without charge"), and who would have to repair the sewing machine used by the whole family in case it broke down (namely, the principal heir).

In view of the fact that old and young live under one roof and that there are no separate households, these and similar provisions are undoubtedly included to prevent, or at least forestall, anticipated friction. It is generally considered important that everything is put down in writing. For example, when a quarrel over an intrafamily loan was taken to court during my stay, one of the farmers remarked: "The minute I found out that nothing had been written, I knew there was going to be trouble." Of course, an intimate knowledge of the parties involved seems a prerequisite for such a prediction. After all, whether or not there is going to be friction, or rather, to what extent, depends as much on the overall feelings of family members toward each other as it does on what is, or is not, written. On the whole, relationships between old and young, and between the principal heir and his siblings, are probably most tense around the time that the transfer of the family holding takes place. The local records allow some insights into the nature and extent of these intrafamily problems.

Initially, there is the period when the designated heir to the holding starts to get restless as he passes into his 30s and his father does not seem ready to step down. If he has a girl who has promised to marry him, he is liable to get even more restless. If everything goes well and the *Altbauer* decides that the time has come to relinquish control, a family council will be convened to work out the details of the transfer arrangements, sometimes including the prospective inlaws. After agreement on the various points has been reached, the parties to the contract will set a date with the mayor's office for the reading and signing of the contract. There are a number of contracts in the records—none of recent date, however—which bear the notation that signing did not take place because of an outbreak of renewed quarreling. Obviously, some of the agreements that were reached in family councils were not to everyone's lasting satisfaction. These particular contracts were usually signed 2 or 3 years later, with or without alterations. There are other contracts in which alterations or amendments were inserted after the respective contract had been in force for some time, such as reducing the number of free meals to which a working sibling was entitled while he or she was ill, or the pledge of parents that they would work to the best of their abilities and without claim for compensation. There are cases in which a father has taken a son to court for nonpayment of the transfer price, or for falling behind in the payments. In one case a father forced his son into a bankruptcy auction and only the fact that no serious buyers could be found kept the land from being auctioned off. There have also been complaints of siblings against the principal heir, mostly about lack of compliance with various provisions in the transfer contract regarding their rights in the house. The most colorful case is that of a blacksmith–farmer who sold his holding to another blacksmith (probably no kin to him). These two fought a protracted war over many small but irritating items, such as changing locks on the door of the seller's room, or not allowing him to store his firewood in or around the house or yard. Although firewood was provided for in the contract, a place where it might be stored had not been stipulated; and, while the buyer referred stubbornly to the "nonprovision" in the contract, the seller pleaded with the village council: "Am I to store my firewood in the clouds?"

Of course, these are only cases that reached the village or district court; we may presume that there have been many inheritance-related quarrels handled within the family. On the other hand, it is also reasonable to assume that not every family has experienced significant problems in this regard (at least this is the impression I got after interviewing a number of people on this subject). Even so, the atmosphere surrounding inheritance procedures is highly charged, as almost everyone will admit. When I caught a few glimpses of the intrafamily, small-scale power struggles in preparation for inheritance arrangements, some of the old cases in the records seemed to come alive. There is, however, a new element which has entered into the inheritance picture: the problem experienced by some farmers of getting one of their children to take over the farm rather than turn to a non-farm occupation. This has prompted a general attitude among the young—especially if there is no potential competition from siblings—which culminates in the phrase: "If he doesn't do it my way, he can keep it." For those who are in line to inherit a farm of relatively small size, or one that needs a heavy outlay of capital to bring buildings and machinery up to par, the decision to earn one's living in some other field than farming often seems to be the only sensible one to make, even though many of the older people may bemoan the fact that with their withdrawal from active work there will be no renewal of ties between their heirs and the family land.

6

The Socioeconomic Structure

The two most important factors governing the socioeconomic structure of the rural community are the size of agricultural holdings and the occupations of heads of households. Most of the households in the two communities of this study have been integral parts of family farms; local land registers and published statistics show that up to the Second World War, the total number of households equaled the total number of agricultural holdings.[1] However, in some of these households the major source of income was not derived from agriculture, but from the specific craft practiced by the head of household. Furthermore, after the Second World War, we find that some households are not attached to agricultural holdings. A knowledge of both of these factors is therefore essential for the construction of the complete picture. Both size of holdings and occupations of heads of households are presented in graphic form for selected years in Figures 23–26.

In the discussion that follows, I shall first concentrate on conditions as they existed around the turn of the century, taking the data published for 1907 as a point of departure. Where possible, conditions during the last century will also

[1]"Agricultural holding" (*land- und forstwirtschaftlicher Betrieb*) is officially defined as "each holding whose proprietor or manager is utilizing an area of at least 0.5 ha, wholly or in part, as tillage, meadow, pasture, forest, fishpond, garden, nursery, orchard, or vineyard. It is immaterial whether the proprietor operates the holding on a full-time or part-time basis; and whether he operates it for profit, or only to satisfy his own needs [Baden-Württemberg, Statistisches Landesamt 1964b:8]." The most recent statistics draw a new distinction in separating holdings under 1 ha with a gross income of less than 4000 DM per annum from all others (see Baden-Württemberg, Statistisches Landesamt 1972b).

be taken into consideration. Next, I shall discuss structural differences between the two communities. Concluding this chapter will be a discussion of the extent to which the "traditional" structure has been modified.

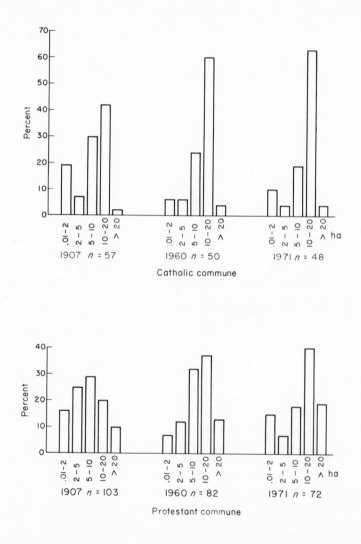

FIGURE 23. Percentage distribution of agricultural holdings by area of cultivated land, 1907, 1960, and 1971. Data from Königlich Statistisches Landesamt (1910); Baden-Württemberg, Statistisches Landesamt (1964b); author's census January-February 1971.

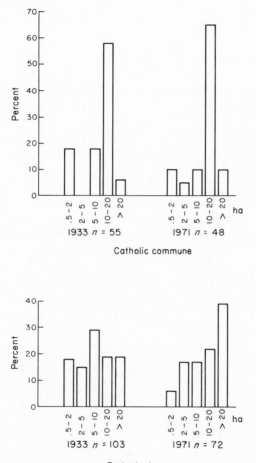

FIGURE 24. Percentage distribution of agricultural holdings by total size (i.e., including forested land), 1933 and 1971. Data from Württembergisches Statistisches Landesamt, 1935; author's census January-February, 1971.

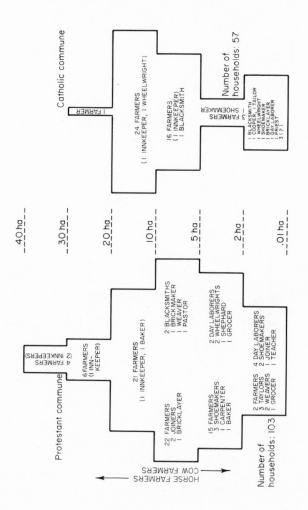

FIGURE 25. Occupations of heads of households, with households arranged according to size of agricultural holdings, 1907 (scale: 1 household = 36 mm²). Data from Königlich Statistisches Landesamt (1910) and local family registers.

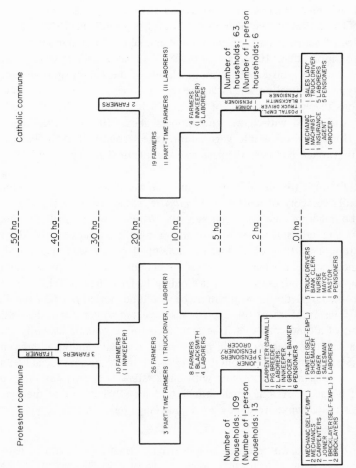

FIGURE 26. Occupations of heads of households, with households arranged according to size of agricultural holdings, 1971 (scale: 1 household = 36 mm²). Data from author's census January-February 1971.

Conditions Around the Turn of the Century

Full-time Farmers

The local population was split into two major factions: Households that worked more than 10 ha of cultivated land were clearly set apart from those that worked less than 10 ha. As arbitrary as this division might seem at first, it rested on the observation of two phenomena in evidence until the 1950s: restrictions on choice of marriage partner and type of animal power used in farming. Over a period of more than 100 years, about 80% of all marriages were contracted between partners who came from households of the same major-size category. As to type of animal power, local livestock records show that with only three exceptions involving deviations of less than 1 ha, farmers below the 10 ha line worked their land with cows, and farmers above 10 ha worked theirs with horses. Horses had come into vogue during the second half of the last century; before that, oxen had been the preferred work animal among many of the larger farmers.

Thus, although we find full-time farmers on both sides of the 10 ha line, the smallholder category of *Köbler*, or *Kleinbauer*, has always been set off distinctly from the medium and large farmer, the *Bauer*.[2] When small farmers, day laborers, and craftsmen started to form a significant segment of the village population, a pattern of endogamy developed which was maintained by a pronounced status consciousness based on economic criteria. As we saw in the last chapter, the principal heir to a holding had to "buy off" his parents and siblings—the larger the farm, the more he would be in need of cash capital at the time of transfer. Much of this capital was expected to come into the holding in the form of a dowry, so that it became almost an economic necessity that the son of a well-to-do farmer would marry a girl of equal standing with a generous dowry. Status consciousness found expression in many areas of social life, and to marry *standesgemäss* (in keeping with one's estate or status) was the expected form of behavior. As one small farmer told me: "When one of them married below his status, why, everybody got a good laugh out of *that*!"

---

[2]*Bauer* (the traditional "peasant," now better translated as "farmer") connotes both occupation and status, although over the last 60 or 70 years the emphasis has gradually shifted more toward occupation.

The *Reichserbhofgesetz* of the Third Reich elevated the term *Bauer* to the level of "title of honor" (para. 11.1). Only the owner of a holding that remained undivided when transferred from one generation to the next (a so-called "*Erbhof*") was allowed to use this title in connection with any kind of official transaction where his occupation would be listed. Owners of holdings that were left subject to partible inheritance, or those which were either below the minimum size of one *Ackernahrung* (see Footnote 3) or above the maximum size of 125 ha, were denied the title *Bauer* and were held to call themselves *Landwirt*, a status-neutral term meaning "agriculturalist" (see Dölle 1939:30-38, 70.).

The status group of *Bauern* was subdivided into medium and large farmers. This division was not as clearly defined as the major one, but according to local informants, farmers with holdings of around 20 ha and more occupied an elevated status position and were often referred to as *Herrenbauern* (*Herr*–lord, master). They communicated their status in various ways, such as leaving most of the farming to servants and going to the inn while others were still working, leasing hunting rights, wearing clothes of better quality, and occupying special pews in church. Only *Herrenbauern* would own an elegant chaise for transportation to church or town; for a lesser *Bauer* to do so would have been presumptuous. There was also a gradation in the number of horses kept on the farm. The medium farmer usually worked with a team of two horses: the larger farmer had three or more. For example, the largest farmer in the Protestant community (who worked 37 ha of cultivated land in one of the hamlets) kept five horses. Although the horse was thus a status symbol as well as a work animal, as a rule the number of horses that were kept stood in a well-balanced relation to the amount of land worked. Conditions such as those reported from Poland, where a "fantastic number of horses" were kept in relation to the crop yields, had no place in the local scheme of social and economic values (Warriner 1965:158).

One further distinction between medium and large farmers was the number of hands required to run both farm and household. Depending on the size of the holding and the number of family members available for work, farmers kept from two to six male and female servants (*Knechte* and *Mägde*), who themselves formed a hierarchy within the household according to sex, age, and type of service performed. In addition to these servants, day laborers would be hired for all tasks that required a greater input of manpower than could be furnished by the household itself. Perhaps a somewhat special position should be accorded those farmers who also operated an inn, as their requirements for servant help were at times a little higher. Farming, however, seems to have constituted the major source of income for the innkeepers. As the records for the last 150 years indicate, innkeeping met with various degrees of success. In some cases, innkeepers were forced to sell their holdings to satisfy tenacious creditors; in others, inns were merely shut down as uneconomic and their proprietors turned their efforts exclusively to farming; and in a few cases innkeepers seem to have done reasonably well.

Let me now turn to the small-holding type of full-time farmer who, around the turn of the century, went by the official designation of *Köbler*. This term originated in patrimonial times and designated a small-holder peasant who fulfilled his obligations of statute labor with his hands rather than with the team of oxen or horses which the *Bauer* had to furnish. The term *Köbler* continued to be used in the records until the First World War. After the war, the term *Landwirt* appeared in its place (see Footnote 2). Colloquially, and for obvious reasons, the two factions of full-time farmers were referred to as *Kühbauern* and *Gäulbauern* (cow farmers and horse farmers).

The average size of a cow farmer's holding was 7.5 ha; the lower limit was usually held around 3 ha. Whether or not a family could live from farming only 3 ha of cultivated land depended on the circumstances, such as family size, distribution of land as to quality and convenient location, and the degree of competence of the individual farmer with which he managed the available resources.[3] The records show that some of the smallholders received a little extra income by taking on certain communal offices, such as that of night watchman, field watcher, village forester, grave digger, and mole catcher, among others. There were also opportunities for extra income that are not reflected in the records, such as performing forest work for the larger farmers during the winter.

Day Laborers

As a rule, the holding of a day laborer was too small to maintain a family on farming alone, and he often also lacked the team of cows necessary for plowing. He derived most of his income from working for the larger farmers on a daily-paid basis. Day laborers did not form a separate social group, however. Besides the fact that the number of day laborers' households was quite small (6% of all households in the Protestant community in 1907, and even less in the Catholic village), there was a high degree of social mobility, which is reflected in the rate of intermarriage between the families of day laborers, cow farmers, and craftsmen, as well as in the relative frequency with which day laborers managed to buy enough land and livestock to become classified as cow farmers.

Craftsmen

In 1907, 20% of all heads of household in the Protestant community practiced a craft. If we want to rank-order those households on the socioeconomic scale, both the type of craft practiced and the size of the attached holding have to be taken into consideration. For example, shoemakers and tailors generally derived a smaller income from the practice of their particular craft than did joiners, carpenters, wheelwrights, and blacksmiths. However, if a shoemaker had enough land to provide for most of his family's needs from the proceeds of farming, and

---

[3] In 1953, the *Ackernahrung* for both communities was officially set (as published by the Bureau of Statistics) between 8 and 10 ha. The *Ackernahrung* is held to be the minimum area of cultivated land required to maintain a family of four to five adults from the proceeds of farming. The actual land area may differ from community to community depending on soil conditions and other criteria. Because the overall standard of living was lower around the turn of the century than it was in 1950, it is conceivable that a family may have then subsisted on considerably less than 8 ha. With today's specialization in farming, however, land area alone is no longer a valid criterion for measuring the lower limit of the economic viability of a family farm.

a wheelwright had considerably less land, their economic positions would be more equal. A few among the iron- and wood-working craftsmen who had more than 5 ha of land seemed to have enjoyed the same economic position as some of the medium and even larger farmers. Exactly how much of a craftsman's income might have come from farming and how much from the practice of his craft is difficult to establish, however. That depended not only on the amount of land worked, but also on the fluctuations of trade. The craft of weaving, for example, was already depressed around the turn of the century and had completely disappeared from the local scene by the end of World War I.

Recruitment into the Various Categories

In view of my earlier remarks on group endogamy, it is not surprising that recruitment into the ranks of medium and large farmers was primarily by birth. In only 5% of all local cases over the last 150 years was a farmer recruited from outside the ranks of his status group. For example, in a few cases it happened that a farmer would find himself both in financial difficulties and with only a daughter for an heir. The dismal financial situation would keep many desirable suitors away, and, once the daughter was over 30, suitors were even harder to come by. In such a case, a cow farmer's son was welcome as long as he brought enough capital to bail out the holding. It also happened that a cow farmer managed to move up into the ranks of the horse farmers by acquiring additional land.

In the case of recruitment into the ranks of the cow farmers, the percentage of recruitment by birth diminished progressively moving from larger to smaller holdings. The factor of frequent intermarriage between the families of cow farmers, day laborers, and craftsmen has already been mentioned. Also, although one generation might hold enough land to be classified as cow farmers, circumstances during the next generation might force the head of household into the position of a day laborer. With at least equal frequency, a move in the reverse direction would take place, too.

A prerequisite for recruitment into the ranks of craftsmen was the successful completion of a prescribed period of apprenticeship. It stands to reason that the sons of craftsmen were more likely to become craftsmen themselves than the sons of farmers. In some instances, principal heirs followed consistently in the footsteps of their fathers. For example, the two men in the Protestant village who operate, respectively, the smithy and the repair shop are both descended from an unbroken line of blacksmiths, going back at least six generations. Succession in the families of some of the other craftsmen has been less consistent. The amount of capital invested in tools and shop equipment possibly had some bearing on whether or not the principal heir to a craftsman's holding would learn the same trade as his father. To give an example of the changes that may take place from generation to generation, the following represents a succession of male principal heirs in one of the local households (the dates in parentheses refer to the respective year of birth):

1. blacksmith and cow farmer (1767)
2. cow farmer (1806)
3. day laborer (1829)
4. shoemaker (1864)
5. cow farmer and road maintenance man (1900)
6. laborer (1941)

Some 170 years ago, the holding of this particular family comprised 3 ha of cultivated land: toward the end of the last century it was down to 1 ha. Then a slow build-up began, and, from 1950 to 1969, the size of the holding increased from 6 ha to almost 9 ha. The present owner inherited the holding in 1969. Being single, he prefers the steady wages of a worker (which he earns in one of the nearby breweries) to the almost impossible task of running a farm without the help of a wife. A few parcels of land have been sold, but most of it is leased out to other farmers.

Another example refers to the succession of four generations of principal heirs and represents one of the rare cases in which a cow farmer made the ranks of the horse farmers:

1. shoemaker (1816)
2. bricklayer (1856)
3. cow farmer (1881)
4. horse farmer (1914)

When the present owner of this holding took over from his father in 1952, he inherited 7 ha of cultivated land. Now he owns almost four times that much and, in addition, works about 25 ha of land on a lease basis.

The Two Communities Compared

The preceding description has been patterned primarily on the Protestant community; there are, however, some deviations from this pattern in the Catholic community which need to be commented on. First, there are some differences in the distribution of holdings by size. In the Catholic community, the greatest concentration of holdings has been in the 10–20 ha range. This may be attributed, to some extent, to the structure of the Protestant hamlets and their relatively large districts, where 7 out of the 10 holdings in the commune larger than 20 ha were located. However, in the Catholic village in the last century there were at least 4 more holdings larger than 20 ha, until they became partitioned in various ways.[4] We also find comparatively fewer households of day laborers and cow farmers in the under 5-ha range than in the Protestant community (namely, 4 against 23 households; see Figure 25, p. 90). This seems to be a reflection of the relative lack of large holdings. As most of the daily-paid labor was required on farms over 20 ha, and practically all of this labor was furnished by day laborers and cow farmers with holdings under 5 ha, it seems reasonable to conclude that a higher percentage of households in the latter category might not have been economically viable in the Catholic community.

Second, the division between cow farmers and horse farmers was apparently not as pronounced as in the Protestant community; for instance, it does not find expression in the local records insofar as the term *Köbler* is rarely used. Both types of farmer were usually referred to as *Bauer*, even though the livestock inventory clearly shows that all farms under 10 ha worked with cows. There have also been more cases of intermarriage between families of horse farmers and cow farmers than in the Protestant community. This factor is reflected in the differential rates of village endogamy (see Chap. 4), with at least a 10% higher rate of endogamy in the Catholic village.

Although there seems to have been a somewhat lower threshold of status distinctions in the Catholic community, these distinctions were nevertheless well-drawn in the cognitive social map of the villager. Every small farmer remembers some of the disadvantages under which he or his father had labored vis-a-vis the horse farmers, and there are numerous stories of the oppressive behavior exhibited by some of the *Herrenbauern*. On the other hand, Protestant smallholders were much more outspoken in their comments on past relationships. Larger farmers would mostly talk around the subject when asked about the relationships between large and small farmers in the past, although one of them stated that this had been a "dark chapter" in the history of the community and that over the generations a certain amount of hate had built up on the part of the small farmers. Although I did not find any hate, there were some expressions of bitterness and resentment, which were rarely, however, directed

[4]Following is a breakdown of these four cases:

1844. One 23-ha holding was divided by a father among his youngest son on the one hand, and, on the other, his second son and one daughter. The latter two sold their share piecemeal to various local bidders in 1855.

1861. Half of one 25-ha holding was handed over by a father to his oldest son; the youngest son received the other half in 1872.

1871. One farmer sold his 24-ha holding to various local bidders and moved to a nearby town with son and daughter.

1884. A 28-ha holding was inherited by an oldest son who stayed single and worked the holding with his two unmarried brothers. Among the three brothers, this largest holding in the village was gradually "drowned in alcohol" over a time span of some 30 years.

against large farmers as a group; in fact, some of them were expressly lauded for their fairness in dealings with the small man. Much of the bitterness came from people who had been *Knechte* or *Mägde* ('servants') of some of the larger farmers, and the overall conditions under which they had to live and work were—especially in retrospect—miserable indeed. (Having once eaten the bread of a *Knecht* myself, I find it easy to empathize.)

In comparison, the lot of Catholic servants seems to have been a little brighter, which may be partly attributed to the source of recruitment. In the Protestant community, servants were partly recruited from the outside and partly from the households of local smallholders. Noninheriting sons and daughters of horse farmers would rarely offer their services to other farmers in the community but would try to obtain work on larger farms away from their home village, unless they went to the city for other jobs. In the Catholic village, servants were also recruited from the outside and from the households of local smallholders, but, not infrequently, sons and daughters of horse farmers would work as servants for other farmers in the village who fit into the same size category. Under those circumstances, social distance was not as pronounced and treatment might be expected to have been less harsh.

The Structure Today

Up to some 30 years ago, the subsistence basis of both communities was almost entirely agricultural. Full-time farmers and day laborers derived their incomes completely from work in agriculture: the craftsmen were, in turn, dependent on the farmers as their customers, besides being part-time farmers themselves. In earlier days, even the teachers and the clerics would work the land set aside for them as part of the compensation for their services. This pattern has been changing, even though little of this change is reflected in the physical appearance of the villages. The difference between now and then is noticeable mainly in the mornings and in the evenings when some of the villagers leave for, or return from, their jobs in nearby communities. These changes in the occupational structure are the result of large-scale, socioeconomic developments which have altered many relationships, especially during the last 2 decades.

Now, there are no longer agricultrual day laborers. Only large estates can afford to pay the kind of wages that might entice a man, or a husband–wife team, to work full-time on someone else's land. Gone are also the full-time farmers with holdings under 5 ha. These smallholders (or their sons) are now working in nearby industry, or they are pensioners who work part of their land to supplement their pension as well as to keep productively busy.[5] The shops of

---

[5]Some of the holdings under 2 ha, shown in Figures 23 and 24, fall into this category; that is, their respective owners have leased most of their land to other farmers.

some of the craftsmen have disappeared for the same reason as have the small farms: it makes no sense to eke out a living at barely subsistence level, when working for wages can ensure a decent standard of living. As I discussed in the previous chapter, most of their land has been leased by smallholders to larger farmers, rather than sold. In only two or three cases were entire holdings put up for sale, either because the heirs have long moved to the city and are not interested in holding on to the land, or because mounting debts dictated a sale. On the whole, land is a commodity which still retains much of its former social value, but it is also seen in terms of a buffer against possible future hardships. The effects of two major wars and ensuing economic upheavals are still very much discussed and on everybody's mind; then, ownership of agricultural land proved to be the best safeguard against possible starvation, and those people who had put their trust in their savings had to watch them being wiped out by inflations and currency reforms.

Those local craftsmen who are still in business for themselves are doing quite well. Mechanics and blacksmiths are kept busy repairing farm machinery, and there is a steady demand for the services of local joiners, carpenters, and bricklayers. Most of the rural dwellings are over 50-years old and lack modern conveniences, such as bathing facilities and central heating. There are kitchens and living rooms that need remodeling, and larger windows are now favored to let in more light. All of these innovations are generally considered both desirable and necessary improvements; it is of special importance to the younger generation that housing standards are raised more nearly to the level of those in the cities. What girl, or so the question goes, would like to marry into an antiquated household? There is also some new construction; in 1971, two new houses were being built to take the place of two old ones—one of them largely upon the urgings of a bachelor son who did not cherish the thought of being left without a wife for lack of suitable housing. In the Catholic village, the last house of the type in which the cattle are stabled on the ground floor was being converted— the cattle were moved to separate stables and their former quarters remodeled into kitchen and living room space. Then there are also stables and barns that have to be kept in repair, or new ones that have to be built. In short, the available work keeps the local craftsmen busy, especially in view of the fact that some of them still farm their small holdings.

The status distinctions that once grouped local households into two major factions are largely breaking down. Farmers are no longer consciously determined to restrict the selection of a marriage partner to girls from their own group (although that is where most of the girls who are willing to marry a farmer still come from). Tractors have replaced cows and horses, thus eliminating visible distinctions out in the fields between former cow and horse farmers. The economic distance between farmer and worker has decreased considerably, as I shall discuss in the next chapter. Compared with conditions in the past, the personal workload of the larger farmer has increased. In the old days, it was the

Herrenbauer who could afford some leisure time, repairing to the inn for a glass of wine and a puff from the meerschaum while others were still working. Today it is the erstwhile servants and day laborers and smallholders working in industrial jobs who have the edge on the farmer when it comes to weekends off and paid vacations. However, status in the local hierarchy is still largely determined on the basis of overall economic standing and landed property, which means that a farmer who is doing fairly well will rank several notches above a worker. However, now as in the past, a man's behavioral characteristics (that is, his *Charakter*), may considerably add to, or detract from, his economic standing in establishing his place in the local status hierarchy.

7

The Dynamics of
Family Farming: Part 1

More than 90% of all agricultural land in the Federal Republic of Germany is owned and operated by individual farmers and their families. Today, the fate of all of these enterprises is tied in large measure to the structure of the European Economic Community, to its agrarian policies and long-range planning, as well as to the economic and fiscal policies of its individual members. The effects of these various policies on the local farmer are modified, to some extent, by government intervention on the national level. These interventions may pursue the aim of stabilizing domestic food prices by subsidizing certain products (as, for example, to offset the effects of a French butter surplus), or they may try to help the farmer in more direct ways by paying him compensation for certain losses (for example, those incurred through the reevaluation of the *Deutsche Mark* in relation to the U.S. dollar). These acts of intervention can not be equated, of course, with the kind of protection that gave German agriculture a virtual monopoly of the internal market in the 1930s. The goal of official federal German agrarian policies has been to strengthen only those farms with the potential resources to provide their owners with an adequate level of financial returns on investments in capital and labor.[1]

However, despite the fact that agricultural labor productivity has increased five to seven times during the last 2 decades—representing the largest single increase among all branches of the national economy—there has been a widening disparity of achieved income between the industrial and the agrarian sectors (see

[1]For excellent discussions of German pre- and postwar policies, see Warriner (1965), and Franklin (1969).

Wirth 1970:37). In order to keep this gap from widening even further, the farmer has to keep increasing his productivity—he can not afford to stand still. Today's farm families have to cope with socioeconomic pressures of considerable magnitude, and the discussions in this and the next chapter will deal with the local responses to specific aspects of these pressures.

Patterns of Land Use and Production

The Shift from Grain to Meat

The local farmers have long practiced the kind of mixed agriculture in which animal husbandry is combined with the production of grain, root, and fodder crops. Wheat now constitutes the major grain crop, followed by barley, rye, oats, and maize. In addition to the field crops, meadows are cultivated and cut twice a year; the harvested hay provides the bulk of the fodder for the stabled cattle during those months when green fodder is not available. Meadows now constitute about 40% of the cultivated land, an increase of almost 10% over their proportion some 70 years ago. The extent of the tillage has correspondingly declined, and so has the area utilized for the production of grain. This has been more than offset, however, by increases in the yield per hectare; for example, the yield of wheat has almost tripled over the last 100 years (Wirth 1970:7). The area utilized for root crops has remained stable; that for fodder crops has increased by about 25%.

In addition to these slight shifts in land-use patterns, there has been a shift in the disposition of grain. Up to 10 or 15 years ago, as much as 70% of the grain harvest was sold; today, between 60 and 75% of the harvest is used by the farmers to feed their livestock.[2] Stimulated by the growing demand for meat by a population that now enjoys a higher standard of living than ever before, there has been a shift in emphasis from the production of grain to the more intensive production of meat and milk. Figure 27 shows in- and decreases in the livestock populations of each community, and Figure 28 charts the livestock inventory of four different farms for select years.[3]

---

[2]Wheat prices have actually declined over the last 20 years. Some farmers have been able to make a little extra money on their wheat by selling it instead of using it as feed, and then buying back denatured wheat. The profit in this move amounts to 2½%, which is the difference between the 8% value-added tax (*Mehrwertsteuer*) received by the farmer with the sale of his products, and the 5½% tax he pays on animal feed.

[3]In 1969, West Germany's population consumed 37.3 kg of pork and 21 kg of beef per person, or a total of 128.5 lbs (see Wirth 1970:59). In Baden-Württemberg, meat consumption (including poultry) increased by 100% between 1953 and 1969 (Baden-Württemberg, Statistisches Landesamt 1970b:87).

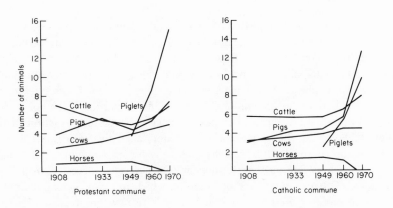

FIGURE 27. Number of livestock per ha of cultivated land. (Note: Figures for 1908 and 1933 list piglets together with pigs; those for 1949, 1960, and 1970 show piglets under 8 weeks separate from pigs.) Data from Königlich Statistisches Landesamt (1910); Baden-Württemberg, Statistisches Landesamt (1964b and 1972b).

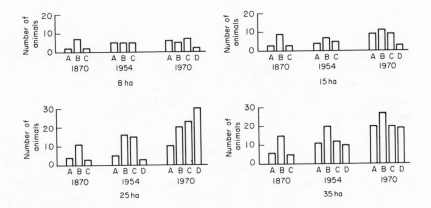

FIGURE 28. Livestock inventory of four select farms of 8 ha, 15 ha, 25 ha, and 35 ha in size (1870, 1954, and 1970). Key: A: cows (milch and breeding); B: other cattle (including calves); C: pigs; and D: piglets under 8-weeks old. Note: Piglets are converted at the ratio of three piglets to one other animal. Data from local sales and contract books, and livestock censuses; Bürgermeisteramt.

Capital and Space

Although the shift to increased livestock production has not necessitated any major structural changes in existing methods of farming, there are certain prerequisites that have to be met to accommodate that shift. Next to the acquisition of suitable animals, the most fundamental one is the availability of buildings to house the animals. During the first stage of expansion, farmers rearranged existing stable space to accommodate more animals, and this is the point where most of them have stopped. The next step involves the construction of new buildings. Some of the farmers who have not taken this step think that the financial burden involved is not justified in view of a number of calculable variables (such as approaching retirement age, lack of a successor, insufficient labor, etc.). Others simply have no space on which to build. Their buildings are so close to those of their neighbors that they have nowhere to go. To solve this problem in the interests of improved farming efficiency as well as complying with a standard of housing, the government has encouraged farmers to relocate from the tightly clustered villages to the surrounding fields and has offered 1½ and 2% loans for the construction of new buildings. However, there are only two farmers in each community who have done so (the two from the Catholic village have actually relocated merely to the village outskirts), and there are several reasons why the response has not been greater. The first has to do with money, the second with fear of isolation, and the third with the existing arrangement of fields. The first two points need no great elaboration; many farmers simply do not want to assume a relatively large financial burden in the face of what they see as an uncertain economic future, and there is also a general dislike among villagers of "living out there like a recluse," unable to observe what goes on in the village, even though relocation would involve a distance of no farther than 1 mile.[4] The last point has to do with the fact that field consolidation has not yet been carried out, thus making it difficult to chose an advantageous site for relocation.

Although field consolidation (*Flurbereinigung*) has officially been recognized as both necessary and desirable for at least the last 100 years, it has become an especially pressing issue since the widespread introduction of tractors and expensive agricultural machines and implements.[5] To haul machinery from one end of

[4]For a discussion of many of the problems that arise in connection with relocation, see Schöck (1971 & 1972).

[5]For example, the local land register shows that in several instances involving the sale of land during the second half of the nineteenth century, official permission to conduct these sales could only be obtained by pledging that the land would not be sold to someone who was, in principle, against field consolidation. The minutes of the respective commune councils also show that during the first half of the present century, several votes were taken on whether the local farmers wanted field consolidation or not, with the majority always voting "nay."

the commune district to the other in order to reach one's scattered fields is unproductive activity, and the same applies to the frequent turning necessary in working a field of relatively small size. In the past, there may have been some degree of justification for having one's fields scattered over the entire district— according to the local farmers, if the crops failed in one end of the district due to a combination of adverse weather conditions, topography, and type of soil, one could always expect the crops at the other end to come out a little better.[6] Under present methods of cultivation this factor would be negligible, indeed, and the installation of a new drainage system as part of the consolidation task would minimize the problem of waterlogged meadows and fields.

After a district is scheduled for consolidation, a government team would move in, survey the entire district, take soil samples, and finally redraw existing property lines so that each holding ends up with three or four parcels of contiguous land instead of the present 20 or 30. Adequate access roads would do away with quarrels about rights of access over someone else's land. Understandably, individual farmers have no say in the final allotment as this would lead to endless disputes. However, care is taken to ensure that the overall value of a farmer's land is as close as possible to what it was before.

Despite the generally acknowledged advantages that field consolidation would bring, a majority of local farmers consistently voted against requesting the government to carry out the work. Only recently has the vote come out in favor of consolidation, but quite a few of the farmers are still unhappy, primarily about the financial burden they will have to bear. The costs of field consolidation including drainage are estimated to come to an average of 2400 DM per ha, of which the government will pay about two-thirds; the rest of 800 DM per ha can be paid off in yearly installments of about 50 DM per ha. Much of the resistance has been by smaller farmers and those with uncertain prospects of succession, even though consolidation and drainage of their land would render it more valuable and more desirable to prospective lessees or buyers. Some measure of consolidation has been carried out by the farmers themselves, through exchange and realignment of individual parcels of land.[7]

---

[6]One of the officials of a field consolidation team, who grew up on a farm, suggested to me that there was also a certain amount of intrinsic satisfaction in being able to work a parcel of land in one day.

[7]The current program of field consolidation, started in 1951, is a formidable undertaking that will take many more years to complete, at a considerable cost to the government. By 1969, out of a total of 1,813,000 ha of cultivated land that had been in need of consolidation, 865,000 ha, or 47.7%, had been consolidated (with another 85,533 ha consolidated in 1970 and 1971). However, out of these 865,000 ha, a total of 268,000 ha, or 31% of the consolidated area, was already in need of a second consolidation. This has brought the total successful consolidation down from 47.7% to 32.9%, leaving 67.1% of the total area still in need of consolidation (Baden-Württemberg, Statistisches Landesamt 1970b:89-90; 1972c:107).

A New Emphasis on Controlled Production

In addition to those prerequisites primarily involving the outlay of capital, there is also the question of quality of labor input. Although every farmer has learned early in life how to take care of his livestock, modern methods striving for more controlled production call for a much closer supervision than is usually applied. To increase his profits per unit of product, a farmer has to try and cut his losses as much as possible. For example, by using rule of thumb it is relatively easy to overfeed one's livestock when a lesser amount of feed would result in the same increase of weight at the same rate of time. But this kind of control requires a certain amount of recordkeeping and exact weighing of feed because differing amounts have to be fed from week to week. Many a farmer finds this too cumbersome. Some of the younger farmers, especially those who have spent a few semesters in agricultural school, are more willing to experiment. Their training also provides them with some of the tools to run a more closely controlled enterprise. Older farmers tend to be more cautious, and when some of the ventures of the younger ones do not work out there is a lot of discussion and "that's what I expected" shaking of heads. Of course, there is no clear-cut division between young and old in this respect, merely a general pattern.

Making Ends Meet

Income from Farming

A statement on income or profits from farming can be rendered here only in approximations, as it is difficult to determine accurate figures for each farm. This has probably less to do with the unwillingness of individual farmers to divulge information, which is almost universally considered sensitive for one reason or another, than with the fact that most of the farmers do not engage in formal bookkeeping and are therefore unable to come up with exact information. Farmers do, as a rule, keep a record of receipts and purchases, and, although they may thus be in the position to determine the ratio between those two, they still have no idea of their true incomes unless they keep books and balance all items, such as amortization of machines and buildings, fluctuations in the livestock inventory, interests, capital costs, and so forth. Indeed, four farmers told me that they had not the slightest idea how much income they derived from their farm, claiming that they had never sat down to try and figure it out. As they do not have to pay income tax, there is actually no compelling need to work out their incomes. So far, only large farms that meet certain structural criteria are compelled by the state to keep proper books, although the government is trying to induce more farmers to do so. For example, any farmer who now wants to obtain a subsidized loan has to have kept books for a specified period of time before he will get the money.

On the basis of informaton furnished by local farmers, I arrived at an approximate yearly net income for farms above 8 ha, which ranged from 2000 DM to around 24,000 DM for 1969-70. (Of especial help in arriving at these figures were those farmers in the two communities who kept books—in one case I was even shown a computer print-out covering one year's operation.) As might be expected, there is a correlation between size of holding and income, although some of the farmers are considerably above or below the average income in their size category. This is not surprising in view of my discussion of capital and space; because the farmers derive about 80% of their cash income from the sale of livestock and milk, it stands to reason that those who have been able to provide for adequate stable space are much better off than those who have not been able to expand, even though their crop resources would make it profitable for them to do so. As indicated before, none of the farmers in the two communities have to pay income tax, which is applicable only if the net income exceeds 25,000 DM per annum.[8] The only substantial tax paid (except sales tax) is that on real estate, which amounts to an average of 5% of net income.

So far, none of the farmers have specialized in only one branch of production —they are all of the opinion that it is better to stand on two legs than one. Beef cattle and cows are the most reliable sources of income because the prices for beef and milk do not fluctuate as much as those for piglets and fattened pigs. On the other hand, cattle take much longer before they are ready for the market, and, with the proper spacing of sows which produce 2-3 litters a year, the farmer can make frequent trips to the weekly pig market, where a crate full of 8-week-old piglets can be converted into ready cash. If the price of piglets drops and shows no signs of recovery in the near future, the farmer can always sell a few of his sows and go easy on the piglet production, relying on his cattle to keep him afloat. A farmer who specializes in only one line of production, say fattened pigs, has no room to manipulate when pig prices fall. His operations are more streamlined because he has to attend to only one kind of production process, but he runs a higher risk and is more liable to end the year with little profit or even a loss. He also has to rely more on purchased feeds rather than on what he grows on his own land, and there have been cases in which the sale of pigs has brought in, say, 40,000 DM, with the purchase of piglets and feed requiring an outlay of 30,000 DM (Wirth 1970:51). Such cases are well known to the local farmers, and they cite these in justification of their resistance against urgings from the Ministry of Agriculture to streamline operations and specialize in one product only. However, some farmers may lean more toward one line of production than another. For example, one farmer fattens about 400 pigs per

---

[8]"Net income" equals deduction from receipts of all operating costs, including taxes, interests, amortizations, etc.; also deducted are allowances for wages and room and board, for helping family members of 2448 DM and 1800-2400 DM per annum, respectively.

year, but he also keeps 10 cows and as many steers; another keeps 50 head of
cattle and only 10 or 15 sows as a sideline for piglet production.

In general, the local farmers tend to view their economic future in pessimistic
terms. Year after year they have to pay more for industrial goods and services
while the prices they are able to get for their own products remain relatively
stable. Compared with 1958, grain prices in 1970 were down 12%; those for
animal products were up 8%. On the other hand, machine maintenance costs
went up 29%, and costs to purchse new machines went up 12%. Between 1962
and 1970, building costs increased by 41%, with the largest jump of 20% occurring in 1969 and 1970 (for the preceding figures, and those on wages, following, see Baden-Württemberg, Statistisches Landesamt 1970b:19;20). This
trend runs parallel to a steady rise in industrial wages. As more than one farmer
complained to me: "Do you know that the worker is now getting more than the
farmer? That isn't right—it's like standing the world on its head!" Between
November 1958 and November 1969, hourly wages for craftsmen rose by an
average of 158%, those for industrial workers (skilled and unskilled combined)
by an average of 113%. During the same period the cost of living index rose by
only 28%. In other words, the worker has scored some real economic gains while
the farmer is falling behind.

A straight comparison of net income between the worker and the farmer
shows that many of the local farmers are not so badly off. Roughly, the average
farm household, which achieved a net income (in 1969) of 7300 DM, was on
approximately the same level of income as the average working man's household.[9] Any farmer whose income was substantially below that figure might have
been better off working for wages rather than farming—that is, all other things
being equal, which of course they are not (one of them being the often-cited
contention that being one's own boss has its rewards, too). Of all the differences
between the two types of household, the most significant is probably the fact
that the farmer often has to plow back a considerable portion of his net income
into the farm, while the worker is potentially free to spend his money on items
of personal consumption.

Outside Income: A Differential Pattern

As we have seen, one way for a farmer to increase his income is to step up his
rate of productivity. Another way, which to some extent may run parallel to the
first one, is to seek outside employment in exchange for wages. As I have

[9]This figure of 7300 DM has been arrived at by deducting average costs for rent, household power (i.e., utilities), taxes, health insurance and social security, and 80% of the
average costs for food from the average working family's gross income of 15,600 DM per
annum (see Baden-Württemberg, Statistisches Landesamt 1970b:186-187). The above
deductions approximate those of the farmer before arriving at net income.

pointed out in Chapter 2, this has become a familiar pattern in more industrialized parts of Baden-Württemberg where there is also a considerably larger
percentage of smaller farms. Whether or not, and to what extent, a farmer can
stay away from his farm to work on some outside job depends mainly on three
factors: the type of farming, the size of the enterprise, and the availability of
family help. In the case of extensive farming, most of the work can be done
during a few weeks of the year, conditions for outside employment are the most
favorable. Mixed agriculture, however, is a year-round proposition. Stabled
animals require daily care, and because the farmer grows most of his own feed he
has to spend considerably more time on his holding (for example, green fodder is
fed from spring to fall and has to be cut almost daily). Here it is the overall size
of the enterprise in terms of land worked and number of animals kept, in
combination with the availability of family help, that sets certain limits to the
amount of time a farmer can afford to spend away from his farm.

Figure 29 shows the distribution of outside income for heads of farm households with holdings between 10 ha and 22 ha of cultivated land (the standard
category of 10–20 ha has been here extended to include the two holdings in the
Catholic village which are over 20 ha). Farmers above and below this range need
not here be considered, for they are either very unlikely, or very likely, to
engage in outside work (thus, of the 10 farmers in the Protestant community
with holdings over 22 ha, only 1 reported occasional income from forest work
earned during the winter). Of interest is the category in between, for it is here
that the factor of size carries less weight than in the categories above and below.
Interestingly, the distribution in this middle category shows significant
differences between the two communities.

First, there is the large percentage of Catholic farmers engaged in occasional
outside work. Employment is not permanent nor necessarily consecutive, but
the men in this category earn additional income ranging between 10 and 49% of
their net income from farming. Of the 18 farmers in this category, four derive
their additional income primarily from jobs in the building industry, especially
from roofing work. In some cases, employers will pick them up and transport
them to the job site and back. Sometimes this site is several driving-hours away,
requiring overnight stays with all expenses paid. The other 14 farmers get their
extra income mainly from working for the commune. Most of the work is
performed in the communal forest (Fig. 30), although more recently a considerable input of labor has gone into the construction of field and forest roads. The
wages paid for this kind of municipal work are considerably lower than those for
construction laborers (3.60 DM per hr, versus about 6.20 DM per hr), but there
are definite advantages in staying close to home. There is also the assurance that
work will be available during the slack winter season when housing construction
is largely curtailed; those who work on outside jobs during the summer are
usually not considered for communal work during the winter. In comparison,
there are only four Protestant farmers who derive occasional income outside of

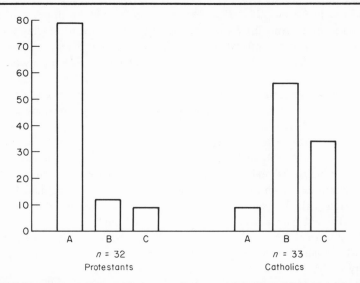

FIGURE 29. Incidence of outside income, farmers with holdings 10-22 ha in size (1971). Key: A: No outside income; B: Income from occasional outside work; C: Income from steady outside work. Data from author's survey, 1971.

FIGURE 30.   Farmers planting trees in communal forest.

farming. This income is primarily derived from work performed in nearby factories during the winter months. The Protestant commune has considerably less work to offer, owning very little communal forest. It seems, therefore, that we may ascribe the much lower percentage of occasional income earners at least in part to this particular lack of employment opportunity. The potential labor pool, however, is the same in either community, at least by the criterion of size of holdings—farmers who engage in occasional outside work can be found right up to the limit of 22 ha.

A somewhat different situation prevails in the category of farmers who work at a steady outside job; these men are employed for at least 7 consecutive months of the year, and the income derived from these jobs amounts to more than half of their net income from farming. The 11 farmers (34%) who fall into this category in the Catholic village are matched by only 3 farmers (9%) in the Protestant community. All of the Catholic farmers are employed by road construction companies; the distance from the village to construction sites generally does not exceed 20 miles. Earnings are around 6.20 DM per hr, and "bad-weather money" amounting to between 60 and 75% of regular wages is paid for thosy days when rain, snow, or excessive frost puts a halt to construction activities. As weather of this type can be expected to last an average of 2 months per year, the men enjoy the advantage of drawing some pay while catching up with maintenance work at home. They also take time off from work during peak periods of agricultural activities. In the Protestant community, two of the three farmers who hold steady outside jobs are truck drivers, and one works as a construction laborer. The question arises: Why this difference between the two communities? Could it be a reflection of structural differences?

There is indeed an upper limit in the Catholic community which stands at 16 ha above which we do not find any farmers who hold steady outside jobs; the average size of the 11 holdings mentioned above is 12.85 ha. This particular limit also applies in the Protestant community, where we likewise find 11 farmers with holdings under 16 ha, none of whom hold outside jobs. However, three of them have to be excluded because of illness or advanced age, leaving eight potential wage earners. A check of their operations reveals that they do not seem to require a higher labor input than their Catholic counterparts; that is, they neither keep more livestock nor own more forest.[10] A survey of available family

[10] The average distribution of the number of livestock and the amount of forested land per farm is as follows

	Catholics	Protestants
Forest	1.80 ha	1.0 ha
Cattle (total)	15.09 head	14.75 head
Cows	5.09	6.63
Pigs	12.00	11.88

labor shows no significant differences; a comparison of age shows the Protestant farmers slightly older on the average (45 years versus 42 years). In sum, there are no significant structural differences which might account for the relative numbers of part-time farmers.

Native opinions differ as to the merits of working at outside jobs. Predictably, those who do not are critical of those who do, and the latter provide arguments in justification of their own positions. Following are some of the statements made on the subject.

1. *Farmers who hold jobs outside the community* (Catholics):

> *If I can make 6 mark per hour, why shouldn't I take it? That doesn't mean I'm giving up farming.*

> *I have never been satisfied with my occupation as a farmer. In fact, I have never really wanted to become a farmer. But the main reason I work is that we badly need the money.*

> *All around one, the standard of living has been rising, and, if one doesn't want to be left behind, one has to have money, and the income from farming is not enough.*

> *As long as my parents can help to take care of things, I'll go to work and accumulate credits for social security so that no matter what happens I will have a pension later on.*

> *Sometimes I leave at four o'clock in the morning and don't come home till half-past nine at night, and the next morning I'm back farming, and you know why? Because I have a wife and six children!*

2. *Farmers who do not hold outside jobs* (three Protestants, three Catholics):

> *We are of the opinion that if you do something you do it right; not that you chase after something else and your own business deteriorates.*

> *If I take an outside job, there is bound to be something which is left undone at home. The fields won't suffer so badly, but there will be more damage in the stable. If I want to take care of my stable properly, I have to spend at least 5 hours in it every day [8 cows, 4 other cattle, 5 sows].*

> *I think that working at an outside job is counterproductive. During the 6 months of summer, I have to fetch green fodder daily and I have to feed for 2½ hours in the morning and then again in the evening. If I don't stick to the long feeding times. I can't expect a high yield, which means there won't be any profit, in which case I might as well quit.*

> *They have said to me, "You should have kept your son home to work the farm, then you could have taken a job."*
> *I said, "I, take a job? I have always been my own boss and I'm not ever going to place myself under someone else." There is really no reason why I*

should go to work, either. If my farm could not bring in enough to satisfy my own and my family's needs, that would be bad, indeed.

If you have a farm, you have to be able to put your all into it. If I go to work and can't completely take care of my livestock—for instance, if hot fodder is being fed—there can be a great amount of damage. I think I have as much money as those who go to work. If one goes to work and wants to catch up in a hurry at night and a machine gets damaged—that can cost a lot of money. Or when it rains on the hay during the day, all the work that went on before was for nothing. And then there are those who don't like it at home and would rather work somewhere else, and maybe there is an old grandmother or grandfather who complain about this, that, or the other thing that hasn't been done right, and so they might say, "It's better if I go away and bring home some money so they keep quiet."

Whether this thing is going to work out all right that some are working on the outside, I don't know . . . A lot of work is left for the women to do. If they would take proper care of their farms, they would probably have as much money as they have now. As it is, there is more damage done and the women become drudges, too. That's why the farmers can't get wives any more.

The above quotations reflect that there is general agreement among full-time farmers, Catholics and Protestants alike, that a farmer should take care of his farm and little else. The most convincing arguments against part-time farming under the prevailing production patterns came from farmers who have fairly accurate figures on relationships between labor input, overall farm management, and ultimate profits. On the other hand, those farmers who work at outside jobs are convinced that they are adapting to economic pressures in the best possible way. In terms of the structural changes now affecting European agriculture in general, and the German family farm in particular, the question of full-time versus part-time farming is but one aspect of a transitional stage. In terms of this specific investigation, the question arises whether the observed differential pattern is but a reflection of purely idiosyncratic behavior which would average out if the investigation were extended to cover a greater number of communities, or whether we have found indications that this pattern is the function of particular cultural factors with ultimately more general applicability. An answer to this question will be considered after the presentation of further data.

The *Bäuerin*: Cornerstone of the Family Farm

The importance of a woman in a farm household is difficult to overestimate. Besides filling the role of mother and housekeeper, she also shoulders the burden of partnership in the family enterprise, actively participating in many phases of farm work. Her work day covers 15 hr or more. She is the first to rise in the morning, and, after the evening meal when her husband grabs his coat and heads for the inn, she settles down to some more housework. It is not that she is held in the position of chattel or slave to her husband, it is simply that the work has to be done and that often there is no one else to do it. The last servants left in the 1950s, and since then both *Bauer* and *Bäuerin* have been largely on their own. Any additional help comes from family members (or one of the refugee women who stayed on after the war); depending on the particular point in the developmental cycle in which each family finds itself, there may be older children and/or aging parents and sometimes an uncle or aunt. Older people who can still contribute their share of work are now appreciated as never before. As one farmer put it coyly, "*So 'ne Oma muss man sich warmhalten!*"

Wives whose husbands work on outside jobs carry an especially heavy load, even though the comment by one of the farmers that "everything has to be done by their wives" is somewhat exaggerated. The men try to do as much work as possible, cutting green fodder in the early morning hours before going to work and doing more chores after getting home in the evening, but it is nevertheless true that much of the work is left to the women to take care of. Of course, the women do not all share the same degree of hardship, which varies mainly with the number of small children who have to be looked after and the overall size of the enterprise. Some women seem to be more or less at peace with the prevailing conditions; others complain bitterly.

The same holds true for all women, not only for those whose husbands hold outside jobs—the amount of work that has to be done differs from household to household, and so does the amount of consideration wives receive from their husbands. For example, some farmers take their wives along to the fields by habit, even if little help is needed. There are other farmers who don't do this, and I have heard some criticism from Catholics and Protestants alike. Said a Protestant farmer in one of the hamlets:

> *I noticed that in* [the Protestant village] *there are a number of women who have to run behind the drill, or uncouple the wagon so the husband does not have to get off the tractor. I think that isn't right. It can be done differently, because we do it differently, too. But some men are like that, and if one should mention something to them, they say, ". . . well, my wife wants to get out, too." But whether that is true or not—I don't know . . .*

My own questioning of some of the women brought out that in many cases they would much prefer to stay home and take care of things around the house, but their men need them and there is not much they can do. To a certain extent, this seems to be a post-servant phenomenon; after the servants left, some farmers adjusted to do much of the routine fieldwork by themselves; others did not. Without malice, the wife of one of the farmers in the latter category told me: "I guess we have become *die kleinen Knechte* of our men; it's just that they always have to have someone around."[11]

To find out more about women's views on men and farming, I asked 34 women whether they felt that the introduction of tractors and more efficient machines had made farming easier for them, and whether they felt that their husbands appreciated their work. Answers to the last question were evenly divided in both communities between those who thought that their work was being appreciated and those who thought that their husbands took it for granted and did not really see how much they worked. Five of the women did not want to commit themselves either way. Answers to the first question brought out a slightly differential pattern: More than half of the Protestant women thought that the work had become easier; two-thirds of the Catholic women thought that it had not become easier, or only in limited ways. The major contention here was that despite the machines, working hours had not decreased because there were now fewer hands to share in the work. Women over 30 would remark that the machines have destroyed the old work rhythm and were causing a lot of nervous tension—the machines now dictated the tempo and everything had to be done in such a great hurry; besides, the proper handling of a machine required greater concentration, and when a machine broke down the tension would mount. The women generally agreed that riding a tractor can be the cause of certain kinds of physical distress, especially back trouble. Some women commented disapprovingly that it has been the machines that have made it possible for their husbands to take on outside jobs. On the other hand, several women in the Protestant community mentioned that the machines have been especially welcome when relieving them from overly hard physical labor, such as loading manure. (Comment from a woman who had moved into the community from another region: "Where I come from, women would have never loaded manure.") It seems that on the whole, women who are more involved in field-work and the handling of machines are also experiencing certain discomforts and take a more negative view; those who have experienced the machines capacity to do certain types of work, and thus lessening the workload, see the machines in a more positive light.

Parenthetically, the old division of labor under which certain farming tasks

[11]In the hierarchy of male servants in a farm household, the *Kleinknecht* ranked below the *Grossknecht*. I do not want to create the impression, however, that farmers' wives did not work in the fields when they still had servants. Müller claims (1938:57) that as a consequence of economic developments during the nineteenth century (more intensive cultivation, a higher level of market orientation, etc.), there arose a belief among the German farming population that a *Bäuerin* who did not help with the fieldwork was no proper *Bäuerin*.

were once routinely assigned to either male or female has now given way to ad hoc solutions. For example, with the introduction of milking machines, quite a few males are now milking their cows, a task formerly performed by females (except on large estates where there might be professional male milkers). On the other hand, there are now several women who can carry out all phases of cultivation by themselves, including the once distinctly male task of plowing.

On the whole, the women work very hard. Unfortunately, most of them do not take as good care of their health as they should. (Neither do the men.) One or another physical discomfort may have bothered them for some time, but by the time they get around to see the general practitioner (who has his practice in a small town 5 miles distant but will come to the village if called), it is usually too late for general treatment and they have to be referred to a specialist. A visit to a specialist usually requires 10 hr absence from work and is therefore often postponed. This is an old pattern, and although every family is now covered by one or another type of health insurance (which in the past was rarely the case, the farmer being a "free entrepreneur"), the old pattern tends to persist. Apart from inoculations and periodic visits by a pediatrician under the auspices of the department of public health, the concept of preventive medicine has not yet taken hold, nor is it freely propagated; very few of the people would see a doctor unless they were ill.[12] Dental hygiene leaves much to be desired, too. There is one area, however, in which women are much better off than before: since the 1920s, deaths attributable to childbirth have gradually declined to zero. This seems to be the major reason why women, on the average, now tend to outlive men (Figure 31).

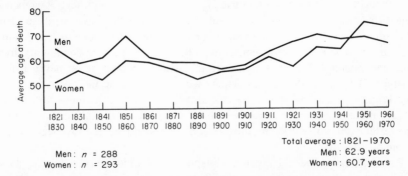

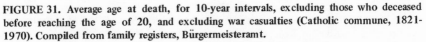

FIGURE 31. Average age at death, for 10-year intervals, excluding those who deceased before reaching the age of 20, and excluding war casualties (Catholic commune, 1821-1970). Compiled from family registers, Bürgermeisteramt.

[12] For example, when we took our 4-month-old daughter for a routine checkup to a pediatrician in a nearby town, this overworked and nervous man was somewhat disturbed and at first failed to grasp our intentions: "If the child is not sick, why are you bringing her to me?"

Some Observations on the Plight of
the Bachelors

What happens if a farmer cannot get a wife? The answer to this question is fairly straightforward: Unless he can avail himself of other female help, he will find it next to impossible to go on farming for very long. In the past, cases of farmers unable to get a wife have been very rare. Not so today. I took only one or two days of residence in the Catholic village before I became aware of what was described to me as the greatest local problem: The phenomenon of a number of bachelor farmers with little hope of finding wives. Life on the farm is synonymous with long hours of hard work, and, as the complaint goes, "The young girls of today just don't want to work any more."

This issue became of special interest to me when I found that it does not present as acute a problem among the Protestant farmers: The percentage of bachelor farmers over 31 years of age is 5 times as large in the Catholic community as it is in the Protestant community (28% versus 5% of the respective total number of farmers).[13] There are 12 Catholic bachelor farmers with a median age of 34, who run their farms with the help of a mother or aunt whose median age is 67. That means, within the next 10 years, 28% of the farms in the Catholic village will very likely cease to operate in their present form, unless wives can be found. Both the bachelors and their elders stated that this was the most vexing problem in their lives, as the following quotations illustrate.

I like farming and my farm is profitable, but when one does not get a wife and the old ones die—that's the end.

If I want to go on farming, I have to have a wife. On my own, I can't do it. The work in the fields and in the stable, and on top of it housework—that's too much!

If I had a wife, everything could go on. So much has been invested in the farm and so far everything has worked out all right, but if my mother dies—I can't work the farm on my own.

(A mother) *My biggest problem is this: If a wife would come in here the whole thing could go on. It's not only that the holding would be preserved, but what is he going to do once he is on his own? When one dies these days, one doesn't even know what is going to happen.*

---

[13] The average age at first marriage for men over the last 150 years has been 31.3 in the Catholic community, and 30.3 among the Protestants; therefore, I have excluded bachelors below the age of 31 because they still enjoy a 50% probability or more of getting married. (By late 1974, none of the bachelors who figure in this analysis had managed to find a wife.)

(A widowed mother) *Our biggest problem is that we don't have a young wife and that I don't see or know how this is going to go on. Now that we have invested so much—we have built and he has attended winter school—and now it seems that it was all for nothing. I have tried everything; I have looked and listened, but those who fit agewise have all left, and for the real young ones he is too old. They all want a worker—a man who works in a factory and builds himself a little house has a much better chance than a farmer.*

The villagers know that this problem is not confined to their region alone, but that it constitutes an "occupational hazard" among farmers nationwide.[14] Many a farmer's daughter is far more attracted to a nonfarm household with its prospects of a more leisurely lifestyle than to a life of work on the farm. As to the high proportion of bachelor farmers in their midst, the villagers offer various explanations. In some cases they blame the parents: When their sons were thinking about marriage at a time when girls were still available, the parents actively discouraged them because they did not want to transfer control of the farm before they were ready to retire. Another view has it that the young men did not make themselves *präsentabel* to the girls; instead of paying more attention to courting, they would get on their motorcycles and do the rounds of pubs in nearby villages and towns. Then there are also the usual references to particular personality traits: this one is too "smart" for the girls, that one got involved in a game of family intrigue, the other one tried to hold out for a girl with money, and those over there behave like wooden statues in the presence of girls. These observations more or less describe the hazards of courting as they have always existed, except that the introduction of the motorcycle entered a new note by providing the young men with increased mobility which may have helped to disrupt some more traditional, community-oriented types of diversion. There is every indication, however, that these factors applied equally in the Protestant community—there were motorcycles there, too, and parents who were reluctant to retire, and young men who felt awkward in the presence of young women. The question remains: Why should the bachelors in one community have fared better than those in the other?

The answer, in my view, has to do with the potential number of girls who were willing to marry a farmer, and that potential has been greater among Protestants than among Catholics. Why was it greater? Here we have to focus attention on the percentage of farmers' daughters who have received some formal training at agricultural and housekeeping trade schools (so-called *land und hauswirtschaf-*

[14]Based on nationwide sampling conducted in 1968, it was found that only 42% of farmers' daughters between the ages of 17 and 28 were willing, in principle, to marry a farmer. Thirty-three percent were willing if certain conditions were met, and 25% declined to marry a farmer under any circumstances. The corresponding figures for daughters of nonfarmers (but residing in rural communities) were 4%, 32%, and 64% (Planck 1970:116).

tliche Fachschulen), especially in view of recent findings that show there is a positive correlation between such received training and the willingness to marry a farmer (see Planck 1970:118). It turns out that over the last 12 years only 3 girls from the Catholic village have received such training, as against 5 times that many girls in the Protestant community. According to various informants, similar conditions (i.e., a higher rate of formal training among Protestant girls compared with Catholic girls) have prevailed in those communities constituting the main reservoir of prospective marriage partners. It seems safe, therefore, to postulate that the number of farmers in a community who do not find a wife will vary with the number of girls in the potential marriage pool who are, in principle, willing to marry a farmer, and that the number of girls who are so willing will vary with the number of girls who had formal training in agricultural and housekeeping subjects. Not surprisingly, data I obtained during various interviews indicate that girls with formal training feel a certain degree of professional challenge vis-a-vis their future role as mistress of a farm household, as well as confidence that this training will help them to better organize their work, while there is a tendency for girls without such training to see the role of a farmer's wife primarily in terms of the hard, long hours of work.

Of course, we now have to ask ourselves why it is that more Protestant girls have received formal training. We may assume that the decision to seek formal training is made in an environment in which positive attitudes toward farming as a life-time vocation will generally outweigh negative attitudes.[15] Indeed, when we look at this environment, we do find other indicators that support this assumption. For example, out of 47 farmers in the Protestant community with holdings over 8 ha, there are 26 (or 53.3%) who have attended the *Landwirtschaftsschule*, as against 3 out of 40 farmers (or 7.5%) in the Catholic community.[16] In view of the higher percentage of larger farms in the Protestant community, it might be important to point out that the above distribution is not a function of size: Four out of 10 farmers with holdings over 20 ha have had no formal training, yet there are 3 farmers with holdings under 8 ha (not included in the above figure of 26 farmers) who did. This clustering of farmers in the Protestant community who have received formal training might be perceived as the mirror image of farmers in the Catholic community who work at outside jobs. In more generalized terms, there is a tendency among Protestant farmers to concentrate their efforts on farming and to develop all available resources to that end, yet there is a tendency among Catholic farmers to divide their work potential between farming and nonfarming activities. From an economic standpoint,

---

[15] I asked 60% of the Protestant farmers, and 80% of the Catholic farmers, whether they were on the whole satisfied with being a farmer by occupation. More than half of the Protestants claimed they were, as against 25% of the Catholics.

[16] The three closest schools of this kind are government-operated, coeducational schools located at distances of 5, 11, and 15 miles from the two communities.

both approaches are entirely rational, but this qualitative difference in attitudes toward farming as a profession, which, in exaggerated opposition, might be termed "professional" versus "nonprofessional," does lead to certain social consequences, such as the differential scarcity of potential wives. The complex interrelationships between these attitudes and their ideational background will be discussed in Chapters 10 and 11.

8

The Dynamics of
Family Farming: Part 2

In the introduction to Chapter 7, I mentioned that agricultural labor productivity in Germany has increased 5 to 7 times between 1950 and 1970. This remarkable increase is the result of an overall reduction in the agricultural work force (which has taken place without a decrease in gross production), and of the progressive modernization of the family farm. These two factors have acted on each other, but their relative weight has varied from farm to farm—in some cases, initial moves towards modernization preceded a reduction in the work force; in others, modernization was initiated as a consequence thereof. From a wider perspective, however, modernization has proved to be inevitable, and those farmers who have not been able, or willing, to commit the required capital resources have either been "phased out" or are living a marginal existence. The discussions in this chapter deal with two areas of agricultural modernization: motorization (usually referred to as "tractorization"; see, e.g., Franklin 1969 & Schwarzweller 1971) and mechanization. In both of these areas, we shall analyze the ways in which the local farmers have met the demands of a changing economy.

Tractorization

The number of tractors operated in the area around the two communities before the Second World War was quite small. The local savings and loan association in the Protestant community had acquired a tractor in 1937, which was then rented out to farmers for certain types of work, such as long-distance and

121

heavy-duty hauling, or pulling the reaper-binder in harvesting suitable fields. Its heavy weight rendered it largely unsuitable for the performance of general field-work, however. On the other hand, one could find more tractors in Mergentheim County which is characterized by more extensive wheat farming; there the tractors were less hampered by small-sized fields and adverse topographic and soil conditions.

In the years following the war, it was primarily the larger farmers who felt the progressive labor shortage most. Thus, the first local farmers to acquire tractors were the two largest farmers in the Protestant community. Both bought their first tractor in 1949, one year after the currency reform; before that reform, manufactured items were either in very short supply or not available at all. After this initial move, it took another 10 years before each farmer in the Protestant community had acquired at least 1 tractor (Figure 32). During the first 5 years, tractors were acquired exclusively by horse farmers; by the end of 1954, 65% of the horse farmers owned a tractor. In August of 1955, the first of the cow farmers bought one, too; and in 1960, three cow farmers closed the circle of first-tractor acquisition in the Protestant community. By that time, several farmers who had been among the first to buy a tractor had already acquired their second one, mostly because the first one was not powerful enough and/or lacked the hydraulic system required to operate the more complex machines and implements.

In comparison, the Catholic farmers started and completed the process of tractorization several years behind the schedule of the Protestants. By the end of 1959, when 96% of the Protestant farmers had acquired at least one tractor, only 40% of the Catholics had done so. Interestingly, almost half of those 40% were cow farmers. In fact, the first—and only—Catholic farmer who acquired a tractor in 1954 was a cow farmer. The last to buy tractors were horse farmers; out of 19 farmers during the last 3 years of first-tractor acquisition, only 2 were cow farmers. This stands in marked contrast to the Protestant community, where 62% of the horse farmers had become tractorized before the first cow farmer acquired a tractor, and where the tail-end of tractorization was formed by cow farmers. It is therefore the intra- as well as the intercommunity patterns that are different.

As I have indicated, the leadership in tractorization was taken by the two largest farmers in the Protestant community; partly in response to the labor shortage, and partly as the first conscious step in a modernization of their enterprises by following nation-wide trends. Industrialization before World War I had started to deplete the ranks of agricultural labor, but the years of depression after the war created more potential farm labor than the farmer could employ. During the 1930s, labor started to drift to the cities again, despite an initial attempt by the Nazi government to keep everyone who had been employed in agriculture on the land. New machines and implements that were introduced

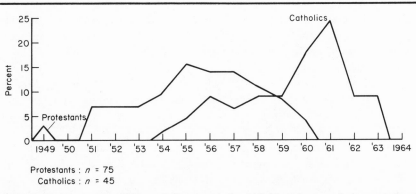

Protestants : n = 75
Catholics : n = 45

FIGURE 32. Year of acquisition of first tractor by individual farmers, in percentages of number of farmers in each community. Data from author's survey 1971.

during the first 2 or 3 decades of the century, such as the reaper-binder and the electricity-powered threshing machine, helped to considerably shorten the work hours connected with the grain harvest. During the First as well as the Second World War, the labor shortage was alleviated through the employment of prisoners of war and other aliens. (For an extensive analysis of farm labor in Germany, see Wunderlich 1961.) The influx of refugees after the war in 1945 again provided the farmer with sufficient help, but it was fairly clear that this would be only a temporary situation. Those farmers who closely followed overall agrarian developments knew that the time for a large-scale mechanization of the family farm had come.

After the "leaders" in the Protestant community had shown the way, others soon followed, although not necessarily in the order of size category or degree of actual need. As one farmer remarked: "When the tractors started to come in, people said, 'If he can buy one, I'll show them that I can buy one, too.' And so the whole thing gathered momentum all over the community, and envy and jealousy did a good deal of pushing, too. There was practically no other way but to go along." The first cow farmer to buy a tractor had felt very daring in following the "big ones." "At first there was talk: 'How is such a thing possible? Where did the *Kühpritscher* [cow drubber] get the money?' But soon everyone of the cow farmers followed along and it was sure a great relief to be independent of others." The relative gains in the area of time-saving conferred by the possession of a tractor were indeed greater for the cow farmers than for the horse farmers. Cows were so much slower than horses, they could not develop the same power and were useless for long hauls to and from the warehouse and for work during the time of winter snow. On those occasions, the cow farmer had to turn to the horse farmer for a loan of his horses, for which he would usually reciprocate in the form of work performed on the latter's holding. For these types of exchanges, more or less stable bonds had formed between two or more farmers, although these bonds were subject to manipulation by either side.

In sum, individual motivations to acquire a tractor at a particular time were often multifaceted and ranged from a response to compelling economic needs and long-range planning to a sense of rivalry and competition and the desire to be more independent of others.

The Catholics observed what their neighbors were doing, but they held that it did not make sense to spend money on a tractor when the work could be done more cheaply with a team of draft animals. Besides, they were still not quite convinced that the soil might not become compacted too much through the constant use of tractors. This pattern of communal "abstention" from the tractor was broken in 1954 by one of the cow farmers. A Swabian from further south, where small holdings were dominant, he had married into a cow farmer's holding in late 1953, full of ambition to become a "proper farmer." He had gone through several years of high school education and had worked as a machine adjuster in a knitting factory. His first project on his way to becoming a proper farmer was to replace his team of cows with a much more efficient tractor. He recalls the widespread derision (fully corroborated by his erstwhile antagonists) with which the other farmers in the village greeted his venture. "*Der Rein-geschmeckte* [derogatory term in southern Germany for a resident of non-local origin, especially one with a different ethnic background] wants to show off his education; he wants to prove to us that he is something better!" They tried to prove to him that working with draft animals was cheaper, for not only did one save the costs involved in the purchase and maintenance of a tractor, but also the expenses for improved implements which one would have to buy.

The following year, in 1955, two other farmers decided to take the same step. One was a cow farmer who had just become married and had taken control of the parental farm; he also decided that his tenure might best be initiated by giving the cows a rest and getting the work done much quicker with a tractor. The other one was a horse farmer of "marginal" standing in the community.[1] It was not until the year after that the two largest farmers in the village decided to each buy a tractor. For 2 years they had received daily demonstrations of the tractor's efficiency, watching as the neighbor on his tractor was bringing home his first load of fodder while they were still harnessing the horses. A little prodding from the younger generation also seems to have helped them make up their minds that the time for a tractor had come. Most of the horse farmers held out a few more years; in fact, more than half of them did not become tractorized until 1961 through 1963. We may speculate that had it not been for the outsider's determination to become an efficient farmer, tractorization might have been postponed a few more years. Here as in the Protestant community, the pattern was to take one's clue from the larger farmers in the acquisition of

---

[1]He was marginal in the sense that he was born in a city to the south and had inherited the farm via his mother's sister; but even more so, because he had remarried a Protestant woman.

new tools, unless one wanted to appear presumptuous. We have also seen, however, that stratification along socioeconomic lines was not as rigid in the Catholic village as it was in the Protestant community, so that it became comparatively easy for the second cow farmer in the village to buy a tractor before the "big ones" had made a move, after the first cow farmer to do so had taken the brunt of the socially sanctioned ridicule. In contrast, the first cow farmer in the Protestant community to acquire a tractor still felt quite daring to make such a move, even though more than half of the horse farmers had already bought a tractor.

The argument by the Catholic farmers that working with draft animals was cheaper was certainly justified, as far as rough calculations go; it was only when some of them were confronted with the sudden loss of a horse which would have to be replaced that the subject of immediate savings could no longer be seen in the same light. The major reason why their arguments in favor of the retention of animal power seemed to make sense, however, is the fact that the average Catholic farmer could avail himself of a larger pool of relatively inexpensive family labor than the average Protestant farmer. As long as the Catholic farmer had more helping hands on his farm, he did not feel such a strong need for efficient, labor-saving devices. The benefits that could be derived from a larger family included those members who had left to reside in the city, as many of them could be relied on to turn up for harvest-time work. In sum, the time schedule of tractorization may be seen as having been dependent, to a significant degree, on family size; and family size (as demonstrated in Chapter 4) has been influenced by the respective religious affiliation. Thus, religious affiliation has had an unanticipated effect upon the respective modernization time schedules of our two communities.

In generalizing this point, we are led to the conclusion that on the average, Catholic farmers have been slower to modernize their operations than Protestant farmers, at least wherever they operate in a similar environment. To test this hypothesis, I looked at the statistics of two counties and found tentative support. In Künzelsau county, we find 20 predominantly Catholic, and 29 predominantly Protestant communes (excluding the county seat). These communes contain 881 and 986 holdings, respectively, above 5 ha of cultivated land. By 1960, 93.1% of the holdings in the Protestant communes were tractorized versus 66.5% in the Catholic communes.[2] Künzelsau county is very similar in its overall

---

[2] Baden-Württemberg, Statistisches Landesamt 1964b. The statistics show the total number of tractors (including one-axle tractors) which are individually owned, by commune. I arbitrarily divided the number of tractors shown into the number of holdings over 5 ha of cultivated land, reasoning that most of the smaller holdings acquired a tractor relatively late, if at all (as has been the case in the two communities of this study). The results are therefore approximate, but I would expect that the actual distribution does not deviate significantly from the averages worked out here.

agricultural structure to that of our two communities. The other county where Catholics and Protestants live side by side in about equal numbers is Mergentheim, but here the statistics are inconclusive. Mergentheim county has a much higher incidence of extensive wheat farming, and by 1960, 100% of the holdings in the Protestant communes and 97.2% of the holdings in the Catholic communes were in the possession of tractors. In other words, if there was a differential time schedule here, too, it has to be sought at an earlier date; unfortunately, the only year for which published statistics on the distribution of tractors are available is 1960. To answer our question, we would therefore have to resort to the commune-to-commune collection of data.

Mechanization and Co-ownership

It would be inaccurate to claim that the mechanization of the family farm had to wait for the tractor. To a certain extent, mechanization had already revolutionized many phases of agricultural work. There had been steam- and electricity-operated threshing machines which did away with the drudgery of threshing the grain by hand or with the help of oxen; there had been implements such as seed drills and reaper-binders which constituted tremendous improvements over previous methods of broadcast sowing and of cutting with sickle or scythe and tying of sheafs by hand. However, the tractor brought with it the potential for a whole range of sophisticated time- and labor-saving machines and implements that need more than the power of draft animals to become operable. It is generally conceded that in the initial stages of the post-war modernization process the main concern of the recovering, agricultural machine industry had been to fill the overwhelming demand, so that quite a few machines were but hastily designed, soon becoming obsolete after only a few years of use, thereby putting an extra burden on the farmer. Thus, farmers who had postponed the acquisition of a tractor were often spared the unanticipated necessity of having to buy new machines before the recently acquired ones were amortized.

The point is that since the introduction of the tractor, the farmer has invested his capital in farm machinery to a greater extent and over a shorter period of time than ever before. The possesion of a tractor constituted an immediate improvement in the speed with which the farmer could now carry out many phases of his work, but while some of the implements, such as seed drills and reapers, could be adapted to the tractor after a few modifications had been carried out in the local smithy, others, such as the horse-drawn plow, became obsolete and had to be replaced with newly designed implements. (I ought to mention, however, that many of the farmers hung onto their horses a few more years after acquisition of a tractor so that the transition to the new phase was not totally abrupt.) Some of the machines and implements found in today's farmyard are in almost everyday use, such as the automated loading wagon which eliminates the hard work of loading fodder, hay, or straw by hand. Others are in use only a few days—sometimes only a few hours—out of the year, and thus represent capital investments that bring a very low rate of return.

To ameliorate this unfavorable situation, many farmers own certain machines and implements in common. For example, a group of five farmers may get together and decide to buy a beet seed drill which is only used a few days of the year; each partner contributes toward the purchase price in proportion to the amount of land that he usually sows to beets. Thus, various items are owned by groups of 2–15 farmers; they include tanks to carry liquid manure, implements for planting and seeding, weeding and harvesting beets and potatoes, various other types of seed drills, grain blowers (to blow grain from the ground level up to the attic for storage), implements for turning hay and pushing it into rows, chain saws, weedkiller sprayers, fertilizer spreaders, and self-driven combines. Some of the more expensive machines, such as combines and automatic potato harvesters, were being subsidized by the government to up to one-third of the retail price when purchased by groups of farmers, with the stipulation that the farmers would submit reports on the utilization of these machines for a period of 2 years. However, quite a few farmers prefer not to own such expensive machines as combines at all, but have someone else come and do the work for an agreed fee per hectare. Such is the case with 43% of the farmers in both the Protestant and the Catholic village, who pay some of the other farmers to harvest their grain for them. On the other hand, although 37% of the Protestant farmers own a combine individually, only 5% of the Catholic farmers do so, but 53% of the latter are co-owners of combines, against 20% of the former.

This brings me to the observation that a greater number of machines and implements of various types (except those in frequent use) are co-owned by a greater number of farmers in the Catholic village than in the Protestant village. Here we might look at the following figures. Of 28 agricultural machines and implements on which I took a farm-to-farm survey, 13 were most commonly co-owned to various degrees of frequency. By counting the number of times each of these items were individually owned by 1 farmer only, I found that on the average, 50.5% of the Protestant farmers owned all of these items individually, against 32% of the Catholic farmers. On the other hand, Catholic farmers were involved in the co-ownership of machines and implements to twice the extent that the Protestants were. The underlying figures are summarized in Table 9, and the networks of bonds of co-ownership are graphically rendered in Figures 33 and 34.

Table 9 is based on a comparison between the farmers in the Catholic village and the farmers in the Protestant village only, as inclusion of the Protestant hamlets would have been problematic in terms of spatial proximity. Structural conditions in the two villages are not very different. In the Protestant village, 30 farmers with holdings over 5 ha work an area of 462 ha of cultivated land, an average of 15.4 ha per farm. In the Catholic village, 42 farmers work an area of

Table 9

EXTENT OF CO-OWNERSHIP OF MACHINES AND IMPLEMENTS[a]

	CATHOLICS	PROTESTANTS
Total number of farms over 5 ha	42.0	30.0
Number of types of machines and implements co-owned	13.0	12.0
Farm-to-farm bonds generated by co-ownership:		
Total number of bonds	547.0	192.0
Average number of bonds per farm	13.0	6.4
Range per farm (total bonds)	(0–28)	(0–14)
Range per farm (counting multiple bonds as one bond)	(0–18)	(0– 8)
Number of farms with zero bonds	1.0	2.0

[a]Data from Author's survey: 1971.

505 ha, with an average of 12.0 ha per farm. The distribution of co-owned machines turns out to be functionally independent of the size of holdings. Thus, there are no obvious structural reasons why the farmers in each village should engage in the co-ownership of machines to a differential degree. It is possible, of course, that they harbor divergent views, in principle, on the advisability of such action. The following quotations from various interviews bear directly on this issue.

(Catholic farmer, 5 bonds) I don't care much for cooperative ventures—it isn't worth the trouble. When the machines are new, it's not so bad, but when the repairs start . . . The machine breaks down and the one who has used it last puts it away, and when the next one comes and wants to use it, he finds it does not work. I even bought my own combine; I can drive out whenever I want to—I don't have to heed anyone else and that way it always works best.

(Catholic farmer, 14 bonds) Three of us own a combine, seven a potato harvester, two a cultivator for beets, and five a weedkiller spray. Those are the things you don't need very often, and, on the whole, it works all right, but the more people that hang on one machine, the more sloppiness there is. Those machines and implements that I own alone, I can hook onto the tractor, and I know they are going to work; but if there are several guys—the next one comes along, wants to pick it up, and finds something amiss.

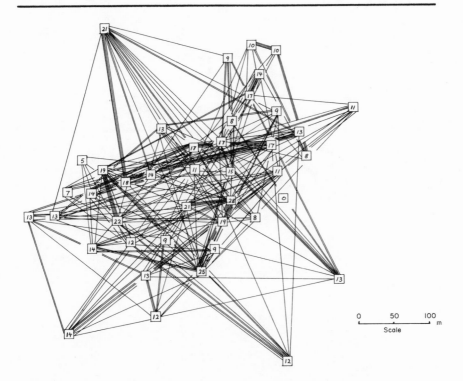

FIGURE 33. Bonds between individual farms generated by co-ownership of machines and implements, Catholic village. (Figures in squares are total number of bonds per farm.)

(Catholic farmer, 10 bonds) Two of us own a combine, which works out quite well. One of us threshes till three, and the other one till seven or eight. But when there are three, it becomes difficult, especially when the weather is bad and you have to stop off and on.

(Catholic farmer, 13 bonds) Even though we only share the combine among three—if one wants to use it, the other one wants to use it, too. Everyone looks at the weather and wants to have it when the weather is nice. Twelve of us own a beet seed drill; one wants to pick it up and drive out into the fields and what do you know—it doesn't work. But the guy who had it last didn't say anything. That kind of thing takes a lot of time—one has to go up to the smithy and get it fixed.

(Protestant farmer, 10 bonds) Well, if you are in a position to buy things on your own, you save a lot of annoyance. There is always talk about how much money one can save—that is true enough—but one buys a lot of trouble, too. If the weather would always be good, there would be no problem, but especially during the last few years it's always been variable,

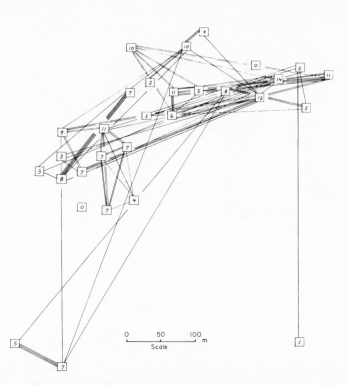

FIGURE 34. Bonds between individual farms generated by co-ownership of machines and implements, Protestant village. (Figures in square are total number of bonds per farm.)

and if there are some in the partnership who are quite inconsiderate—nobody talks about the cost of frayed nerves.

(Protestant farmer, 3 bonds) I am against co-ownership in principle. If you share the machines, they break down more often and nobody wants to be responsible.

(Protestant farmer, 9 bonds) There are four of us who share a seed drill, a cultivator, and a weedkiller spray. My neighbor up that way buys everything for himself. Take for instance yesterday—he used his beet seed drill for 2 or 3 hours. That thing once cost 2000 Mark, and the rest of the year it just stands around. Sometimes we borrow a machine from the neighbor over here, but only if we really can't help it; usually, after you have borrowed something, it breaks down.

The above quotations suffice to show that there are no great qualitative differences of opinion on the subject in the sense that they would set the Catholics and the Protestants clearly apart. Most of the farmers I talked to agreed that it would be preferable to enjoy exclusive ownership of all the machines that are needed, but that such a course made little economic sense. A few were of the opinion that they were willing to pay the price of exclusive ownership in exchange for peace of mind. But how, then, do we account for the greater involvement of the Catholic farmers in this kind of cooperative venture? An answer to this question involves an analysis of the field of social interaction. In my view, it is the differential patterning of face-to-face interaction that may be held responsible, to a significant extent, for this difference in cooperative involvement. To anticipate a point which will be discussed in the next chapter: there is a substantial difference between the two communities in the amount of time, the number of occasions, and the number of participants in face-to-face interactional situations in which topics such as cooperative ventures can be discussed. Thus, the differential co-ownership network densities are primarily a reflection of the differential patterning of social relations, which, in turn, are based on different organizational principles.

9

Social Interaction

In this chapter I shall concentrate on certain aspects of social interaction that I feel are relevant to my major theme as well as necessary for the presentation of a balanced ethnographic background. The first section deals with patterns of face-to-face interaction among, primarily, farmers and attempts to demonstrate that the observed differential patterns may be seen as the basis on which the farmers tackle certain economic problems. In the second section, I have endeavored to widen the focus by examining a broader range of social relations in cooperative as well as conflict situations within each community, and the third section analyzes social interaction between the two communities. Finally, a fourth section deals with voting behavior as an aspect of differential religious affiliation.

Dimensions of Face-to-Face Interaction

It is Sunday morning in the Catholic village, any ordinary Sunday morning of the year. The clock strikes three quarters of the eleventh hour and the ten o'clock morning mass is drawing to a close. The church doors open and the worshipers emerge; first some of the children and teenagers, then the women and the men. The young folk disperse in little groups; the women exchange some small talk and then head toward their kitchens to prepare the noonday meal of roast pork, noodles, and potato salad. The men form two or three groups and discuss the latest events—the weather, the state of the crops, the cow that had twins last night who both perished, the falling pig prices, the threat of lay-offs in industry which is a sure indication that gloomy days are ahead, and the latest move of the Social Democrats towards rapprochement with the East which proves once more that Willy Brandt is a traitor ready to sell out to the Communists. Gradually, a majority of the men start to drift off to the inns for the traditional *Frühschoppen* ("early half-pint" of beer or wine) and a continuation of the discussions (Fig. 35). The rest of the men make their way home, and 45 minutes after the mass has ended, the area around the church is empty. The noise level in the inns is rising, blending with the banging of pots and pans in the

FIGURE 35.   Group of men in Catholic village assembled after church.

kitchens. Around noontime, there is a general drift from the inns toward home, sometimes not as fast as a wife might wish: "My God, isn't that scoundrel ever going to come home?" After the meal, some of the men lie down for a nap, others head back to the inn. Here and there a family gets into their car to visit relatives or to go sightseeing. After the kitchens have been cleaned up, the women have a few leisurely hours, settling down with some knitting or sewing by the tiled stove or out in the sunshine. This is also the time to visit friends in the village, or to entertain visiting relatives from the city or country. When the weather is favorable, small groups of girls and women walk along the roads leading out of the village, sometimes pushing a baby pram between them. In the late afternoon or evening, a requiem mass may be read, attended by some of the women but few of the men. The inns are filling up with men who feel the urge for more companionship. Sometimes a card game gets going between three or four men, but mostly there are discussions. With six or eight men sitting around a table, several discussions may be carried out simultaneously, forcing everyone, in turn, to shout a little louder so that his voice might be heard. Agricultural topics outnumber all others. Anything that can be turned into a controversy is especially welcome, and it is amazing how fervently the pros and cons of a certain machine or the qualities of a certain field can be discussed. Next in line of discussion are local affairs, followed by national politics. All of the farmers are staunch Christian Democrats; if an outsider has something good to say about Chancellor Willy Brandt he will find a unanimous front turned against him. After a while some of the men may get up and go across the street to the other inn to test the degree of liveliness over there. By the end of the day, the vast majority of the male villagers have been able to inform themselves on what their fellow villagers think on a wide range of topics.

Now let's switch to the Protestant village. The church bells are ringing out the Sunday morning service, the doors open and the worshipers emerge (Fig. 36). On an average Sunday there will be about 20 men and 30 women and a handful of teenagers, no more than about 20% of the local parishioners. Unlike the Catholic village, the men do not form discussion groups. Afrer a few greetings and en-quiries about each other's well-being, the people disperse and hurry home. Some

FIGURE 36.   Protestants leaving church on Confirmation Day.

of the women may stop off at the general store across from the church to buy a few items they forgot the day before. Ten minutes after the church service has ended, the square in front of the church is empty. The inns are rather quiet; there are no groups of men in discussion assembled at their *Frühschoppen*. Later in the afternoon and evening some of the men meet for a game of cards or for an exchange of news and views, but, unless there is a special occasion, they never amount to a majority of the local men as in the Catholic village. Because the two inns in the Protestant community are dispersed between the village and one of the hamlets, there is little drifting back and forth in pursuit of the "action." Although the Protestant village is larger than the Catholic village, one gets the feeling on an ordinary Sunday that it is almost deserted.

This Sunday pattern of face-to-face interaction has its sequel in the quality of the weekday pattern. Take the milk pick-ups in the mornings. In the Protestant village there are two locations, the upper and the lower village, where the milk truck stops to make a pick-up (Fig. 37). The farmers line up in the order of their allotted numbers and exchange a few greetings and news items with the persons next to them. When the truck comes, the hand carts with the milk cans are pushed forward, the milk is sucked into the tank with the exact amount recorded on a chart, and from another nozzle one or two of the now empty cans are filled with skimmed milk. As each person has been served, he or she will pick up the cart and push on home. Not so in the Catholic village. Before the milk

FIGURE 37.   Milk pickup in Protestant village.

FIGURE 38.   Milk pickup in Catholic village.

truck comes to make its pick-up by the church wall, the men and women stand around in loose groups and talk (Fig. 38). They do not have numbers that require them to line up in a set order (they are served by a different dairy cooperative); when the truck comes they fall into line. After the truck has left, many push their carts aside and assemble for the daily morning discussion (unless there is pressing business during periods of peak agricultural activity). There may be as many as 20 initial participants (women do not stay behind) before the group gradually diminishes in size. A group may last up to an hour, and in the winter some men may repair to one of the ongoing stills or to the warmth of the smithy. How different this is from the customary pattern in the Protestant village was underscored one weekday morning in March, when a prominent man from the Protestant village happened to pass through the Catholic village (a rare occasion as the Protestants have little business in that direction). He had noticed such a discussion group by the church wall long after the milk truck had left and asked me whether something out of the ordinary had happened. When I told him that this was the usual pattern, he was quite astonished and exclaimed: "Just imagine—and all of them able-bodied men!"

Let us once more turn to the inns and see what goes on there during the week. The ones in the Catholic village have a reputation for doing business any day of the week. The two inns in the Protestant community are closed on Mondays, and there were other evenings when I found both places practically empty. In the inns of the Catholic village there is always some nightly companionship to be found, even though there may be times when the guest and the publicans are alternately falling asleep over their beers, exhausted from a long day's work. There is a contingent of five or six regulars who can be relied on to show up almost every night. Apart from the regulars, there are evenings when many of the local farmers are assembled, sometimes for a specific occasion. For example, 1 evening per week an officer from the bank in the nearest Catholic village comes up to one of the inns to conduct local business. Another evening is set aside for the barber. Or the vet may have conducted a difficult delivery, and he and the owner of the cow as well as the handful of interested neighbors who had come to lend a hand may repair to the inn to recuperate from the event. One night every other week—except for the busy summer months—the men from the choir drop in for refreshments after their practice sessions. The choir is made up of men from both the Catholic and the Protestant community, and the men take turns practicing in either location. There are other nights when some of the Protestants can be found in the Catholic inns; especially some of the young people prefer to enjoy themselves away from the gaze and out of earshot of their elders. The same holds true for the Catholic youths who prefer establishments in other villages. Then there are also men from surrounding communities who occasionally drop in for an evening of companionship.

The most popular beverage is beer; some men prefer wine, others wine mixed with mineral water or lemonade. A guest may also order a soft drink—either because he is a teetotaler or because he doesn't care for an alcoholic beverage that particular night—and nobody will make any disparaging remarks. The times that I have seen a man urge another one to drink fall into the category of pranks, and to buy a drink for others is reserved for special occasions. The rule seems to be that once in the inn, everyone has at least two drinks of whatever kind. Sometimes, when a man has already consumed the amount of alcoholic beverage that he feels is good for him while the lively conversation entices him to stay, he may follow up with a soft drink. The regulars usually consume between 4 and 6 pints of beer per night. I have never seen any hard liquor consumed in either of the two inns in the Catholic village; with the village boasting 16 stills in which the farmers distill plum, apple, and pear brandy, there seems to be no need to go to the inn to buy one's schnapps.

Usually, food is not consumed by the locals who go to the inn after their evening meal, but they will nibble at snacks placed on the tables. (Thus, one of the publicans has a predilection for chocolate wafers placed on the tables and dutifully consumed, and I just wonder in how many other inns around the world men will drink good, strong beer while nibbling at chocolate wafers.) On Saturday nights, however, some of the men will order a supper, such as fried chicken, various sausage meats, or cooked and smoked pork ribs (*Ripple*). Sometimes two or three of the women accompany their husbands to the inn on a Saturday or

Sunday night. This does not change the usual tenor of the proceedings; men shout as loud as ever to make themselves heard, and the same general kinds of topics are discussed as always. No switch in verbal decor is actually necessary, unlike in Anglo-Saxon countries it is not customary among the men to use four-letter words with sexual connotations, and to say "shit" every once in a while is quite acceptable—and so is the ubiquitous invitation "*doa leck's mi am Oorsch*" which is used by men and women alike.[1]

Every inn has its distinctive flavor, and one of the major ingredients is the personality of the innkeeper. One of the inns in the Catholic village is run by a bachelor in his 30s and his elderly mother. They are both very warm and friendly, but he is a rather quiet man who hardly ever leads in a conversation. It is in this inn where the barber and the banker conduct their weekly business. The other inn is a better money-maker, mainly because of the different personality of its owner. He is very lively, a hearty drinker, and enjoys initiating and leading conversations. Some of his stories are quite tall, but nobody really minds because people come to be entertained by one another as much as to drink their beer. Neither of the two inns has an exclusive set of customers who will not visit the other inn, except in cases of temporary feuds, when the two parties involved can stay out of each other's way by visiting separate inns.

The inn in the Protestant village is run by two widows. There are no weekly scheduled meetings, but once a month the local savings and loan association will pay out the milk money to those who desire to pick it up there. For some, this is largely the extent of their visits to the inn, apart from special festive occasions. The other inn is just outside one of the hamlets at the edge of a forest and run by one of the larger farmers and his family. The old inn was torn down a few years ago and a new one now stands in its place. A back room features a juke box which seems to attract some of the teenagers from surrounding localities. The picturesque location of this inn also invites those on a Sunday outing to drop in, and for more than 100 years many of the Catholic villagers have come here at least once a year after a traditional walk through the forest.

We now might want to ask why the Catholic men are such better patrons of their inns than the Protestants are of theirs. Some of the Protestants are ready with a simple answer, which centers around the fact that many of the Catholic farmers enjoy some outside income. As one Protestant farmers stated with conviction:

You know why they work on outside jobs? So they can drink! That is important to them. Whenever we drop into their inns after choir practice, we

---

[1]In literary German: *Leck mich am Arsch*. This popular saying was elevated to literary status by Johann Wolfgang von Goethe in his play *Götz von Berlichingen* (Act 3, Scene 17). Götz, an Imperial Knight of robber-baron fame who had his possessions not far from the two communities of this study (he also became involved in the peasant uprisings of 1525), extended this invitation to enemies who wanted him to surrender (Pistorius 1731:121).

always find the same ones squatting there. We don't do that here. Well, on
Sundays there are a few at the inn, but mostly the older ones; but the young
ones . . .

And one of the publicans remarked:

They can afford to go to the inn because they go and work on outside jobs;
here the farmers don't have any money.

Although it may be true that for some men weekly wages are easier to spend
than the monthly milk check or the receipts from livestock sales, there is general
consensus that the Catholic inns were at least as well frequented when none of
the farmers had any outside income. On the other hand, even the Protestant inns
were once better frequented than they are now. We therefore have to look for
other explanations, and I propose to do that after sketching in a few more
points.

There are some other indications that social interaction among Protestant
farmers follows somewhat different patterns. For example, it is considered quite
alright in the Catholic village to enter another man's stables when looking for
him, which among Protestant farmers is generally considered bad form. The
Catholic farmers are rather well-informed on how much livestock each of them
keeps, but some of the Protestant farmers try to keep that a secret from all but
their closest friends. This may or may not stand in some relationship to the fact
that the Catholic farmers have their own local cattle insurance association (in
existence some 35 or 40 years) and the Protestants do not. They used to have
one, too, but it was discontinued in 1960, and there are conflicting reports as to
why nobody wanted to take over after the person who had been in charge quit
his job. Some say that the paperwork required by the county bureaucracy kept
people from wanting to handle the job; others say that there had been some
internal problems that had to do with the lack of cooperation on the part of
some of the members. Briefly, this is the way it works in the Catholic village:
Each head of cattle 6 months and older belonging to a member of the association (all but one farmer in the village are members) is insured against death
through illness other than epidemic diseases, after its existence has been reported
to the association. Compensation for animals usually works out to about half of
their live value. For example, a good cow costs on the average around 1500 DM,
but the top compensation paid by the association is 800 DM. This limitation is
seen as a safeguard against any possible negligence on the part of those who
might feel: "Well, it doesn't matter all that much if the cow dies—I am insured."
Upon the death of the animal, two or three men of the association get together,
estimate its value, and decide how much they are going to pay. These payments
are made from the periodic contributions of the members, with each farmer

paying a stipulated sum of money per head of reported cattle in his stables. It stands to reason that continued uncooperative behavior on the part of some of the members may put a considerable strain on this kind of local voluntary association.

There also seems to be a higher level of competitive spirit among the farmers in the Protestant village. Some of the farmers prefer not to discuss their experiences with new methods and techniques, or new machines, with any of the other farmers. It was claimed that some of the fieldwork, such as spreading fertilizer, has at times been done surreptitiously under the cover of night, so that the neighbor could be confronted with a good stand of crops without knowing the extent of the input. Although this is a rather extreme and idiosyncratic form of one-upmanship, the general trend was sufficiently confirmed. At times I found that it was helpful to talk to both husband and wife together, for the chance that one would remind the other of a committed lapse. For instance, as I was trying to get confirmation from one of the Protestant farmers about the general trend toward secretiveness, I met with a round denial that such was the case. Whereupon his wife reminded him, "But you didn't tell so-and-so when he asked you what you did with your wheat, either." He then conceded that he thought it best to tell as little as possible, and he also related that a few days ago he had completely misled some outsider who had gone around asking the farmers how they utilized their skim milk. Another example of secretiveness is the weekly pig market; when one farmer asks another one how much he received for his piglets, chances are that the answer will not exactly hit the mark. I also felt that conversations at the Protestant inn somehow reflected this general trend of competitiveness; they seemed to be more guarded and at the same time more probing and more aggressive than those among the Catholics. Needless to say, not every farmer in either community fits the general pattern (in fact, some fit quite well into the pattern of the other community), but the actors themselves realize that there is a differential distribution of traits between the two communities. Incidentally, there seems to be no correlation between the size of a locality (within the range here under discussion) and the degree of cooperativeness. In a survey of eight hamlets in the surrounding area, I found that farmers in three of the hamlets cooperated to a significant extent; in the other five, cooperation and social interaction were restricted to a bare minimum. There is a local saying about this type of hamlet: "*Wenn's acht Baure hat, brauchet's neun Türe um in die Kerch 'nein zu kommen*" ('When there are eight farmers, they'll need nine doors to get into the church').

To summarize the foregoing observations: The Catholic farmers engage in fairly frequent and prolonged face-to-face interaction encompassing relatively large groups of individuals and are involved in cooperative ventures to a greater degree than their Protestant counterparts. On the other hand, face-to-face interaction among the Protestants takes place less frequently and among relatively small groups of individuals, and cooperative ventures are less extensive and individualistic behavior is more prominent. From a slightly different angle, we might say, that the Catholic farmers exhibit more cohesiveness as a group than the Protestant farmers. In my view, the degree of cohesiveness and cooperative action is linked to a significant extent to the degree of involvement in the communal aspects of religion.

Let me approach this from the secular end. We have seen in Chapter 8 that there are no significant structural reasons why the Catholics should be involved in the co-ownership of machines to a greater extent than the Protestants. I have now just described the greater frequency and intensity of face-to-face interaction among the Catholic farmers. This kind of interaction provides an effective platform for the launching of extensive cooperative ventures such as the one referred to. I am not saying that the Protestants could not possibly generate the same network density if they wanted to, even under the given conditions of the lesser frequency and extent of their face-to-face interaction, but the fact is that they have not done so. On the other hand, the Catholics have developed a denser network despite the fact that they dislike the negative features of co-ownership as much as the Protestants. Their frequent exposure to each other, however, has the net effect of joining more people in cooperative ventures. In other words, the fact that so many people are present at so many occasions provides the logistics for denser networks. It is no coincidence that the man with the largest number of bonds (28) is the lively publican. His counterpart in the Protestant village (with 14 bonds) is the leader of the trombone choir. An investigation might bring out that each of these two men interacts more frequently with a larger number of farmers in his respective community than any of the other farmers.

To establish fully the linkage between certain forms of cooperative behavior and religous behavior, I now have to connect the latter with the differential pattern of secular assemblage. We might conceive of the Sunday morning church service as the foil against which secular interaction is patterned. Almost all of the Catholic farmers gather every Sunday morning, participate in Holy Communion, and recite as a group the basic tenets of their common faith which binds them together. The feeling of communitas which is reinforced every Sunday morning is carried over into secular situations of which large and frequent assemblages constitute an extension of the religious gatherings. On the other hand, many of the Protestant farmers participate in the Sunday morning church service rather infrequently and are, therefore, not "stimulated" to form relatively large and frequent gatherings in a secular setting. What is absent here is the foil, or point of reference, provided by a religious gathering that encompasses most of the community, and I shall return to this theme in my discussion of the religious factor in Chapter 10.

Intracommunity Patterns of Conflict and Cooperation

Although Chapter 5 included a discussion of some of the forms of intrafamily conflict, I want to present a brief sketch of the most prevalent forms of conflict between the members of different households within the same community, and the ways in which these conflicts are resolved. An outside investigator working in a small community can not expect to observe more than a few conflict situations within the short time span of one year; he has to get most of his information from what the local people tell him, or from any records that may exist. In the sketch that follows, I shall first look at the written records and then report on answers to interview questions and on my own observations.

Records of the village court have been preserved in the Catholic village, spanning the period from 1828 to 1932 (similar records were apparently discarded in the Protestant commune). In these records, which are supplemented by the minutes of the village council, are contained all cases brought before the court (consisting of the mayor and two elected villagers), either for arbitration or for punitive action. The court had jurisdiction over misdemeanor offenses and was authorized to levy a fine, order restitution when applicable, or commit an offender to spend a few days in the village jail. The defendant had the right to appeal the decision to the district court (*Amtsgericht*). When the complaint dealt with a more serious offense, such as causing bodily injury, statements from the parties involved would be taken down and forwarded to the district court. If the complaint involved disputes over ownership of land, or over rights of access and similar property rights, the case would be examined through consultation of pertinent records and the hearing of witnesses. If one or both of the parties involved were not satisfied with the resulting decision, or the suggested arbitration, they could take their case to the district court.

The more numerous cases are more or less evenly divided between disputes over land, and disputes over access and related rights. For example, during the 30-year period from 1828 to 1858, when the village consisted of 56 households, there were 20 cases in each of the preceding categories. Decisions or arbitration in cases involving property rights were usually handled successfully at the village level; only 3 out of 20 cases went to the district court. These property rights dealt with access to parcels of land surrounded by other parcels, the right of turning a team of draft animals over an adjoining field at the end of a furrow, restrictions on where run-off water could be drained, access between houses in the village, and so forth. In most of these cases, the court could either rely on entries in the land records or on the testimony of older men to the effect that a certain right had existed "since time immemorial." In some instances, the court found that two men were simply making life difficult for each other and ordered them to cease and desist under penalty of a fine. Cases involving disputes over ownership of land, however, were more difficult to resolve, and three-fourths of them found their way to the district court. In some cases the records were not clear or no entries had been made in the land register after land had changed hands; or there were mix-ups after land auctions when someone claimed that he had really meant to buy this piece and not that one, and that he had signed the contract in error; or when a man claimed he was drunk when he sold another man a piece of land, or where border markers were found to have been removed or reset. In the latter case it was obligatory that the district court be notified because tampering with border markers constituted a criminal offense.

The preceding two categories are followed by 11 cases of disputes over owner-ship or rights to property other than real estate, and by 9 cases of nonpayment of debts. The property disputes were mostly over trees; for example, when three men owned one parcel of forest and two claimed that the third one had cut and sold a few trees without their knowledge and consent, or when a man cut a tree and another one claimed that it had stood on his land. Some men would refuse arbitration and take their case to the district court even though the monetary value of their claim might not exceed the equivalent of three or four chickens. We may assume that such an action was the capstone on a series of squabbles between two households which are not reflected in the records.

There follow four cases of theft of crops and three cases of assault and battery, all but one involving the same party. The evidence given at such occasions indicates that incidents of this nature were not always reported. I would also like to point out once more that the sample given does not include cases involving relatives from the same household, or disputes between villagers and outsiders.

During the Nazi regime, local courts were allowed to lapse, but they were revived, in Baden-Württemberg, in March of 1949. The new courts were given the name of *Friedensgericht* ('peace court') with functions similar to the old village court. However, these peace courts were declared unconstitutional and dissolved in November of 1959. It was held, among other things, that they did not guarantee equal protection, as it would be next to impossible in a small community where people knew each other's affairs rather intimately to provide a hearing before neutral or disinterested persons. Nonetheless, the position of *Gemeinderichter* ('village judge') remained. As a rule, it was filled by the mayor who had jurisdiction over minor civil cases brought to him for arbitration, in-volving disputes up to a value of 100 DM, and after 1962, 300 DM. In 1971, the parliament in Stuttgart decided to abolish this office as of the end of the year, contending that it had outlived its usefulness as a result of changing socioeco-nomic conditions, citing as evidence that between 1966 and 1969, only one-fourth of all the judges had cases brought before them.

The majority of cases dealt with during the 10 years of local "peace court" concern violations of traffic laws (such as riding a bicycle without lights) which are not relevant here. Beyond that, the records of the Catholic village show two cases of libel, both involving the same parties; those of the Protestant commune show a few complaints about trespassing animals, four cases of libel, two cases involving access rights, and one which revolves around the temporary boycott of the village inn. Except for one case in the Protestant community, cases such as libel were successfully arbitrated and did not reach the district court.

Let us now turn to the current situation. As part of an interview directed at heads of farm households, I asked: What, in your opinion, are the major causes that lead to tension around here? I followed up with questions about extent and resolution of the respective conflict situations. With one exception, the same kind of tension-producing situations were named by the men in both communities, at about the same rate of frequency. These are (in order of frequency): (1) driving over someone else's land; (2) envy about material possessions or personal fortunes of others; (3) getting involved over acts committed by children; (4) plowing an additional furrow into a neighboring field; (5) slander; and (6) (mentioned in Protestant community only) trespassing of animals. According to this testimony (which was reinforced by statements made by some 80 men and women during taped interviews at a later date), infringement of property rights is still the most prevalent, overt cause of conflict situations. Almost all of these cases, however, are now handled informally between the parties involved, sometimes with an assist from the mayor as arbiter; everyone claimed that to take such a small matter to the district court would indeed be extravagant. Rather, the offender would be told off at a suitable occasion and the matter put to rest. On the whole, it is claimed that people attach less importance to infringements of property rights than in the past. As I did not try to obtain access to the records of the district court, I do not know how many cases involving local complaints were brought before it, but I was informed about the actions of three farmers in one of the Protestant hamlets who had reported each other for minor infractions of the building code and were subsequently fined.[2] Incidentally, disputes over ownership of land, which were so prevalent during the last century, have largely disappeared, partly because there has been very little sale of land during the last 5 decades and partly because of better record-keeping, even though once in a while parties to an exchange of land seem to have neglected to effect the necessary entries.

Most of the overt causes of strife and conflict are relatively small matters, but many of the local people think that envy has a great deal to do with any of the conflict situations. Interestingly, among the farmers it was only the larger farmers in the Protestant community who mentioned envy as a potential cause of conflict; none of the medium or small farmers thought to bring it up. Could it be that they strongly feel themselves a target of envy because they have more,

[2] There were a few others cases that were brought to my attention, such as a paternity suit in the Protestant village, and a suit between relatives in the Catholic village about repayment of a loan.

and that the others do not mention it because to them it was such a touchy point that they do not want to admit its existence? (We did see, however, that two or three of the smaller farmers mentioned envy in connection with tractorization, albeit not necessarily in reference to themselves.) Or is it that the large farmers themselves are much more aware of feelings of envy because the competition is so much keener among their own group? To relay the general tenor, here are some brief quotations:

> *Tension and conflict among the people here is mostly caused by envy and it works this way. When I buy a new machine tomorrow and the neighbor gets to see it, his eyes will turn big: "Oh, look, he bought himself a new machine!" Now you just look at him, because now he is envious. That's the envy of the have-nots, and now the circus starts. When you meet them they'll turn a little to the side, or if the children did something they'll be right on your back, or they wait for a chance to throw at you that you have more money—some people have a terrible time with their envy!*

> *The causes for many quarrels are the same for man as for beast and this is never going to change—envy, mutual envy. And envy produces hate. The other one has more, has this and that, and each watches constantly what the other is doing and just waits that the other one is doing something wrong.*

> *Envy plays the greatest part in many of the conflicts. If people were considerate of each other—but if everyone thinks he has to have the most and he wants to suppress the other and wants to add another furrow and another furrow and doesn't want to give it back and my field gets ever smaller and his field gets ever larger—that's when the problems mount.*

Although the first remark refers to the envy of those who rank lower on the economic scale than the one who thinks he is the target of envy, the last two remarks refer to interaction between large farmers of about equal standing. Envy is therefore not confined to, or solely generated by, material differences between the "rich" and the "poor." Jockeying for a slight advantage over a competitor with equal resources may generate more tension than fretting about someone who has considerably more. I should add that some of the women were also very outspoken on the existence and disruptive effects of envy—independent of the ranking of their respective households on the economic scale.

Although much of the conflict takes place between two individual parties, the existence of factions plays a part in the alignment of forces, as well as being an indicator as to who is most likely going to have a fight with whom. For example, cutting across all other divisions in the Catholic village are two factions: the "Nazis" and the "anti-Nazis." These had their beginnings in the 1930s, when a handful of local farmers decided to throw their support to the existing regime, while a larger group decided to remain as passively resistant as possible under the prevailing conditions. The majority of farmers in-between had more quietly aligned themselves with either one or the other side. The "Nazis" wielded considerable power; among other things, they had a say in who was or was not going to be drafted into the armed forces. Most of the villagers claim that despite all the hate and bitterness once generated between these two factions, they are now no longer functional. Some actions in recent years, however, in which opposing forces were lined up along these factional lines, and my own observations, indicate that this factionalism will still surface, even if on a more limited scale. Discussions at the inn will often bring out which side a person had stood on. One incident during my stay brought out that in case of friction, support is expected to be furnished by members of one's own group. One of the villagers, an "anti-Nazi," had his nose broken one Sunday evening in one of the inns by a member of the opposite faction, more or less as the result of a misinterpretation of his arm movements during a heated debate over personal virtues. He reported the matter to the police (as a preliminary step to recover at least medical expenses from the assailant) and began marshaling support along factional lines. When one of the key witnesses did not agree with his own version of the event, he went around complaining bitterly about this let-down in his own camp.[3]

I might add that physical violence is generally shunned and that the above case, which was almost an "accident," is the only one that came to my attention during my 1-year stay.[4] Villagers were generally unhappy about the incident: "If only those guys, or one of them, had been from another village." Fights give a village a bad name, and although people love to spar verbally and may attack each other by way of gossip and rumor-mongering, physical violence is held to exceed the bounds of propriety. I assumed, therefore, that the villagers would be interested in having the case settled out of court, but I was surprised to find out that there were no mediators. Everyone claimed that no matter who the person was that would try to mediate, he would automatically be placed in the other camp by either one of the contestants and people were therefore unwilling to get involved in any way.[5] The case was abruptly resolved when one of the men was killed—slain by his tractor when it overturned on him on a steep slope.

[3]The present identities are mainly based on past affiliation or nonaffiliation of a man, or his father, with the Nazi Party. The ideological perspectives of some individuals from either faction do not necessarily differ greatly from each other.

[4]There are no records or memories of homicides. The "goriest" incident I came across took place on August 28, 1839, at half-past six in the morning, when a farmer had his ear pierced by a pitchfork-wielding father-in-law who was avenging his daughter for having received a box on the ear.

[5]This aversion toward becoming a mediator, and thereby running the risk of being identified with the interests of either party, may account for the fact that (with one or two exceptions) I was never introduced by a person who already knew me to a person I had not yet met. Almost all of the local contacts had to be initiated by myself.

The fact that people live at such close quarters and that most of them are engaged in the same occupation is instrumental in generating many of the conflicts. The villagers find it generally unpleasant to have to avoid someone because of an ongoing feud, and it is difficult to stay out of each other's way in such a small place. Furthermore, there are always times when help is needed and it is therefore unwise to have too many quarrels going for too long. There are numerous small occasions when a man needs to call one or several others to lend a hand, as well as larger occasions involving more or less the whole community. For example, people who built a house or barn up to 10 or so years ago claim that they saved a large part of the labor costs because their fellow villagers pitched in without pay to do most of the work. The old-established pattern of reciprocal assistance would normally include almost all of the local households, so that the construction of a new house or barn became a communal affair. During the last decade, availability of unpaid labor has steadily decreased. Not only can households no longer furnish as much manpower as before, but people can now make money working on outside jobs. This has brought about a new attitude toward helping a fellow villager without compensation on a larger project, and I was told that even relatives now expect to be paid for their help at construction jobs.

Some of the villagers see the fact that so many of them are related to each other that it is a means of keeping a check on too much strife. In the words of one farmer:

> *It's like this: one knows the other and there are differences of opinion and some yelling and driving over another man's fields, but there are no serious problems and people help each other and by and large get along with each other. And then, too, many families are related to each other. If it quakes at one end of the village, it rattles at the other end, too—kinshipwise, that is—even though relations may span several generations. For example, the A's up there, they are an older generation, they are related to the B's, and the B's are related to the C's back there, and the C's again to the D's over there, and the D's are related to the E's, and the E's are related to us, and my wife comes from the G's down there—and so it goes around and around. My wife is from the village, my brother has his wife from the village, my sister has her husband from the village, and only my little sister married down to* [neighboring Catholic village]. *Now if you carry this back over several generations, you'll find that the whole village is related to each other.*

[Letters substituted for names by author.]

Of course, many of the kinship bonds referred to would cancel each other out, exactly because of their extensiveness. Furthermore, most of these bonds are not usually recognized by the villagers in a functional sense. When I asked them whether they have any relatives in the village (to find out to what extent they recognized "relatives"), most people would only go as far as naming second cousins ("Our parents are *Geschwisterkinder*," i.e., children of siblings). Only a few would name those that had to be traced further back than grandparental sibling pairs, or great-grandparents, mainly because they assumed that this infor-mation might be helpful for my work, not because they would usually think of them as relatives. I found that some of the most active social intercourse and mutual assistance can be found between households connected through marriage in the present generation.

In concluding this section, I want to point out that my emphasis on patterns of conflict, or instances of conflict, should not be construed as reflecting the kind of situation in which "village social life goes on in a context of envy, mutual distrust, and conflict," as has been variously observed in Mediterranean and Latin American communities (Aceves 1971:118, and subsequent remarks). Although it is true that there are always a few households in every generation that might fit this pattern, they never constitute a majority (except in the case of small hamlets). From my point of view, life goes on within a context of mutual accommodations and pragmatic considerations, in which the well-being of the community as a whole is not ignored. We may very well here touch on basic differences of personality along large-scale cultural divisions, but this point is beyond the scope of my investigation (see Quigley 1973:319).

Intercommunity Relations

Up to the 1930s, contact between the two communities was minimal. Some of the Catholics would pass through the Protestant community on their way to market or to the warehouse; they might exchange a few greetings or even stop off at one of the inns, but social contact remained rather superficial. According to testimony from both sides, everyone was very much aware of the different religious affiliation of the other. The Catholics generally looked down on the *Ketzer* (heretics), and some of the Protestants were irked by this show of re-ligious superiority. In retrospect, there is a widespread feeling that the clergymen were actively seeing to it that their flock remain on their side of the fence, keeping social barriers intact. Beyond some name-calling, differences in religious affiliation apparently did not lead to active conflict, however. The general lack of social contact was seemingly paralleled by peaceful relations.

The Third Reich brought some of the individuals a little closer. Four or five of the Catholics joined the S.A. (storm troopers) and the Nazi Party, and found themselves rubbing shoulders in the same unit with their Protestant neighbors. A few friendships have developed out of these contacts which have lasted into the present, with Protestants having come over several years ago to help a Catholic build his house, for example. Most boys over the age of 10 joined the Hitler Youth and had to go to the Protestant village or a nearby town for their regular meetings. Today, the men who had been in the Hitler Youth recall that there were certain problems, such as when a Sunday morning meeting conflicted with attendance at church; the Catholics would usually go to church and were subsequently upbraided for not coming to the meeting. There were also physical fights, many of them started over taunts as to religious affiliation. It is questionable, however, that religion itself was of any great importance in these fights, because it was usually the custom in many regions of Germany that youths from different villages would fight each other, even if the denomination was the same.

Although a few individuals had thus established closer contact with each other, social interaction between the two communities remained at a minimal level. The Second World War, and especially post-war events brought some changes, however. The flood of refugees from eastern regions of Germany had to be distributed among the towns and village, bringing a number of Catholic families to the Protestant community. The Catholic village was successful in restricting intake of refugees largely to the same denomination. For example, when a Protestant refugee family from a nearby village made an application to move into a vacant flat, an entry in the minutes of the commune council, dated December 1949, lists several reasons why the application could not be accepted, concluding that "last but not least, it should be mentioned that a residence permit cannot be granted because of the denominational differences." Thus, although the Protestants reportedly somehow benefited from having Catholics living in their midst, learning to shed some of their prejudices (after an initial period of upset), the Catholics in their village remained separate and withdrawn.

A series of events which started in 1967 has considerably changed this withdrawn position. During that year the number of elementary school students dropped below 15, and the county school board decided that for the new school year the children would be transferred to the neighboring Protestant community and the school in the Catholic village would be closed. This was a blow for the whole village (especially after a new school house had been built in 1963 at considerable expense), for to take the children out of the village and away from the supervision of the parents was a novel situation. There was also considerable trepidation among the villagers about sending the children to school in a Protestant village, but their fears were somewhat allayed when it turned out that the children did not experience any problems.[6]

---

[6]Up to about the middle 1950s, the schools in either community had been *Konfessionsschulen*, i.e., the teachers had to be of the same denomination as the children and instructions were partly geared to the respective ethics of Catholicism and Protestantism.

With the end of the school year in July, 1971, the Protestant community had to close down its school, too, as part of a move by the ministry of education to close all schools where the low number of students did not warrant the separate instruction of grade levels. Since then, the children from the Protestant community have been attending school in the neighboring Protestant community with which their own commune is presently going to merge (see Chapter 3), and the children from the Catholic village are attending school in the neighboring Catholic community, likewise slated for a communal merger.

The first year that their children attended school in the neighboring Protestant village also brought with it an occasion for closer contact among the adults. The state-run radio station in Stuttgart had been producing a series of 1-hr programs for broadcasting on Sunday mornings; each of these programs would feature one particular town or village in Baden-Württemberg with performances by its choir and brass band, interspersed by information on its points of interest and history. Such a production was planned for the Protestant community, but it turned out that the local choir was too small. Contact with two neighboring Protestant communities proposing a possible consolidation of choirs brought no results. The teacher then suggested that the neighboring Catholics be approached, and the children helped to propagandize the scheme. Subsequently, the two local choirs merged, and the teacher (who had formerly taught in the Catholic village) became the conductor. Since then, between 10 and 20 men from each community have come together for weekly choir practice, except for the busy summer months. They sing together at festive occasions in each other's community and, on special holidays, in each other's churches. This point is of some importance; a person who has been raised to consider only his or her own Church as the only legitimate one will often entertain certain notions about the religious practices of the "opposition," but once the heretofore strange service has been witnessed on a number of occasions, most of the former misconceptions tend to disappear.

A considerable relaxation of negative attitudes has followed these events, as everyone is well aware, and this relaxation has certainly been helped by the fact that the Protestant mayor, who serves both communities, has been a great success with the Catholic villagers. His business acumen and the energetic efficiency with which he handles the local affairs have earned him everyone's admiration. Before his taking office, village leaders had adhered to a communal policy of maintaining an overly conservative budget. Field and forest roads of the Catholic commune had remained in a rather primitive state long after those in the Protestant commune had been graded and partially blacktopped. The introduction of new types of farm machinery had put a premium on the existence of good field roads, and, although most of the Catholic farmers were generally unhappy about the excessive amount of wear and tear on their machines caused by the bad condition of the roads, the leaders could not be moved to embark on a plan of rehabilitation. This became one of the first tasks of the new mayor after he took office in 1969. He "shook up" the commune council and embarked on a comprehensive program of repairs and new construction (with the work, in 1974, being completed). This action has benefited the community as a whole and has been gratefully acknowledged by all.

One last point that has brought the Catholics a little closer to the Protestants is the fact that, over the years, more and more children of Catholic families who have moved to the city have married Protestant partners. However, the tabu on having a Protestant marry into the village has so far proved a very powerful one. Two of the local bachelors think that they would be brave enough to marry a

Protestant girl should the opportunity present itself. As one of them saw the situation:

> *According to the new regulations proclaimed by the Church, it is no longer the case that, if children have not been baptized into the Catholic faith, the Catholic partner in a mixed marriage is automatically excommunicated. Nowadays, after a bishop has given his consent, one can get married in a Protestant church or by a registrar—both actions are binding. Of course, in rural areas there are certain problems. The families are much more conservative—not so much the young people, but the older generation. When the bishop decrees a new regulation prohibiting something, all of the older people are complying; but if he relaxes a law and allows something which used to be prohibited, they just don't want to believe that this is now permissible and the old prohibition done away with. In this respect, the older generation is very shortsighted. If there were already two or three who had married a Protestant girl, then the problem would not be so great; but to be the first one in the village requires a thick hide and a lot of courage. Actually, the situation is quite ridiculous, but it takes time before these things are demolished.*

It is apparently very difficult for the older generation to discard traditional attitudes of religious segregation, but not all of the younger generation are in favor of mixed marriages, either. One ought to remember that young and old have to get along in the same household; given the climate of potential friction which exists under these conditions, many are afraid that the presence of a Protestant daughter-in-law might further complicate intergenerational relations.

Voting Patterns

When I examined available statistics before going to the field, I noticed two differences in the voting patterns of Catholics and Protestants. The Catholics were giving their votes almost exclusively to candidates from the Christian Democratic Union (CDU), and the Protestants would split their votes primarily between the CDU and the Free Democrats (FDP). Secondly, the Catholics showed a consistently higher voter participation, or turn-out, than the Protestants (Table 10).

Considering the generally conservative orientation of farmers in conjunction with the religious and economic factors, it is not difficult to see why the Catholics would feel drawn to the CDU. The older generation had voted for the *Zentrum* (the Catholic Center Party, 1870–1933), whose predominantly Catholic membership included Silesian industrialists, farmers from southern Germany,

Table 10

VOTER PARTICIPATION AND DISTRIBUTION OF VOTES CAST FOR MAJOR PARTIES IN PERCENTAGES
OF ELIGIBLE VOTERS, AND NUMBER OF VALID VOTES CAST, RESPECTIVELY[a]

Election	VOTER PARTICIPATION		PARTIES VOTED FOR:						
	Cath.	Prot.	CATHOLICS			PROTESTANTS			
			EDU	FDP	SPD	CDU	FDP	SPD	Misc.
S 1952	93.3	58.2	95.4	4.1	0.5	50.2	25.3	2.5	
S 1956	94.6	66.3	95.0	2.8	1.1	50.7	38.1	4.9	
S 1960	83.1	50.7	99.4	0	0.4	25.7	67.8	5.3	(GDP) 20.0
F 1953	99.0	71.3	96.9	2.0	0.5	57.5	18.5	2.5	
F 1957	92.5	62.1	96.2	1.6	1.6	35.1	56.8	1.6	
F 1961	95.3	84.9	96.6	2.2	1.1	22.1	76.2	1.2	
F 1965	91.1	65.4	98.3	0	0.6	47.1	45.5	7.0	
F 1969	91.0	67.3	98.1	0	1.9	53.8	25.8	8.1	
S 1972	88.1	68.4	97.5	0.6	1.8	59.8	16.7	23.0	(NPD) 11.8

[a]Data from Baden-Württemberg, Statistisches Landesamt (1964c, 1966, 1970a); *Hohenloher Tagblatt* (Dec. 11, 1972).
Key S: State Parliament (*Landestag*) Baden-Württemberg.
     F: Federal Parliament (*Bundestag*).

153

and workers from the Rhineland. Beyond the religious factor, this party had appealed to the farmer because of its pursuance of a protectionist policy in favor of German farm products. To some degree, the CDU is the successor of the old Center Party, although its base is considerably broader and its appeal is directed as much toward Protestants as it is toward Catholics. In the Protestant communities, on the other hand, most of the votes (before the advent of the Nazis) had gone to Conservatives and Democrats. The Free Democrats of the postwar era have drawn their main support from the ranks of entrepreneurs, both large and small. The history of the party includes alternate formations of coalition governments with either the CDU or the Social Democrats (SPD), both on the level of the *Land* government in Stuttgart, and the federal government in Bonn.

As I mentioned before, very few of the farmers have much use for the Social Democrats whom they see as pledged to help the worker by promising him lower food prices and higher wages, which, in turn, translates into higher expenditures and lower incomes for the farmer. The Catholics apparently have to do little soul-searching as to whom to give their votes at election time. In answer to questions in structured interviews, as well as in informal conversations, time and again I would hear the same theme:

> *We vote for the party rather than the personality or the promises of a particular candidate; this is really the only way we can vote. Of course, voting the Christian ticket does not mean that we vote straight Catholic— many of the candidates around here have been Protestants. But the SPD is a worker's party, and workers want to live cheaply, and we want to make a little money and that is difficult to reconcile; besides, we don't care for the kind of policy which will lead to collectivization and takeover by the Communists in the east. As for the Free Democrats and their liberal and shifty ways—we prefer the Christian ticket.*

At the same time, none of the farmers harbor any illusions about the fact that they are a minority group in the power game of state and national politics:

> *It stands to reason that our political representatives can't do too much for us. Those few farmers who are left, they can't give them everything. Germany is an industrial country and policies are made accordingly. But you can tell when election time draws close—that's the time we can usually expect a few things to come our way.* [7]

[7]This does not mean, however, that German farmers are taking everything in stride without any protest, as demonstrations of farmers riding their tractors into various cities have shown (see, for example, 1971 reports in the *Württembergisches Wochenblatt für Landwirtschaft*). Also, the German Farmers Association (*Deutscher Bauernverband*) does exert a certain amount of influence on national and EEC policy-making; see, for example, the treatise by Ackermann (1970) on the DBV and European grain prices.

In the Protestant community, the Free Democrats were able to draw a considerable number of votes, not only because of the local conservative-democratic (pre-Nazi) tradition, but also because of the appeal and seeming competence of particular candidates. Their popularity was at a peak in the early 60s, but toward the middle of the decade they started to lose ground. The 12% of voters who came out in favor of the "neo-Nazi" National Democrats (NPD) in the federal elections of 1969, further detracted from the diminishing percentage of votes for the FDP. During my stay in 1971, it became clear that the FDP was bound to receive even fewer votes in the 1972 elections. Some people argued that it made little sense to waste one's vote on a party that was becoming ever smaller, losing political support everywhere; others—especially those with a more conservative bent—took exception to the FDP having formed a coalition government with the SPD, which they saw as a disastrous turn toward the left. The outcome of the federal elections in 1972 indeed proved that support for the FDP had dwindled further. The CDU has not, however, emerged as the full beneficiary of this desertion; although I do not know who cast the 23% of votes for the SPD, I suspect that this represents the local blue collar workers, many of whom had previously seen the Social Democrats as alien to their way of rural existence.

The other area of differential voting behavior has been the percentage of voter participation. An explanation for this difference eluded me for some time. In my observations I did not find any overt indications that the Catholics were noticeably more interested in politics than the Protestants—neither the quantity nor the intensity of discussions that dealt with political topics seemed to be measurably different. Political meetings (for example, when Dr. Jenninger [CDU], member of the *Bundestag*, came to conduct an election talk with a scheduled question and answer period) certainly did not turn out a larger percentage of Catholics.

The clue to a possible explanation of this difference came rather late during my stay, in October 1971, when elections for seats on country and commune councils were held. This brought home to me a factor which I had completely overlooked: Elections in Germany are always held on a Sunday. The local pattern now started to fall into place: The Catholics combined their attendance at church with a walk to the polling booth at the *Rathaus* to cast their votes. As we shall see in Chapter 10, church attendance among Protestants is considerably lower, so that for most Protestants the act of voting requires an effort on its own. It therefore seems reasonable to conclude that the percentage of voters per commune will vary with the number of habitual churchgoers.

To test this hypothesis for other rural communities, and assuming that reports from various informants were correct and church attendance there followed similar patterns, I checked the results of past elections for the two counties of Hohenlohe which combine the largest number of denominationally differentiated communes, selecting only those, however, whose inhabitants are at least 70% either Catholic or Protestant. As Table 11 shows, the results clearly dupli-

Table 11

VOTER PARTICIPATION IN PERCENTAGES OF ELIGIBLE VOTERS IN
COMMUNES WITH POPULATIONS PREDOMINANTLY (I.E., MORE THAN 70%)
CATHOLIC OR PROTESTANT[a]

	MERGENTHEIM COUNTY			KÜNZELSAU COUNTY		
Election	Cath.	Prot.	Total county	Cath.	Prot.	Total county
S 1952	86.1	64.3	68.0	92.1	70.6	76.6
S 1956	89.5	68.3	74.4	92.2	67.4	77.0
S 1960	79.8	57.5	62.4	84.6	58.4	66.6
F 1953	87.8	79.2	85.1	96.6	81.0	87.5
F 1957	91.8	77.5	82.2	93.2	76.4	84.0
F 1961	93.3	77.8	84.5	95.7	79.3	86.6
F 1965	92.4	78.7	84.5	94.6	77.5	85.7
F 1969	84.9	77.5	79.6	89.0	76.5	82.1

[a]Data from Baden-Württemberg, Statistisches Landesamt (1964a, 1964c, 1966, 1970a).
Key S: State Parliament (Landestag) Baden-Württemberg
       F: Federal Parliament (Bundestag)
  Number of Communes: Mergentheim: Catholic–15; Protestant–33; Total–61
                        Künzelsau: Catholic–20; Protestant–13; Total–51

Table 12

PERCENTAGE DISTRIBUTION OF VALID VOTES (ERSTSTIMMEN) CAST FOR
MAJOR PARTIES IN COMMUNES WITH POPULATIONS PREDOMINANTLY
(I.E., MORE THAN 70%) CATHOLIC OR PROTESTANT IN THE FEDERAL ELECTION
(BUNDESTAG) OF SEPTEMBER 28, 1969[a]

MERGENTHEIM COUNTY	NUMBER OF VALID VOTES	CDU	SPD	FDP	NPD
Catholics (15)[b]	4,919	80.5	12.4	3.4	3.7
Protestants (33)[b]	7,966	48.7	21.6	16.0	13.4
Total communes (61)[b]	21,944	61.3	21.4	9.2	8.0
KÜNZELSAU COUNTY					
Catholics (20)[b]	5,140	87.7	7.8	2.2	3.1
Protestants (13)[b]	2,728	40.9	24.1	25.1	9.8
Total communes (51)[b]	16,898	58.0	24.9	10.2	6.6

[a]Data from Baden-Württemberg, Statistiches Landesamt (1964a, 1970a).
[b]Figures in parentheses refer to respective number of communes.

cate the pattern found in the two communes of this study. Furthermore, as a glance at Table 12 will point up once again, it is the Christian Democrats who have benefited from the presence of Catholics to a larger extent than from the presence of Protestants. In view of this correlation between church attendance, voter participation, and votes cast for the CDU, it is easy to predict that, if the voting day were shifted to a weekday, the rural vote for the CDU would suffer a significant decline.[8]

[8]For a discussion of politics, voting patterns, and religion, see Dahrendorf (1969, Chaps. 7 & 21).

10
The Place of Religion

This chapter endeavors to present a description and analysis of various manifestations of religious behavior. We shall look at religious practices and the degree of involvement on the part of the participants, as well as discuss the opinions and attitudes of both clergy and laymen. This will be done by presenting each community separately, and by looking at the scene through the eyes of the clergymen, the parishioners, and the investigator. An overall interpretation on a comparative basis will be rendered at the end of the chapter.

As a point of reference, here is a recapitulation of the respective denominational distributions:

CATHOLIC COMMUNITY

Total resident population (January 1971)	256
Roman Catholics (98%)	250
Protestants (2%)	6

The Protestants in the Catholic community comprise two families who moved in during the last decade (one to buy a house and lease the general store, the other one—a mixed marriage—to rent the vacant rectory) and one woman who married one of the local farmers 20 years ago (see Chapter 8, Footnote 1, p. 124).

PROTESTANT COMMUNITY

Total resident population (February 1971)	388
Protestants (91%)	354
Roman Catholics (9%)	34

The Catholics in this Protestant community comprise one farm family in one of the hamlets (whose members have resided there for many generations) and 30 persons who came into the community after the war, most of them as refugees. Those 30 persons are distributed over five Catholic families, and nine families of mixed marriage (in three of those nine families, one partner is native to the community).

Of the Protestants, 321 persons (83% of the total population) are members of the *Evangelische Landeskirche in Württemberg*.[1] Another 28 persons (7%) are members of the New Apostolic Church,[2] and 4 persons (1%) belong to a sect of fairly recent origin (the *Spätregengemeinde*, literally, 'late-rain congregation') whose major attraction seems to lie in its faith-healing sessions.

Protestants

The Pastor (Pfarrer)

The Protestant village has had its own church since pre-Reformation times, and the list of known, local clergymen goes back to 1531, twenty years before the Reformation was introduced in the area. Most of the pastors bear names that have a familiar ring in this part of Germany, but it is possible that some came from northern regions. Many of them seem to have been raised in agricultural communities and were, therefore, familiar with all phases of farming. But some of them were from towns and cities and, at times, complained about the burden of unfamiliar farm work on land that had been given to the church for the partial remuneration of the pastor. The Protestant Church still holds some of this land, but the pastors have long ceased to work it with their own hands.

The present pastor is a city man from Prussia. He was transferred to Württemberg 15 years ago, and was eventually placed in charge of the local parish after the previous pastor had died in 1966. He is close to retirement but may stay on

[1]In 1817, a union between Lutherans and Calvinists was effected in various parts of Germany, which took the name *Evangelische Kirche* ('Evangelical Church'). Lutheran, Reformed, and Evangelical churches in Germany were variously constituted as state churches; these unions were dissolved subsequent to the constitutional separation of church and state in 1918. The present *Evangelische Landeskirche in Württemberg* is a member of a federation of churches known as the *Evangelische Kirche in Deutschland* (see Lueker 1954:411-413; 1075-1079 & Hermelink 1949.)

[2]The New Apostolic Church was founded in Germany in 1862, as a movement away from the Catholic Apostolic Church (Irvingites). "The apostles are viewed as the spiritual canals who supplement the Bible with their teaching; complete the work of the Atonement; govern the Church; give efficacy to the sacraments; impose the tithe as due Christ the High Priest and Chief Apostle; and through the laying on of hands, the 'holy sealing,' prepare men for Christ's second coming [Lueker 1954:180-181]."

if he wishes, because there is a shortage of Protestant ministers (in fact, he retired 3 years after the ethnographic present of 1971 at the age of 67). He is also in charge of a neighboring parish with a slightly smaller number of parishioners.

On the whole, the local congregation does not measure up to the pastor's expectations. The following is a paraphrase of his expressed views; his views will be commented upon after we have also looked at the church service and the congregation.

The people here are not very interested in religion. Many desecrate the Sabbath by staying away from church instead of following the call of the bells. Only a few participate in Communion. The confirmands who attend confirmation classes are unable to discuss religious concepts, and they are apt to forget what they have learned from one class period to the next, not the least because there are no religious discussions held in the home. This is hard to understand since the farmer ought to be, and indeed is, closer to God because of his dependence on the forces of nature; he ought to be able to see how little his personal efforts have to do with the end results. Few people take their troubles and problems to the pastor and they are generally reluctant to talk about their spiritual needs. There is a barrier between the pastor and his parishioners which he finds difficult to penetrate. He does not really know what goes on in the community; nobody will tell him, not even the presbyters. He has heard that the priest who has jurisdiction over the local Catholics knows more about this community than he who lives here. He has noticed, however, that the people here do not form the kind of Gemein-schaft *that one would expect in a small, rural community. What seems to be lacking most around here is the respect for authority and the discipline that goes with it. The pastor's primary duty, however, is to bring Jesus to the people.*

The Sunday Morning Church Service

The service starts alternately at nine o'clock, or at half-past ten (the pastor has to conduct a service in the church of the neighboring parish as well), and lasts for an hour. It begins with a prelude performed on the organ or by the trombone choir, which is followed by some hymn singing, a prayer, and a sermon of about 30 min duration. The service is concluded with the communal recitation of the *pater noster* and the blessing of the congregation by the pastor. The sermons follow a pattern of exhortations in which repentence and turning back from the path of sin are the major themes. There is a persistent emphasis on such negative aspects as the vanity of man, his irreligious stance, and his refusal to admit to his lack of faith. Rarely touched upon in these sermons are the positive aspects of religion, such as the strength that emanates from belonging to a spiritual community or the joys that might be experienced even in this life. Neither has there ever been any mention of current efforts to bring Catholics and Protestants together in ecumenical services.

The arguments pursued in the sermons are rarely related to contemporary events and generally lack illustrations drawn from everyday life. When such references are made, however, the congregation is presented with a particular kind of conservative point of view. For example, in an aside on the difficult phase through which agriculture is passing at the present time, the farmer is told to stay on his land and remain a master, rather than go and work in industry and become a slave who can be hired and fired at will. Or, in a brief comment on the state of contemporary society, the congregation is told that democracy is something that many people cannot handle; it is, in fact, a "demon of the people." There are some areas, however, in which the pastor would welcome changes, for instance in the way in which the sexes are segregated in church with the men sitting upstairs in the gallery and the women downstairs in the nave. Every once in a while he pushes this point in a sermon and also chides the congregation for mainly occupying the back rows, quipping that it might be dangerous to come closer to God's word. So far, the congregation has not responded, however, and only on holidays do some of the men (usually nonfarmers) sit next to their wives in the nave. (Segregation according to marital status has been abandoned for some time, and high-ranking families no longer use their special pews; the children below confirmation age have their own service, the *Christenlehre*, which follows that of the adults.)

The sermons of the relief pastor (an elderly gentleman and former refugee who is in charge of a large neighboring parish, helping out when the local pastor is on vacation or ill) are generally more colorful and, in a way, take more cognizance of the fact that they are largely directed at farmers. The pastor excels in waging the traditional war against carnal lust and other worldly pleasures, especially pointing his finger at those who take the pill so they can increase their lustful experiences instead of carrying the burden that is rightfully theirs. The farmer is elevated in one sermon and chastised in the next. He is portrayed in a favorable light when compared with atheistic professors in the city:

> *Behold the farmer who tills the soil and sows the seeds—he knows where it's at. But wait and consider: technology and environmental pollution, including the use of chemical fertilizers and insecticides, spell the downfall of the Occident. Times have changed since the farmer walked behind his horses or cows; now he rides his tractor, his senses blunted through his constant association with machines. The close contact with the earth and God has been lost.*

The Parishioners: Commitment, Attitudes, and Opinions. [3]

The most visible form of participation in religious affairs is attendance at the Sunday morning church service. On an ordinary Sunday, attendance by parishioners over the age of 14 (a total of 257, the basis of computation for the following percentages), averages 46 persons (19 male and 27 female), or 18%. On holidays, attendance ranges from 40% to 65%. There is a core of about 20 persons (8%) who can be relied on to turn up almost every Sunday; another 30% attend occasionally, i.e., about once or twice a month; another 40% attend on all or some of the major holidays; and about 20% not more than once a year, or not at all. Farmers and older people are proportionately overrepresented, although there are usually representatives from each age range. The presbyters, or church elders, are likely to turn up more often than some of the other men, and among some families it is customary that at least one member of the family should put in an appearance in church. There do not seem to be any significant seasonal fluctuations in church attendance that can be linked to the agricultural cycle.

The parishioners claim that church attendance was better a few years ago than it is now. They see the personality of the pastor as an important element in this issue. The previous pastor is described as having been warm, intelligent, unpretentious, and understanding the nature of the farmer. This does not necessarily mean that they find the present pastor completely lacking in all of these virtues. They especially recognize his sincerity, his devotion to duty (he will hold weekly prayer meetings even if only two or three people will come) and his willingness to listen to them, but they also find it regrettable that he stands so aloof from their way of life and from the real issues, and that the "Frau Pfarrer" (the "Mrs. Pastor," an important element in the communal functions of a village rectory) has been unable to establish ties with the members of the congregation. Some parishioners will justify their abstention from regular church attendance by referring to specific points in the sermons to which they take exception; as one of them put it, "If I have worked hard all week and go to church on Sunday, I don't enjoy having my nose wiped!" Others claim that they have too much work to do at home, or that they know beforehand they are going to fall asleep and therefore see no sense in going in the first place. Although one does not have to take all of these explanations at face value, it seems that the personality of the pastor has an important bearing on the extent to which the members of his congregation participate in religious affairs. [4]

[3] Data on sermons and on attendance are based on participation in 22 services over a period of 11 months. Data on religious beliefs, etc. were collected as part of 52 taped, structured interviews (36 males, 16 females), as well as numerous unstructured interviews.

[4] This does not merely pertain to rural congregations. For example, in one study of an urban congregation, it was found that even among those who attended church on a "regular" basis, more than half would only attend when "their" pastor (among three rotating pastors) conducted the service (Köster 1959:34).

Because church attendance is only one manifestation of religious commitment, I asked about 25% of the parishioners (ranging across all categories of church-goers) a number of questions about individual religious experiences and beliefs. For example, three-fifths of the men and four-fifths of the women questioned think that praying can be effective in situations in which we have no absolute control over events. On the other hand, four-fifths of the women, but only two-fifths of the men, believe in a life after death. Almost no one experienced worries at the thought that one day we may be held accountable for our deeds by God (I had asked this question to obtain an indication of possible struggles within an individual as to his or her commitment to religiously inspired duties). I also asked the men where they would place themselves, regardless of their stand toward the church, as to their feelings of religious commitment—among the devout Christians (*gläubiger Christ*), among those who primarily follow because of tradition, or those who go along without conviction (*Mitläufer*). The majority of men saw themselves as motivated by traditional aspects of communal religion; only two admitted to being mere conformists without conviction, and two saw themselves as devout Christians (one of the latter even suggested that only firm believers should be allowed to retain membership in the Church). Many of the interviewees stressed that they thought of themselves as good Christians even though they might not attend church very often, closing with the statement "But in my family everything is in order!" In this they claimed support from the previous pastor who had told them that it was the inside that counted, not how often a person went to church (cf. Fél and Hofer 1969:304-305). Asked to name what they conceived of as their most important duty as a Christian in this life (*Christenpflicht*), the men named (in order of frequency): the keeping of order and of a harmonious relationship within the family; loving and helping one's neighbor; to be honest; to have a good character; to keep the ten command-ments; and to see to it that the family farm is well taken care of. The women named: to love one another, starting with the next of kin; to be honest and open; to live in such a way that one could always "pass the test"; and to trust in God.

Although these data (which will be returned to in a comparison with the Catholics) suggest that there is little antireligious sentiment per se, we may once more look at the various factors from a broader perspective.

There are several reasons why the congregation does not measure up to the expectations of the pastor. One of them seems to be rooted in his personal background of prior pietistic leanings, which apparently induces a stronger com-mitment to lead his flock to an intimate encounter with Jesus than is ordinarily the case among ministers of large, established churches. Another reason can be traced to the persisting notion that the farmer has a "natural" propensity for religion, that his closeness to the soil and his dependence on the elements place him so much nearer to God. Thus, the pastor expects a much higher level of religiosity, of personal involvement in religious issues as well as overall attendance at religious services. But, as Max Weber noted (1963:80-84):

> *The religious glorification of the peasant and the belief in the special worth of his piety is the result of a very modern development. It was characteristic of Lutheranism in particular. . . . In modern Lutheranism (for this was not the position of Luther himself) the dominant interest is the struggle against the rationalism of the intellectuals, and against political liberalism.*

The Lutheran Church has since abandoned this view of the peasant's natural piety and close relationship to God, partly because it could not be substantiated on theological grounds, but more so because of changed sociopolitical conditions. Today, this view is perpetuated primarily by conservative groups outside the Church, who completely ignore the fact that the Church has officially abandoned her previous position (for this and following points in this paragraph, see Ziche 1968). But as we have seen, this does not prevent individual clergymen to think along similar lines. Thus, the warning of the local pastor that the farmers should not leave their land to work in industry is not only a matter of "master" versus "slave" in the conventional sense, but also a matter of tearing one's soul away from God and enslaving it to the devil. And when the relief pastor tells the farmer that his soul is becoming blunted because of his association with mechanical power in place of animal power, he is surely extending the Romanticist notion of a pious peasant struggling against the evil forces of progress emanating from the cities.

There are farmers (as well as conservative nonfarmers) who seem to be similarly convinced of this propagated special relationship that exists between God and the man who tills the land. Often one encounters a mixture of Romanticist notions as contained in the erstwhile position of the Church and those same notions as colored by Nazi ideology. Although Nazi ideology certainly was not propagated to promote the idea of a Christian God, it placed great emphasis on the farmer's special position as the *Lebensborn*, the 'well-spring' from which the nation would be replenished with racially pure individuals, and it did portray him as standing in some mystical relationship to the forces of nature, clothed in the garb of Germanic gods (the diffuseness of this "ideology" and its mixture of old and new is admirably discussed by Fest, 1974). There are also those who see evidence for the farmer's religious propensity in the fact that church attendance is so much higher in the country than it is in the city.[5] Others, however, hold to the opinion that this partial conservation of traditional religious behavior is more a function of the social setting than of any inherent mystical qualities.

[5]Higher attendance rates do not, however, apply uniformly to all rural areas in Germany—see Müller 1962:161.

This "traditional" behavior has indeed been modified to a considerable extent. If the pastor is primarily concerned about filling his church, he is quite right in deploring the demise of discipline and authority, for it was the discipline evoked by the authority of the pastor that had a great deal to do with keeping the church filled in the past. Reportedly, some 50 years ago, the pastor still exerted considerable authority and ruled his flock with a firm hand.[6] Where in the past a pastor would investigate if a violation of established morals by one of his parishioners was indicated, today such affairs are considered entirely private and intrusions by the pastor are not welcome, unless he has been asked for advice. The degree to which a pastor wields authority and is able to influence his parishioners is now more a function of his personal ability rather than his official position. Furthermore, social sanctions against persons who do not participate in religious services seem to operate on a very diminished scale. There is only perfunctory criticism leveled by those who feel more strongly about the role of the Church against fellow parishioners who do not. Ultimately, it is one's own conscience that seems to be the major point of reference.

However lax an individual may be in fulfilling his or her religious obligations, nobody has yet withdrawn from the Church (except to join another denomination), nor does anyone contemplate doing so. Almost everyone still wants the Church to perform the major rites of passage for himself and his family. Several times I was told the story of two men from nearby communities who had died not being members of the Church (they had left her during Nazi times and had not re-joined). Regulations prohibited the pastor from conducting a proper service at the gravesites, and only a few private words were spoken. The funerals took place in silence as the bells did not toll, either. In these villages where church bells are so much a part of daily life, this is indeed a deprivation which nobody wants to "experience." As one of the older farmers remarked: "I don't want to be buried like a beast!"

The Sectarians

From the time the Reformation was introduced until quite recently, all of the local Protestant families seem to have belonged to the official Lutheran Church; sectarian movements, such as the Anabaptists, did not find many converts among the farmers of this region (see Clasen 1965, especially page 177). Around 1925, however, a husband–wife team of peddlers from a nearby town came to peddle their wares and at the same time to win converts for the New Apostolic faith. After an initial conversion of one elderly woman, by 1931 four of the local families had withdrawn from the Church and joined the new faith. Two of the families were those of a shoemaker and of a laborer who had little land of

---

[6]Some studies have shown that although the rural clergy were once accorded first place in the local hierarchy, they are now ranked fifth or sixth. See, for example, Wurzbacher 1954:33, and Wissler 1968:49.

their own; one was the family of a cow farmer; and the fourth that of one of the larger horse farmers. Reportedly, it was the women who were converted first, and they, in turn, got their men to follow suit. Local reactions were largely unfavorable, although status distinctions seem to have had a bearing on collective behavior. Thus, when a woman belonging to one of the poorer families died after having been converted only a short time before her death, the question arose whether the bells should toll at her funeral. The presbyters decided that the bells should not be rung for the funeral of anyone who was not a member of the Church. After the death of the New Apostolic horse farmer, however, there was no general interest to uphold the previous decision, and the funeral took place with the bells tolling over the grave.

Of the original converts, only one person, now widowed, is still alive. The children and the children's children of the converts have married (at least locally) within the faith. A minister stationed at a nearby village comes and conducts Sunday morning services in a rented room in the school. As far as I could determine, the local New Apostolics are not conducting any kind of proselytizing (although there is some activity in other villages), nor are any of them known as being overtly more religious than the other Protestants. Everyday social interaction with the other villagers follows no noticeably different patterns, although the families of the two craftsmen keep very much to themselves, largely by their own choice. When some of the villagers are directly asked their opinions on the sectarians, one might hear such comments as: "I would kick my wife out of the house if she would try to convert me; nobody could convert me—why should I be so simple-minded?" or "Those sectarians are people who imagine that they are better than we are. If I have my church and my beliefs, why should I want something else?" The point that would have to be made, of course, is that the spiritual "needs" of the initial converts had not been met by the established Church and that they were ready to embrace a faith that appeared to stand in a more fundamental relationship to God.

Finally, there are four persons from two of the hamlets who have followed the call of a new sect, the *Spätregengemeinde*. When the organizers of this sect conducted a faith-healing session in a neighboring village a few years ago, the people who attended hoped for deliverance from physical and psychic discomforts. The fellow citizens of the local converts consider this new development to have only peripheral communal significance which is liable to pass soon, as the converts are middle-aged or elderly and there are no children involved.

The Catholics

The Priest (Pfarrer)

For many centuries the villagers did not have a resident priest; religious services were performed by vicars who were sent up from the neighboring Catholic village in the valley. As these vicars had to take care of more than one village and could not officiate every Sunday and holiday, those who wanted to participate in religious services more often had to walk the 4-mile round trip into the valley and back. It was therefore a proud moment when the village received its first resident priest in 1843. Two years prior, a contract had been drawn up in which the village, after elevation to a parish, commited itself to build a rectory, to maintain the church (erected in 1766, after a previous, smaller one was torn down), and to contribute to the priest's remuneration in the form of cash payments and income from glebe lands. The priests were nominated by the King of Württemberg in the exercise of his right of patronage; since 1918, however, they have been nominated by the head of the diocese, the Bishop of Rottenburg (Württemberg).

All of the local priests have been natives of Württemberg except for the last one, a refugee from the East. He left 9 years ago and since then the village has been, once again, without a resident priest. According to most accounts, he was very well liked by a majority of the villagers—he even helped them in such tasks as loading manure—but there were some people who could not get used to the idea that a refugee, an ethnic foreigner, should be in such a position of authority. There were small ways in which life was made difficult for him. For instance, the rectory was in urgent need of certain repairs, but with one excuse or another, these repairs were forever postponed. What brought the animosity to a head, however, was the fate of the chestnut tree which had stood in front of the church since 1774. This tree was in danger of breaking apart and had therefore become a public hazard. The diocese refused to carry appropriate insurance and advised that this was a matter to be handled by the parish (in accordance with the contract of 1841). The priest then wanted to carry through a rescue operation in which staves were to be placed under various branches, but he failed to receive the necessary assistance from the "secular powers," and he finally decided to have the tree removed. This was the signal for his adversaries to place more unpleasantness in his way. It was then that he announced his decision to leave, unwilling to be fought over by two opposing factions (some claim that this rift in the community, separating his followers from his adversaries, followed the lines of the old Nazi and anti-Nazi factions). The point I want to stress, however, is that church attendance reportedly did not fall off during the feud.

After the priest had left, the mayor and councilmen realized the bad state of repairs that the rectory was in; a loan was taken up and repairs carried out at a cost of about 25,000 DM. This proved not enough, however, to entice another priest to settle in the village. One or two came and looked the place over but decided against it. By now the villagers are resigned that they will never have their own priest again. After the last priest had announced his decision to leave, the initial reaction by some of the men had been "Good—now our women can't run to mass everyday any more." But many of the villagers felt deep regret, especially when they realized that they would never get a replacement. Today it is generally claimed that such a display of narrow-mindedness as happened 10 years ago will not be repeated.

The local church is now administered by a priest who resides in a village on the heights across the valley; he takes turns celebrating mass with the priest from the valley. He hails from a village near Stuttgart and, according to the locals, displays the kind of Swabian "pig-headedness" they consider so typical of Swabians in general.[7] On the whole, priest and congregation have few complaints about each other; each side is apparently more or less living up to generally accepted standards of behavior. The priest is well aware of the fact that clerical authority does not carry the same weight that it once did. Of course, the fact that he resides 4 miles away diminishes both his chances of communal supervision and the frequency of contact with the parishioners that a resident priest normally enjoys. Occasionally, there are lapses that would very likely not occur were he physically present, such as when the villagers neglected to obtain permission to work on one particular Sunday during the haying season.

Religious Services

The ten o'clock Sunday morning mass lasts 30–45 min and is read in the vernacular. Sermons take only 10–15 min and usually deal with parables from the Bible. In place of a sermon, a passage from the Bible may be read without commentary; or the priest may read a letter from the bishop dealing with contemporary issues (such as the increase in violence, or crimes against the unborn). When I asked the priest from the valley about the short sermons—referring to the more lengthy ones in the Protestant church—he indicated that this is one area that is given relatively little attention in today's training of priests. He is also of the opinion that it takes a very good preacher to hold the attention of a congregation for more than 15 min—and that there are few good preachers around. In addition to the regular Sunday masses and those celebrated on holidays, there are rosaries and requiem masses which are not, however, as well as attended as Sunday morning mass.

At least three processions are conducted each year: one on Ascension Day (Fig. 39); one on Corpus Christi; and one on *Hageltag* ('hail day'), one week after Corpus Christi. The latter was instituted to commemorate a devastating hail storm which destroyed most of the crops standing in the fields of three adjoining villages in July of 1873. The processions start from the church, with most of the villagers taking part. They wind their way along field roads while hymns are being sung. At several points along the way, usually at wayside shrines, the

[7]To balance the scales, it ought to be reported that the priest found an equally "pig-headed" match in the local sexton, a man who served under three priests and proud of his expertise. He finally tired of insisting that things be done "the right way" and resigned during the year of my stay.

procession comes to a halt and the priest reads a passage from the Bible and then blesses the crops. These processions reportedly do not cover as much territory as they once did, as the priest has to conduct two in one day (one in his own parish)—not that the villagers mind very much. For example, the procession on Ascension Day took place under a hot afternoon sun, and everyone looked greatly relieved when the priest gave the signal to turn back after less than a mile had been covered. When the procession returned to the church for one more blessing, some of the lads went around the church instead of inside and headed straight for the inn to quench their thirst. On certain holidays, smaller groups of villagers used to walk to specific churches or chapels as far as 15 or 20 miles distant, but the last time such a pilgrimage was undertaken was by one of the older men some 5 years ago. Now, those villagers who still want to visit these places use their automobiles to take them there.

FIGURE 39.   Procession on Ascension Day.

The weather has always figured prominently in the life of the farmer, and processions to bless the crops and prayers for favorable weather have certainly held their place in religious ritual. (It is also still customary to ring the church bells when a thunderstorm approaches; see Chapter 3). According to the priest in the valley, church attendance is falling off because due to modern methods of farming (for example, the speed with which a harvest can now be brought in) the farmer can feel a little more relaxed about the weather. Interestingly, when I tried to find out how much faith the local farmers have in the efficacy of prayers and processions, I was told that it was the Protestants who put more faith in these rituals than they, the Catholics did. Some of the Protestants said that there was some truth to that; thus, when there is a bad stand of spring crops due to unfavorable weather, they will say, "Let's wait till the Catholics have had their processions, then things will pick up again".[8]

The Parishioners: Commitment, Attitudes, and Opinions[9]

The ten o'clock Sunday morning mass is well attended, on the average by about 70% of the parishioners. The emphasis here is on fulfilling one's obligations to God; attendance at Sunday morning mass is called the *Sonntagspflicht* ('Sunday duty'; cf. Friedl 1974:39). Those who have to be absent on a Sunday morning are now allowed to accomplish their *Sonntagspflicht* by attending mass in the valley church on Saturday nights. There are a few "peripheral" individuals who attend mass very rarely, but, ordinarily, people who have not attended Sunday morning mass feel compelled to explain to their neighbors why not. Each person has his or her accustomed seat in the church, and it is therefore easy to spot who is missing.

But the morning mass also represents an important marker in separating the work week from Sunday rest. It is probably futile to try and sort out motives for church attendance according to religious and social categories; the comments of one of the younger farmers sum up quite well the feelings of the majority of the men.

Here, only a few misfits don't go to church. But you also have to consider that everyone here has his seat, and when someone is missing everyone else knows. And this is a small place and you can't do anything without the neighbors asking, "Where are you going" or "Where have you been?" And then again, if you don't go to church, Sunday will never come. If I go to church, I am dressed in my Sunday clothes at ten o'clock. Then off to the church, and afterwards to the Frühschoppen. *And the other Sunday I didn't make it, and at noon I was still dressed in my work clothes, and then I had lunch, and afterwards I went back to bed and I never had any Sunday. But once I'm dressed in my Sunday suit, there is order for the rest of the day. I know that in the city many don't go to church; but those who do go, and without any elders to push them, I think those are devout Christians. But here, if I may be honest, here it is more something of a tradition, an old custom.*

[8]For a discussion of religious and magical practices among Catholics and Protestants in the area, see Kramer 1957:100-133 and Renner 1965.
[9]Apart from casual interviews, data were collected as part of 60 taped, structured interviews (37 males, 23 females).

Among other comments on church attendance was the recurrent theme: It is not important how often one goes to church, it is important how one treats one's fellow man; those who prefer to run to church so often (this in reference to occasions other than the Sunday morning mass) are not necessarily better Christians.

As yet, there is no clearly discernible trend as to whether church attendance will fall off in the foreseeable future. Some of the teenagers want a little more color, a little change from the accustomed. They are talking about jazz masses and similar innovations and think that they would like to attend mass in the city as soon as they have their own means of transportation. So far, the traditional patterns of overt communal participaton have endured almost intact, even without the presence of a resident priest. Some of the older villagers say that everything today is too free and easy, that it certainly is not what it was like in the old days when the village was "ruled with an iron hand" by both teacher and priest.[10] They also complain about changes instituted by the Church, which leaves them wondering what to believe and what not (as I alluded to in the last chapter). Well-established patterns do not change overnight, of course. For example, St. Joseph's Day had always been celebrated as a religious holiday; none of the farmers used to work and the children did not have to go to school. This holiday was dropped by the Church beginning in 1971, but, when St. Joseph's Day came around (on Friday, March 19), the farmers were hesitant to treat this as an ordinary workday. They stood around in groups, looking vaguely uncomfortable. A few puttered around in their yards, but by the end of the day I had counted only two who had gone out on their tractors to work in the fields.

Now let us turn from church attendance to other categories of religious commitment. Similar to the Protestants, almost all of the men put themselves in the category of tradition-bound Christians, and only one saw himself as a devout believer. Two-thirds of the men thought that praying could be of help, and four-fifths of the women thought so, too. Two-thirds of the men confessed to believe in an afterlife, versus only three-fifths of the women. Of those with negative answers, most would say nobody has yet returned. Some of the doubters indicated that they had often thought about this question without reaching a conclusion. The discrepancy between men and women might be explained by looking at the quality of the affirmative answers: The ratio of "weak" to "firm" affirmations as to the personal belief in an afterlife was more than 3:1 among males, versus 1:2 among females. The most frequent forms representative of "weak" affirmations were: "Yes, I guess so" and "That's the

---

[10]Everyone still talks about the "rule" of one of the teachers, who ran the local school for 41 years from 1889 to 1930. As the school was strategically placed in the middle of the village, the teacher had a chance to witness much of the public behavior of his charges; for instance, if he spotted a child still out in the street after the prayer bells had tolled at six or seven o'clock in the evening, that child would corporally be punished in class the next day.

way we have been taught, so we have to believe it." Examples of "firm" answers are: "Yes, that I believe!" and "Yes, of course; the way one has to struggle in this life, there has to be a reward, otherwise life wouldn't make sense!" As among the Protestants, almost no one was bothered by the prospect that the time would come when one would be held accountable for one's deeds; the general contention was that if you did your best there was no need to worry.

As to what they conceived of as their most important duty as a Christian, the following points, named by the men and in order of frequency, were: to love and help one's neighbor; to be honest; to be tolerant; to stay with the faith; and to put hate and strife aside. The women named: to love one's neighbor; to live in peace without hate and strife; to look after the family; to pray and work; to believe in God and to bring up the children in accordance with the faith. (Points dealing with tolerance were all brought up by younger people.)

A Comparative Overview

Briefly, what are the major differences in religious behavior between the two communities? As a point of reference, let us look at some of the figures mentioned in this chapter (where "n" equals 100%).[11]

	CATHOLICS		PROTESTANTS	
	%	n	%	n
Church attendance (average on ordinary Sunday)	70	181	18	256
Yes, praying can help				
Men	68	25	59	22
Women	81	21	80	10
Yes, believe in afterlife				
Men	68	25	41	22
Women	57	21	80	10

[11]Although I have not conducted an exhaustive inquiry into the various dimensions of religiosity and have chosen only two items of personal belief for purposes of illustration in the summary, I want to point out that my understanding of religious patterns derives as much from my casual observations and interviews as from my questions that were distinctly aimed at a quantitative evaluation. I might also point out that the structured interviews themselves were conducted in rather intimate fashion, and that the nuances abstracted from the various answers could not have been obtained if a mechanical questionnaire had been used.

Incidentally, Planck, in his nationwide sampling of young persons on the extent of their beliefs in the "value of prayer," arrived at percentages quite close to mine (1970:279).

The three variables listed above may be conceptualized as representing two among several dimensions of religiosity—the first one the ritualistic dimension, and the last two the ideological dimension of religiosity (see Glock and Stark 1965, Chap. 2). To obtain a profile of the ideological dimension that would characterize the two local populations, my questions were aimed not so much at finding out to what extent a person believed in certain tenets of a distinctly Roman Catholic or Evangelical-Lutheran nature (a probe in this direction met with very meager results), but rather to what extent a person believed in a number of Christian tenets in general.

My findings indicate that the differences between Catholics and Protestants along the ideological dimension are rather small; in terms of personal commitment and devotion, it seems unjustified to conceive of a larger concentration of devout Christians in one camp rather than the other. For example, although a larger proportion of Catholic men express belief in certain religious tenets than do Protestant men, we have also seen that this distinction is somewhat diminished when the perfunctory manner in which many of the answers are given is taken into account. This pattern is substantiated by data I gathered in more informal settings than those of structured interviews; most overt expressions of personal commitment to certain religious beliefs are not so much sustained by the impact of religious experiences, but rather by a feeling of loyalty to the religious tradition of one's community (as one of the Catholic farmers remarked, "Somebody has to be on God's side!"). On the whole, the higher incidence of expressed religiosity along the ideological dimension among Catholic men is undoubtedly a consequence of their more frequent involvement in the ritual practices of their Church.

When we look at the women, we find very little denominational difference in this sector of religiosity, but the proportion of affirmative answers exceeds that obtained among the men. Thus, women as a group seem to feel more commited to hold certain religious beliefs than do the men, quite in line with a more generalized cultural pattern, according to which women are traditionally expected to express a higher degree of religiosity than men (cf. Lison-Tolosana 1966:309). The one exception here is the low incidence of belief in an afterlife among the Catholic women; this might be explained by the concreteness in which they pictured such an afterlife. This concrete conceptualization was much less pronounced among Protestant women; for example, I rarely heard them utter the phrase "Nobody has yet come back to report about it!" as I heard so often from Catholic women.

Now, we turn our attention to church attendance as the most conspicuous aspect of religiosity in which the patterns among Catholics and Protestants diverge. Of course, such differential patterns have been noted by other investigators in a variety of settings (see, for example, Glock and Stark 1965:218-221; Greeley 1972:13; Lenski 1963:47-48; & Planck 1970:277). It is also important to point out that attendance records among Catholics themselves show substantially different trends from country to country as, for example, a comparison between Germany, Austria, and the German-speaking areas of Switzerland on the one hand, and France and Italy on the other would show (Banfield 1967:19, Höffner 1961, Wylie 1964:xii;284). Such national or regional differences among Catholics can only be explained by analyzing the sociopolitical processes instrumental in shaping the attitudes of the people toward institutionalized religion. For our present purposes, the local situation may be seen as part of a larger pattern that prevails among German-speaking, rural Catholics: the relatively high frequency of Sunday morning church attendance is supported by a feeling of strong commitment toward fulfilling one's *Sonntagspflicht*. The immediate "pay-off" as perceived by the participants is not only that they have fulfilled their religious duty, but also that Sunday activities will proceed in orderly fashion. We should not overlook the fact that high attendance rates are reinforced and upheld by mechanisms of social sanction such as gossip, which labels those who habitually stay away from Sunday mass as "misfits."

When we consider the socializing effects of this relatively high degree of involvement in the religious practices of their community, we might expect a greater degree of social cohesion and community-oriented attitudes among the Catholics compared to their Protestant neighbors. We have seen, indeed, that an analysis of various patterns of social interaction tends to substantiate such differences, and we shall return to this point in the concluding chapter. I might add that these differences in degree seem to be reflected in the answers given by interviewees when asked what they conceived of as their most important duty as a Christian: among the Protestants, replies centering on obligations toward one's family outnumber those expressing obligations toward neighbors, community, or man at large; the reverse trend obtains among the Catholics. This point is also implicit in those remarks that show that, as a rule, neither Catholics nor Protestants consider church attendance as the touchstone of being a good Christian. Where the Protestant would say, "I'm no great churchgoer, but in my family everything is as it should be!" the Catholic would say, "It is not important how often one goes to church—it is important how one treats one's neighbor." Both show concern about harmonious relations with those around them, yet the Catholic seems to extend this concern to those outside the immediate family more often than the Protestant.

To sum up, the differences in religiosity between the local Catholics and Protestants are not so much an expression of the degree to which they accept or reject tenets of Christian faith, but rather of the way in which they relate to and identify with their respective Churches. The Catholics subject themselves to the ritual demands of their Church in much larger proportions than the Protestants do; they see their participation in those rituals primarily in terms of a traditional duty, essential to upholding the identity of both individual and community as "good Catholic." The discharge of this duty seems largely independent of the personality of the officiating priest. Most of the Protestants, on the other hand, view their religiosity as something personal between themselves and their God, and not as closely tied to their participation in religious services as do the Catholics. The more verbalized aspects of the Protestant church service discussed in this chapter may also be seen as influencing the decisions of Protestants as to whether they should attend church services or not. This difference between the more action-oriented mass and procession of the Catholics, and the more personalistic and verbalized church service of the Protestants, parallels the much stronger identification of the Catholics with their Church in terms of community rather than in terms of adherence to particular Roman Catholics tenets (cf. Stark 1972:95-111, Robertson 1970:182). The fact, however, that the high rate of religious participation among the Catholics is both reinforced and upheld by mechanisms of social sanction (which are largely absent among the Protestants) should not mislead us into assuming that we are no longer dealing with "authentic" religious behavior (cf. Greeley 1970:184).

11

Conclusion

In its broader aspects, this study has presented an analysis of structural changes in two rural communities in Southwest Germany as they have occurred over the last century and a half. At the beginning of this period, we saw two communities of predominantly small and medium peasants engaged in a complex of mixed farming, channeling part of their produce into a marketing network that extended far beyond regional boundaries. Then followed the years of transition, during which the peasants were relieved of their patrimonial obligations toward their aristocratic landlords to assume legal ownership of the land which they had been farming as hereditary leaseholds. And finally there came the eventual dissolution of the corporate body of citizens who held rights to the commons, with the extension of equal rights to all local inhabitants.

Clearly, changes have occurred through the entire period of this investigation, but it is especially the last 25 years that have had the greatest impact on the traditional ways of our two communities. Some of these changes are visibly manifested, others are not. Twenty-five years ago, a person traveling through the surrounding countryside would have passed by many a team of horses or cows harnessed to wagon or plow, but today all of these draft animals have been replaced by motorized power. The gravel and dirt roads that afforded access to the villages have since been black-topped, and even the field roads are no longer rutted and muddy or dusty, but have recently been converted to all-weather roads. The modernization of equipment, facilities, and methods has led to an increase in agricultural productivity, despite a decrease in the number of persons engaged in agriculture. Yields per acre of land have gone up, and the production of meat and milk is conducted along more rationalized lines.

177

As farming has become more capital intensive than ever before, a number of local farmers have not been able or willing to improve their operations beyond the initial stages of recent modernization processes. The number of full-time farmers has decreased, with a further decline expected for several years to come. The socioeconomic forces responsible for this trend are, of course, supra-local; the agrarian policies of state and federal government aim at a relatively painless transition from the "traditional" family farm to the family farm that is completely modernized and run along rational lines, able to hold its own in the changed and changing economic environment. That it is impossible for all of the existing farms to achieve this transition has been clear from the start.

The decrease in the number of holdings and of farmers has become, to a certain extent, a process of natural attrition. A number of small farms are still worked by older people, but their heirs are not interested in carrying on farming on such small units. Some of the farms may go out of existence because their owners are unable to find prospective wives. Other farms, both medium and small, are operated on a part-time basis and it remains to be seen in how many cases this adaptation represents only an interim solution, and in how many others the next generation will find it profitable to carry on this mode of operation. So far, very little land has been sold. In most cases in which people have given up farming or have greatly reduced their operations, the land has been leased to farmers willing to expand; the possession of land is still valued as a buffer against possible future hardships.

Today, almost everyone enjoys a higher standard of living than in the past, although this fact loses much of its significance in the eyes of many of the local farmers when they compare their position with that of wage and salary earners— they are only too aware of the growing disparity in incomes between farming and other sectors of the economy. Mixed farming still requires everyone to put in long hours of work; modern machines have offset the loss of labor, but have not reduced the workload of those on the farm, especially not that of the women. In addition, there is the psychological burden carried by those who have worked hard all their lives to keep the family farm together, and who are now faced with the prospect that the work is not going to be carried on by their heirs.

Declining fertility rates, the loss of servants, and the tendency of almost all the young men and women—who are not slated as principal heirs—to leave the village, have led to a decrease in local population levels of 25 and 30%, respectively, below that of 130 years ago. But the number of households has not declined, and there can be no question that we are not dealing with the kind of "depopulation" experienced by some of the rural regions in Mediterranean countries where the socioeconomic structure as a whole is much less favorable (cf. Frank 1974). Barring a significant reverse in the regional increase of employment opportunities outside of agriculture, local population levels are unlikely to decline further, although an increasing number of households will derive their incomes primarily from nonfarming sources. The loss of the village schools and of local administrative autonomy is also modifying the character of the farming community of yesterday. On the other hand, there can be little doubt that our two communities will retain their separate identity and their overall agricultural character for some time to come.

The Religious Factor

It is within this context that I have attempted to trace the influence of religious factors on the patterning of various categories of institutionalized behavior; the choice of this particular research setting has enabled me to conduct my investigation under closely and systematically controlled conditions. Here we have two discrete communities, structurally very much alike, sharing the same ecological niche, the same ethnocultural heritage, and the same sociopolitical and economic environment. The one major factor that sets them apart is their affiliation with the Protestant and Catholic Church, respectively; thus, for the last 400 years, there has no longer been any intermarriage, and social interaction has subsequently been curtailed.

I proceeded from the assumption that given the high degree of structural similarities, we might expect a corresponding degree of similarity in the patterning of behavioral responses to changes in the larger society, but that any significant divergence in these behavioral patterns might well be a consequence of the difference in religious affiliation. We might now recapitulate the differential patterns discussed in this study, and examine the ways in which they are interrelated.

Let us begin with the clearly established relationship between the explicit stand of the Catholic Church on the subject of birth control, and the sexual behavior of the local Catholic population. Our comparison with the Protestants has shown that the higher fertility rate among the Catholics was sustained in the presence of socioeconomic forces that seem to have been instrumental in lowering fertility rates among the Protestants, locally as well as nationwide. The Catholics were constrained, for the most part, from adopting voluntary measures of birth control through the internalization of religious strictures actively propagated by their Church, charging that those who would wilfully interfere with the natural processes of procreation are perpetrators of a mortal sin. Older Catholic women recalled their acceptance of such constraints, in contrast to most of the Protestant women who felt little or no commitment in this respect, even though their Church was not, in principle, taking a liberal stand. Of course, much of the rigidity of such religious constraints has since been modified. Large-scale socioeconomic changes have exerted pressures, working counter to the internatlization of such values, even influencing the inflexible position of the Church herself. The outcome has been a decline in the fertility rate of the local

Catholics, which precedes the willingness of the Church to make formal concessions to voluntary birth control, but is not necessarily at odds with the opinions of local priests.

One unanticipated consequence of this difference in fertility rates became manifest when we analyzed the differential time schedule of tractorization in our two communities. During this process of changing from animal power to motorized power, the Catholics lagged several years behind the Protestants. As a result of higher fertility rates and larger families, the Catholic farmers were able to draw on a larger pool of relatively inexpensive family labor than the Protestants. The availability of this labor enabled many of the Catholic farmers to postpone acquisition of a tractor for a longer period of time than they might have been able to otherwise. But in addition to this factor, their attitudes are also characteristic of a more pronounced traditionalistic orientation, supported in essence by the overall position of their Church. This orientation seems to have fostered an outlook toward farming that is "less professional" compared to that of the Protestants.

This "less professional" outlook among the Catholics is manifested, for example, in the much lower incidence of advanced training taken by males and females in agricultural and housekeeping subjects. Completely independent of farm size or other structural criteria, considerably more Catholics than Protestants subscribe to the view that the operation and management of a family farm can be conducted without the benefit of advanced training—that is, without thereby incurring an economic disadvantage. (We are here confronted with differential attitudes toward new trends in agricultural policies which envision the "professionalization" of the family farm in every respect.) Among the Protestants, completion of advanced training confers a certain amount of prestige, whereas, among the Catholics, advanced training is often deprecated by remarks such as: "Look at him—he got all this training and he still makes all these mistakes and is no better off than we are."

These differential attitudes toward farming are also apparent when we consider the much larger proportion of Catholics who work on outside jobs in addition to farming their holdings. Here we have a situation of two farmers with potentially equal resources, but while one opts to divide his time between farm and outside job, the other one prefers to put all of his personal labor and management potential into the operation of his farm. We may certainly conceive of the latter as displaying a more "professional" attitude toward farming, which is, of course, closely linked to the fact that his advanced training enables him to adopt a more "rationalistic" approach; in other words, he is both more motivated to apply the skills acquired in school to the operation of his farm, and better equipped to undertake a cost analysis before making a decision. It might be pertinent to point out that here, as in the other analyses, I am not referring to rational versus irrational behavior per se. Each side is convinced that their adaptation to the present economic environment is at least not inferior to that chosen by the other side; in fact, neither side seems to enjoy a distinct economic advantage.

In yet another analysis, we have seen that this "less professional" attitude toward farming has played a significant part in leaving a greater number of Catholic bachelors with slim prospects of obtaining a wife, thereby placing in jeopardy the continued operation of their respective farms. Proportionally, more daughters of Protestant farmers than of Catholic farmers have been available, in principle, as prospective wives for farmer-husbands. The higher incidence of advanced training among the Protestant girls constitutes a motivational factor that may be translated in terms of a "professional challenge" (similar to the situation described for the men), which functions as an incentive for the girls to marry into a farm household. This incentive is largely missing among Catholic girls, who view the prospect of becoming a farmer's wife primarily in terms of the drudgery involved in long hours of hard work. They have preferred to leave the village to work in occupations that guarantee them a regulated number of working hours, with prospects of meeting a potential husband who is not a farmer.

The factor of advanced training in preparation for running the family farm is a more recent aspect of the "professionalization" of farming as an occupation. Well into the twentieth century, farming had been regarded primarily as a way of life and only secondarily as an occupation (see Chap. 6, Footnote 2); one learned all there was to know about farming from one's father. Today, the farmer is expected to master the kind of expertise that will allow him to effectively integrate his enterprise into the larger economy and to conduct his operations along some of the principles of industrial production. Needless to say, most of the skills of farming—especially those that have been developed in adaptation to local conditions—are still best transmitted from father to son, but at the present stage of structural transitions in agriculture, this additional expertise has to be acquired in the form of advanced training.

In comparing the two communities on the score of modernization, I am not saying that the Catholics (on the average) are failing to adopt new approaches to farming, but that they have been doing so at a slower rate and with a differential commitment of human resources.

From variations in traditionalistic orientation, we now turn to those differential patterns that are strongly linked to the degree of communal participation in religious activities. One of these patterns concerns the intensity and extent of face-to-face interaction, which occurs at significantly higher levels among the Catholics. Both Protestant and Catholic villagers enjoy the same potential for social interaction within the setting of co-residence in the spatially narrow confines of their villages, but the level of this interaction is greatly influenced by the congregational pattern of their respective religious communities. In the case of the Catholics, regular and near-universal participation in religious ritual generates a heightened sense of "communitas" (Turner 1969:96), which is carried into the secular realm of the community, affecting both a higher level of social integration and an intensified and more extensive degree of face-to-face interaction. In contrast, the Protestant community lacks the basis for the generation of an equivalent sense of communitas; the sporadic participation of most of the Protestants in the religious activities of their Church is simply insufficient to create the same effect, and there is no secular organization that might serve as a substitute vehicle.

In my discussion of the differential density of co-ownership networks, I have viewed the patterning of face-to-face interaction as a significant factor in the planning and execution of cooperative ventures. I see the larger number of farmers participating in more frequent face-to-face interaction in the Catholic community as standing in a direct relationship to the fact that they participate in the co-ownership of agricultural machines and implements to twice the extent found among Protestant farmers. The most extensive intracommunity venture is the cattle insurance association in the Catholic village, which includes all but one of the farmers. Thus, the greater degree of social integration in the Catholic community seemingly favors activities that include large segments of the community; or, negatively, the integrational factor expressed in the high level of face-to-face interaction may make it more difficult for individuals to withhold their participation in cooperative ventures. We have seen, however, that it still requires strong leadership to translate community-oriented attitudes into the type of action that will benefit the community as a whole; the recent construction of field roads in the Catholic commune under the auspices of the Protestant mayor is a case in point.

Finally, one more differential pattern that we found directly influenced by the level of church attendance is that of voting behavior. The German practice of holding elections on Sundays intersects with the fact that Catholics attend Sunday church services in far greater proportions than Protestants do, leading—almost mechanically—to consistently higher voter turnouts among rural Catholics in the region. Furthermore, Catholics have voted the "Christian ticket" to a much larger extent than the Protestants have, thereby following a long-standing tradition actively supported by their Church.

When we summarize the major differential traits that make up the patterns recapitulated, we emerge with a few key points: a differential level of attachment to the respective Church; a differential level of "traditionalistic" orientation; and a differential level of communal integration. Catholics exhibit a greater degree of attachment to their Church and are thus more likely to internalize the values stressed by the Church, as we have seen in the case of fertility rates. Catholics are more "traditionalistic" in their orientation, especially as reflected in their attitudes toward the *Beruf* ('calling') of a *Bauer*, which is approached by the Protestants from a position that emphasizes to a greater degree the incorpor-

ation of modern, more "rationalistic" elements. Lastly, Catholics exhibit a
higher level of communal integration, as expressed in the higher level of face-to-
face interaction and in the greater number of people who participate in
cooperative ventures.

Underlying these traits are, of course, the prevailing positions of the respective
Churches themselves. Each Church represents a nexus of ideas and values as to
how people should conduct their lives, and thus form the basis for differential
sets of behavior patterns. Even though the Protestant Church has generally maintained a rather conservative position, when the two are compared, the Catholic
Church may be seen as having displayed a still greater degree of conservatism
toward secular affairs and a greater insistence on the maintenance of traditional
values. In addition, the Catholic Church with her emphasis on ritual and on the
constant reaffirmation of the communal bond and the atonement of sin as
celebrated in the mass, has not only been able to maintain a greater feeling of
communitas, but has also been able to retain a greater hold over her charges. The
Protestant Church, on the other hand, has placed relatively more stress on the
role and responsibilities of the individual, and has not been able to wield a
comparable degree of influence over the local congregation.

In sum, if we want to explain the divergent patterns analyzed in this study, we
have to acknowledge the religious factor as the primary force instrumental in
shaping these divergences. There are, of course, reciprocal relationships between
behavior patterns that have their primary locus inside or outside the religious
sphere. For example, a high level of church attendance is very likely reinforced
by a high level of face-to-face interaction—we might expect that social sanctions
against nonconformists can be more effectively carried out via such a high level
of social interaction—but since our two communities represent the kind of
setting in which most of the structural variables can be held constant, it is
possible to trace the causal arrows with greater certainty.

Obviously, some of the patterns dealt with in this study are both relatively
short-lived and have arisen only under particular conditions of change. Thus, the
difference in tractorization schedules spanned only a few number of years, and
one might be tempted to treat this difference as a chance occurrence restricted
to a comparison between our two communities, had it not been the case that
this pattern can be extended to the county level. The underlying factors that
influenced the shaping of this pattern—differential fertility rates, and a differential level in traditionalistic orientation—although longer lived, are nonetheless
subject to change themselves. The relationship between the religious sphere and
other spheres of human behavior is itself a variable, and whether or not hypo-
thesized differences in value orientation between Catholics and Protestants will
be manifested in some of their patterns of institutionalized behavior depends on
the prevailing circumstances (cf. Demerath and Hammond 1969:112). By the
same token, the differences between Catholics and Protestants established in

yesterday's study may be considerably diminished by today, and may have largely disappeared by tomorrow (a view that Lenski holds of his own study in Detroit; see 1971:50).

Whatever tomorrow's patterns may be, this study has demonstrated that contemporary differences in value orientations between a particular population of Roman Catholics and a highly similarly structured population of Evangelical-Lutheran Protestants can both be traced to originate in—or at least to be sustained by—the religious factor, and to exert a causal effect on the differential structuring of various socioeconomic patterns of behavior.

Appendix

FERTILITY RATES PER MARRIED WOMAN, INCLUDING
PREMARITAL BIRTHS, 1800–1969[a]

Date of marriage	CATHOLICS			PROTESTANTS		
	Number of women	*Number of births*	*Average per woman*	*Number of women*	*Number of births*	*Average per woman*
1800–1809	13	83	6.4	16	94	5.8
1810–1819	14	59	4.2	18	76	4.2
1820–1829	17	106	6.2	39	199	5.1
1830–1839	21	126	6.0	26	140	5.4
1840–1849	16	99	6.2	33	193	5.8
1850-1859	15	128	8.4	30	160	5.3
1860–1869	16	106	6.6	29	148	5.1
1870–1879	21	177	8.4	41	179	4.4
1880–1889	14	117	8.3	42	205	4.9
1890–1899	15	87	5.8	20	79	4.0
1900–1909	10	75	7.5	29	115	4.0
1910–1919	17	52	3.1	28	77	2.8
1920–1929	12	41	3.4	29	67	2.3
1930–1939	20	89	4.5	28	68	2.4
1940–1949	11	39	3.5	28	65	2.3
1950–1959	14	50	3.6	23	58	2.5
1960–1969	13	35	2.7	19	43	2.3
Totals	259	1,469	5.7	478	1,966	4.1

[a]Data compiled from local family registers, *Bürgermeisteramt*, and local church registers.
[b]See Fig. 15, p. 62.

Table A-2

FAMILIES RANKED BY NUMBER OF BIRTHS AND SIZE OF FAMILY HOLDING, WITH A CATEGORY FOR CRAFTSMEN, 1820-1969[a]

	Number of births	0.1–5 ha[b]		5–10 ha		10–15 ha		15–20 ha		20 ha		Craftsmen[b]		Totals	
		n	%	n	%	n	%	n	%	n	%	n	%	n	%
Catholics	1–3			5	17	4	7	17	100	3	25			29	19
	4–6			13	43	20	34	17	32	4	33			55	35
	7–9			7	23	15	25	8	15	1	8			32	21
	10			5	17	20	34	11	21	4	33			40	101
	Totals			30	100	59	100	53	100	12	99			156	101
Protestants	1–3	25	40	22	42	23	61	10	45	23	40	40	46	143	45
	4–6	18	29	18	35	7	18	7	32	19	33	23	26	92	29
	7–9	14	23	7	13	8	21	4	18	7	12	14	16	54	17
	10	5	8	5	10	0	0	1	5	8	14	10	11	29	9
	Totals	62	101	52	100	38	100	22	100	57	99	87	99	318	100

[a]Data compiled from local family registers and land registers, *Bürgermeisteramt.*
[b]Numbers too small in Catholic commune to be statistically meaningful. *n*: Number of families (See Fig. 16, p. 64.)

Bibliography

Published Statistics

Baden-Württemberg, Statistisches Landesamt
1952 Gemeinde- und Kreisstatistik Baden-Württemberg 1950. Stuttgart.
1963 Wohnbevölkerung, Erwerbspersonen, Auspendler und Privathaushalte in den Gemeinden; Ergebnisse der Volks- und Berufszählung vom 6, Juni 1961. Bevölkerung und Kultur. Stuttgart.
1964a Gemeindestatistik Baden-Württemberg 1960/61, Teil 1: Bevölkerung und Erwerbstätigkeit. Vol. 90. Stuttgart.
1964b Gemeindestatistik Baden-Württemberg 1960/61; Teil 4: Betriebsstruktur der Landwirtschaft. Vol. 90. Stuttgart.
1964c Die Parlamentswahlen in Baden-Württemberg seit 1952. Vol. 95. Stuttgart.
1965 Historisches Gemeindeverzeichnis Baden-Württemberg; Bevölkerungszahlen der Gemeinden von 1871-1961 nach dem Gebietsstand vom 6. Juni 1961. Vol. 108. Stuttgart.
1966 Die Wahl zum fünften Deutschen Bundestag am 19. September 1965. Vol. 121. Stuttgart.
1970a Die Wahl zum sechsten Deutschen Bundestag am 28. September 1969. Vol. 166. Stuttgart.
1970b Statistisches Taschenbuch 1970, Baden-Württemberg. Stuttgart.
1972a Gemeindestatistik 1972; Heft 2: Bevölkerung und Erwerbstätigkeit, Arbeitsstätten und Beschäftigte. Vol. 185. Stuttgart.
1972b Gemeindestatistik 1970; Heft 4a: Landwirtschaftliche Betriebsverhältnisse 1971; Grössenstruktur, Bodennutzung und Viehhaltung. Vol. 161. Stuttgart.
1972c Statistisches Taschenbuch 1972, Baden-Württemberg. Stuttgart.
Deutsches Reich, Kaiserlich Statistisches Amt
1884 Statistik des Deutschen Reiches. Berufsstatistik nach der allgemeinen Berufszählung vom 5. 6. 1882; Vol. 2. (See pp. 524ff.) Berlin: Puttkammer und Mühlbrecht.

1898   Statistik des Deutschen Reiches. Berufs- und Gewerbezählung vom 14. 6. 1895;
        Gewerbestatistik der Verwaltungsbezirke. Vol. 118. (See pp. 191ff.) Berlin:
        Puttkammer und Mühlbrecht.
Deutsches Reich, Statistisches Reichsamt
1935   Volks und Berufszählung vom 16. 6. 1933; Heft 31: Land Württemberg. (See pp.
        55ff.) Berlin: Verlag für Sozialpolitik, Wirtschaft und Statistik.
1942   Die Berufstätigkeit der Bevölkerung in den Reichsteilen; Vol. 557; Volks, Berufs
        und Betriebszählung vom 17. 5. 1939. Heft 26: Württemberg und Hohenzoll-
        ersche Lande. (See pp. 70ff.) Berlin.
Federal Republic of Germany, Federal Statistical Office
1967   Handbook of statistics for the Federal Republic of Germany. Stuttgart & Mainz:
        W. Kohlhammer.
Königlich Statistisches Landesamt, Württemberg
1910   Württembergische Gemeindestatistik, nach dem Stand von 1907. Stuttgart: W.
        Kohlhammer.
Württembergisches Statistisches Landesamt
1935   Württembergische Gemeinde- und Bezirksstatistik, nach dem Stand von 1933.
        Stuttgart: W. Kohlhammer.

Other Works

Abel, Wilhelm
1971   Landwirtschaft, 800-1800. In *Handbuch der deutschen Wirtschafts- und Sozial-
        geschichte*, edited by Hermann Aubin and Wolfgang Zorn, Vol. 1., Pp. 83–108,
        169–201, 300–334, 386–404, 495–530. Stuttgart: Union Verlag.
Aceves, Joseph B.
1971   *Social change in a Spanish town.* Cambridge, Mass.: Schenkman.
Ackermann, Paul
1970   *Der Deutsche Bauernverband im politischen Kräftespiel der Bundesrepublik: Die
        Einflussnahme des DBV auf die Entscheidung uber den europäschen Getreide-
        preis.* In *Tübinger Studien zur Geschichte und Politik*, No. 27. Tübingen: J. C. B.
        Mohr (Paul Siebeck).
Arensberg, Conrad M. and Solon T. Kimball
1965   *Culture and community.* New York: Harcourt.
Aschenbrenner, Katrin and Dieter Kappe
1966   Grosstadt und Dorf als Typen der Gemeinde. In *Deutsche Gesellschaft im Wandel*,
        edited by Karl Bolte, Pp. 165-232. Opladen: C. W. Leske.
Baden-Württemberg, Statistisches Landesamt
1953   *Der Landkreis Crailsheim, Kreisbeschreibung.* Gerabronn: M. Rückert.
Bader, Karl Siegfried
1957   *Das mittelalterliche Dorf als Friedens- und Rechtsbereich.* Weimar: Hermann
        Böhlaus Nachf.
Banfield, Edward C.
1967   *The moral basis of a backward society.* New York: The Free Press.
Beimborn, Anneliese
1959   *Wandlungen der dörflichen Gemeinschaft im Hessischen Hinterland: eine geo-
        graphischvolkskundliche Untersuchung von sechs Gemeinden des Kreises Bieden-
        kopf.* In *Marburger Geographische Schriften*, No. 12. Marburg: Selbstverlag des
        Geographischen Institutes der Universität Marburg.

Bell, Colin and Howard Newby
1972   *Community studies: An introduction to the sociology of the local community.*
        New York: Praeger.
Bendix, Reinhard and Guenther Roth
1971   *Scholarship and partisanship: Essays on Max Weber.* Berkeley: Univ. of California
        Press.
Bennett, John W. and Gustav Thaiss
1973   Survey Research in anthropological field work. In *A handbook of method in
        cultural anthropology,* edited by Raoul Naroll and Ronald Cohen, Pp. 316-337.
        New York: Columbia Univ. Press (First published: 1970)
Berkner, Lutz K.
1973   The stem family and the developmental cycle of the peasant household: An 18th
        century Austrian example. In *The American family in social-historical perspective,*
        edited by Michael Gordon, Pp. 34-58. New York: St. Martin's Press.
Blake, Judith
1969   Demographic science and the redirection of population policy. In *Population
        studies: selected essays and research,* edited by Kenneth C. W. Kammeyer, Pp.
        378-400. Chicago: Rand McNally.
Bloch, Marc
1970   *Feudal society,* translated by L. A. Manyon, Vols. 1 & 2. Chicago: Univ. of
        Chicago Press.
Bloomfield, Leonard
1965   *Language History.* (Reprinted from *Language,* 1933 edition.) New York: Holt.
Bolte, Karl Martin and Dieter Kappe
1966   Struktur und Entwicklung der Bevölkerung. In *Deutsche Gesellschaft im Wandel,*
        edited by Karl Martin Bolte, Pp. 67-164. Opladen: C. W. Leske.
Bosl, Karl
1971   Gesellschaftsentwicklung, 500–1350. In *Handbuch der deutschen Wirtschafts- und
        Socialgeschichte,* edited by Hermann Aubin and Wolfgang Zorn. Vol. 1, Pp.
        133-168, 226-273. Stuttgart: Union Verlag.
Clasen, Claus-Peter
1965   *Die Wiedertäufer im Herzogtum Württemberg und in benachbarten Herrschaften:
        Ausbreitung, Geisteswelt und Soziologie.* In *Veröffentlichungen der Kommission
        für geschichtliche Landeskunde in Baden-Württemberg,* Vol. 32. Stuttgart:
        W. Kohlhammer.
Cole, John and Eric Wolf
1974   *The hidden frontier: ecology and ethnicity in an Alpine valley.* New York:
        Academic.
Cox, Peter
1970   *Demography.* Cambridge: Cambridge Univ. Press.
Dahrendorf, Ralf
1969   *Society and democracy in Germany.* Garden City: Doubleday.
Demerath, N. J. and Phillip E. Hammond
1969   *Religion in social context.* New York: Random House.
Diesing, Paul
1971   *Patterns of discovery in the social sciences.* Chicago: Aldine.
Dölle, Hans
1939   *Lehrbuch des Reichserbhofsrechts.* Berlin: C. H. Becksche Verlagsbuchhandlung.
Dovring, Folke
1965   *Land and Labor in Europe in the twentieth century: A comparative survey of
        recent agrarian history.* The Hague: Martinus Nijhoff.

Eggan, Fred
1954   Social anthropology and the method of controlled comparison, *American Anthropologist* 56,743-763.
Fel, Edit and Tamas Hofer
1969   *Proper peasants: Traditional life in a Hungarian village.* Chicago: Aldine.
Fest, Joachim C.
1974   *Hitler*, Translated from the German by Richard and Clara Winston. New York: Harcourt.
Frank, Walter
1974   Die sozialökonomische Struktur der Regionen der Europäischen Gemeinschaft, *Sociologia Ruralis* 14, 69-85.
Franklin, S. H.
1969   *The European peasantry: The final phase.* London: Methuen & Co.
Franz, Gunther
1971   *Die Kirchenleitung in Hohenlohe in den Jahrzehnten nach der Reformation.* In *Quellen und Forschungen zur Württembergischen Kirchengeschichte*, Vol. 3. Stuttgart: Calwer Verlag.
Friedl, John
1974   *Kippel: A changing village in the Alps.* New York: Holt.
Ganshof, F. L.
1964   *Feudalism*, translated by Philip Grierson, New York: Harper.
Giddens, Anthony
1971   *Capitalism and modern social theory: An analysis of the writings of Marx, Durkheim, and Max Weber.* Cambridge: Cambridge Univ. Press.
Glock, Charles Y. and Rodney Stark
1965   *Religion and society in tension.* Chicago: Rand McNally.
Gönner, Eberhard
1971   Das Königreich Württemberg; Die Entstehung des Südweststaates; Das Land Baden-Württemberg seit 1952. In *Geschichte der deutschen Länder*, edited by Georg Wilhelm Sante and A. G. Ploetz Verlag, Vol. 2, Pp. 408-445, 735-753. Würzburg: A. G. Ploetz Verlag.
Greeley, Andrew M.
1972   *Unsecular man: The persistence of religion.* New York: Schocken.
Haag, Karl
1929   *Die Schwäbisch-fränkische Sprachgrenze in Württemberg.* Stuttgart: Paulinenpflege.
Hackenberg, Robert A.
1973   Genealogical method in social anthropology. In *Handbook of social and cultural anthropology*, edited by John J. Honigmann, Pp. 289-325. Chicago: Rand McNally.
Hammel, E. A.
1961   The family cycle in a coastal Peruvian slum and village, *American Anthropologist* 63,989-1005.
1972   The zadruga as process. In *Household and family in past time*, edited by Peter Laslett, Pp. 335-373. Cambridge: Cambridge Univ. Press.
Hammel, E. A. and David Hutchinson
1973   Two tests of computer microsimulation: The effect of an incest tabu on population viability, and the effect of age differences between spouses on the skewing of consanguineal relationships between them. In *Computer simulation in human population studies*, edited by Bennett Dyke and Jean Walters MacCluer, Pp. 1-14. New York: Academic Press.

Hardy, Kenneth R.
1974   Social origins of American scientists and scholars, *Science* 185 (August), 497-506.

Hermelink, Heinrich
1949   *Geschichte der evangelischen Kirche in Württemberg von der Reformation bis zur Gegenwart*. Stuttgart und Tübingen: Rainer Wunderlich Verlag Hermann Leins.

Hesse, Paul
1965   *Der Strukturwandel der Siedlungskörper und die Landesentwicklung in Baden-Württemberg zwischen 1939-1961*. In *Jahrbücher für Statistik und Landeskunde, Baden-Württemberg*, 9. Jahrgang. Stuttgart: Statistisches Landesamt.

Höffner, Joseph
1961   *Industrielle Revolution und religiöse Krise: Schwund und Wandel des religiösen Verhaltens in der modernen Gesellschaft*. In *Arbeitsgemeinschaft für Forschung des Landes Nordrhein-Westfalen, Wissenschaften*, No. 97. Köln: Westdeutscher Verlag.

Hoyt, Robert S.
1957   *Europe in the Middle Ages*. New York: Harcourt.

Jankuhn, Herbert
1969   Dorf, Weiler und Einzelhof in der Germania Magna. In *Siedlung, Burg und Stadt: Studien zu ihren Anfängen*, edited by Karl-Heinz Otto and Joachim Herrmann, Pp. 114-128. Berlin: Akademie Verlag.

Keyfitz, Nathan
1972   Population waves. In *Population Dynamics*, edited by T. N. E. Greville. Pp. 1-38. New York: Academic Press.

Klausen, Arne Martin
1968   *Kerala fishermen and the Indo-Norwegian pilot project*. Oslo: Universitetsforlaget.

Knapp, Theodor
1964   *Neue Beiträge zur Rechts- und Wirtschaftsgeschichte des württembergischen Bauernstandes*. Aalen: Scientia Verlag.

Königlich statistisch-topographisches Bureau, Württemberg
1847   *Beschreibung des Oberamts Gerabronn*. Stuttgart und Tübingen: J. G. Cotta'sche Buchhandlung.
1883   *Beschreibung des Oberamts Künzelsau*. Stuttgart: W. Kohlhammer.

Köster, Reinhard
1959   *Die Kirchentreuen: Erfahrungen und Ergebnisse einer soziologischen Untersuchung in einer grossstädtischen evangelischen Kirchengemeinde*. Stuttgart: Ferdinand Enke.

Kramer, Karl-Sigismund
1957   *Bauern und Bürger im nachmittelalterlichen Unterfranken*. Würzburg: Ferdinand Schöningh.
1961   *Volksleben im Fürstentum Ansbach und seinen Nachbargebieten (1500-1800)*. Würzburg: Ferdinand Schöningh.

Lenski, Gerhard
1963   *The religious factor: A sociological study of religion's impact on politics, economics, and family life*. Garden City: Doubleday.
1971   The religious factor in Detroit, revisited, *American Sociological Review* 36, 48-50.

Lison-Tolosana, Carmelo
1966   *Belmonte de los Caballeros: a sociological study of a Spanish town*. Oxford: Clarendon Press.

Lueker, Erwin L. (Editor in chief)
1954   *Lutheran Cyclopedia*. Saint Louis, Missouri: Concordia Publishing House.

Lütge, Friedrich
1937   *Die Agrarverfassung des frühen Mittelalters*. Jena: Gustav Fischer.
1960   *Deutsche Sozial- und Wirtschaftsgeschichte*. Berlin: Springer Verlag.
Mackenroth, Gerhard
1953   *Bevölkerungslehre: Theorie, Soziologie und Statistik der Bevölkerung*. Berlin: Springer.
Meerwarth, Rudolf
1932   Die Entwicklung der Bevölkerung in Deutschland während der Kriegs- und Nachkriegszeit. In *Die Einwirkung des Krieges auf Bevölkerungsbewegung, Einkommen und Lebenshaltung in Deutschland*, edited by Rudolf Meerwarth, Adolf Günther, and Waldemar Zimmermann, Pp. 1-97. Stuttgart: Deutsche Verlagsanstalt.
Miller, Max (Editor)
1965   *Baden-Württemberg*. In *Handbuch der historischen Stätten Deutschlands*, Vol. 6. Stuttgart: Alfred Kröner Verlag.
Müller, Johannes
1926   *Deutsche Bevölkerungsstatistik*. Jena: Gustav Fischer.
Müller, Josef
1938   *Die biologische Lage des deutschen Bauerntums: Ein Beitrag zur Ergründung des Geburtenrückgangs im Bauerntum*. Leipzig: S. Hirzel.
1962   Wird das Dorf zur Stadt? Die neue gesellschaftliche und geistige Situation des Landvolkes. *Schriftenreihe Geist und Zeit*. Darmstadt: Progress-Verlag Johann Fladung.
Neidhardt, Friedhelm
1970   Die Familie in Deutschland: Gesellschaftliche Stellung, Struktur und Funktionen. In *Deutsche Gesellschaft im Wandel*, edited by Karl Martin Bolte, Vol. 2, Opladen: C. W. Leske.
Pelto, Partti J. and Gretel H. Pelto
1973   Ethnography: The fieldwork enterprise. In *Handbook of social and cultural anthropology*, edited by John J. Honigmann, Pp. 241-288. Chicago: Rand McNally.
Pistorius, Wilhelm Friedrich
1731   *Lebens-Beschreibung Herrn Gözens von Berlichingen, Zugenannt mit der Eisern Hand, Eines zu Zeiten Kaysers Maximiliani I und Caroli V kühnen und tapfern Reichs-Cavaliers*, etc. Nürnberg: Adam Jonathan Fleissecker.
Pitt-Rivers, J. A.
1971   *The people of the Sierra*. 2nd ed. Chicago: Univ. of Chicago Press.
Planck, Ulrich
1964   *Der bäuerliche Familienbetrieb: zwischen Patriarchat und Partnerschaft*. Stuttgart: Ferdinand Enke.
1970   *Landjugend im sozialen Wandel*. München: Juventa Verlag.
Quigley, Carroll
1973   Mexican national character and circumMediterranean personality structure, *American Anthropologist* 75, 319-322.
Renner, Heinrich
1965   *Wandel der Dorfkultur; zur Entwicklung des dörflichen Lebens in Hohenlohe*. In *Veröffentlichungen des staatlichen Amtes für Denkmalpflege Stuttgart*, Ser. C: Volkskunde, Vol. 3. Stuttgart: Silberburg Verlag Werner Jäckh.
Riedenauer, Erwin
1965   Reichsritterschaft und Konfession. In *Deutscher Adel 1555-1740, Schriften zur Problematik der deutschen Führungsschichten in der Neuzeit*, edited by Hellmuth Rössler, Vol. 2, Pp. 1-63. Darmstadt: Wissenschaftliche Buchgesellschaft.
Robertson, Roland
1970   *The sociological interpretation of religion*. New York: Schocken.

Röhm, Helmut
1957 *Die Vererbung des landwirtschaftlichen Grundeigentums in Baden-Württemberg.* In *Forschungen zur deutschen Landeskunde*, Vol. 102. Remagen–Rhein: Selbstverlag der Bundesanstalt für Landeskunde.

Rössler, Hellmuth (Ed.)
1965 *Deutscher Adel 1555-1740; Büdinger Vorträge 1964.* In *Schriften zur Problematik der deutschen Führungsschichten in der Neuzeit*, Vol. 2. Darmstadt: Wissenschaftliche Buchgesellschaft.

Saenger, Wolfgang
1957 *Die bäuerliche Kulturlandschaft der Hohenloher Ebene und ihre Entwicklung seit dem 16. Jahrhundert.* In *Forschungen zur deutschen Landeskunde*, Vol. 101. Remagen–Rhein: Selbstverlag der Bundesanstalt für Landeskunde.

Samuelsson, Kurt
1961 *Religion and economic action*, translated from the Swedish by E. G. French; edited and with an introduction by D. C. Coleman. New York: Basic Books.

Schaab, Meinard
1972 Die Herausbildung einer Bevölkerungsstatistik in Württemberg und in Baden während der ersten Hälfte des 19. Jahrunderts, *Zeitschrift für Württembergische Landesgeschichte*, Jahrgang **XXX** 1971, 164-200.

Schlauch, Rudolf
1964 *Hohenlohe-Franken: Landschaft, Geschichte, Kultur, Kunst.* Nürnberg: Glock und Lutz.

Schöck, Gustav
1971 Die Aussiedlung landwirtschaftlicher Betriebe: Probleme der Landwirtschaft im 20. Jahrhundert. *Württembergisches Jahrbuch für Volkskunde 1970*, 84-96.
1972 *Die Aussiedlung landwirtschaftlicher Betriebe.* Tübingen: Tübinger Vereinigung für Volkskunde.

Schremmer, Eckart
1963 *Die Bauernbefreiung in Hohenlohe.* In *Quellen und Forschungen zur Agrargeschichte*, edited by Friedrich Lütge, Günther Franz, and Wilhelm Abel, Vol. 9. Stuttgart: Gustav Fischer.

Schwarzweller, Harry K.
1971 Tractorization of agriculture: The social history of a German village. In *Sociologia Ruralis* **11**, 127-139.

Spindler, George D.
1973 *Burgbach: Urbanization and identity in a German village.* New York: Holt.

Sprandel, Rolf
1971 Sozialgeschichte, 1350-1500. In *Handbuch der deutschen Wirtschafts- und Sozialgeschichte*, edited by Hermann Aubin and Wolfgang Zorn, Vol. 1, Pp. 360-374. Stuttgart: Union Verlag.

Stark, Werner
1972 *The sociology of religion: A study of Christendom; Volume Five: Types of Religious Culture.* London: Routledge and Kegan Paul.

Stycos, J. Myone
1969 Obstacles to programs of population control—facts and fancies. In *Population studies: selected essays and research*, edited by Kenneth C. W. Kammeyer. Chicago: Rand McNally.

Theiss, Konrad and H. Baumhauer (Editors)
1965 *Der Kreis Künzelsau.* Aalen: Heimat und Wirtschaft.

Turner, Victor W.
1969 *The ritual process.* Chicago: Aldine.

Vogt, Evon Z. and Thomas F. O'Dea
1957 A comparative study of the role of values in social action in two southwestern

communities. In *Religion, society and the individual*, edited by J. Milton Yinger, Pp. 563-577. New York: Macmillan.

Wankmüller, Manfred
1969   *Schlitzöhrige Geschichten aus Hohenlohe.* 2 Vols. Gerabronn: Hohenloher Druck-
1970   und Verlagshaus.

Warriner, Doreen
1965   *Economics of peasant farming.* New York: Barnes & Noble.

Weber, Max
1958   *The Protestant ethic and the spirit of Capitalism*, translated by Talcott Parsons with a foreword by R. H. Tawney. New York: Scribner's.
1963   *The sociology of religion*, translated by Ephraim Fischoff, introduction by Talcott Parsons. Boston: Beacon Press.
1892   *Die Verhältnisse der Landarbeiter im ostelbischen Deutschland (Preussische Provinzen Ost- und Westpreussen, Pommern, Posen, Schlesien, Brandenburg, Grossherzogtümer Mecklenburg, Kreis Herzogtum Lauenburg).* Leipzig: Duncker & Humblot.

Weinreuter, Erich
1969   *Stadtdörfer in Südwest-Deutschland: ein Beitrag zur geographischen Siedlungstypisierung.* In *Tübinger geographische Studien*, No. 32. Selbstverlag des geographischen Instituts der Universität Tübingen.

Willems, Emilio
1968   Culture change and the rise of Protestantism in Brazil and Chile. In *The Protestant Ethic and modernization: a comparative view*, edited by Shmuel N. Eisenstadt, Pp. 184-210. New York: Basic Books.

Wirth, Hermann
1970   Die Lage der baden-württembergischen Landwirtschaft um 1970, *Jahrbücher für Statistik und Landeskunde*, 15, No. 2, 5-80. Stuttgart: Statistisches Landesamt.

Wissler, Dieter H.
1968   Berufssoziologische Vorstellungen bei süddeutschen Bauern, *Sociologia Ruralis* 8, 48-57.

Wunderlich, Frieda
1961   *Farm labor in Germany 1810-1945; Its historical development within the framework of agricultural and social policy.* Princeton: Princeton Univ. Press.

Wurzbacher, Gerhard with Renate Pflaum
1954   *Das Dorf im Spannungsfeld industrieller Entwicklung.* Stuttgart: Ferdinand Enke.

Wylie, Laurence
1964   *Village in the Vaucluse*, 2nd ed. Cambridge, Mass.: Harvard Univ. Press.

Ziche, Joachim
1968   Kritik der deutschen Bauerntumsideologie, *Sociologia Ruralis* 8, 105-141.

Zorn, Wolfgang
1971   Sozialgeschichte, 1500-1800. In *Handbuch der deutschen Wirtschafts- und Sozialgeschichte*, edited by Herman Aubin and Wolfgang Zorn, Pp. 465-494, 574-604. Stuttgart: Union Verlag.

Newspapers

Hohenloher Tagblatt. Fränkischer Grenzbote, Der Vaterlandsfreund; Kreisamtsblatt. Unabhängige Tageszeitung für Stadt und Kreis Crailsheim. Crailsheim and Gerabronn.

Württembergisches Wochenblatt für Landwirtschaft. Organ des Bauernverbandes Württemberg-Baden—Mit Bekanntmachungen und Mitteilungen des Ministeriums für Ernährung, Landwirtschaft, Weinbau und Forsten Baden-Württemberg. Stuttgart.

Index

A

Abel, Wilhelm, 5
Ackermann, Paul, 154
Agricultural
  field consolidation, 104–105
  income, 106–108
  modernization, 17, 106–107, 115–116,
    121–131, 177–179
  productivity, 101–102, 177
  relocation, 104
  training, 118–119, 180, 181
Anabaptists, 166
Arensberg, Conrad M., 1
Aschenbrenner, Katrin, 61

B

Bader, Karl Siegfried, 27, 30
Bachelors, 116–120, 181
Banfield, Edward C., 175
Bauer, 77, 92–94, 97–100, 182
Baumhauer, H., 5
Beimborn, Anneliese, 30
Bell, Colin, 1
Bendix, Reinhard, 2
Berkner, Lutz K., 52
Blake, Judith, 63, 65
Bloch, Marc, 11
Bloomfield, Leonard, 9
Bolte, Karl-Martin, 61, 66, 67, 68
Bosl, Karl, 5

C

Capital, 39, 105–106, 178
Choir, 151
Church attendance, 133, 135–136, 142, 163,
    165, 168, 170, 171–172, 173, 174–
    175, 183
Clasen, Claus-Peter, 166
Cole, John W., 52
Collectivization, 154
Communications (Roads), 16, 26, 151, 177
Communitas, 142, 182
Conflict, 31–32, 85–86, 124, 139–141,
    143–152, 168
Cooperation, 128–131, 140–141, 143–152,
    182
Co-ownership, 126–131, 182
Courts, 143–145
Cox, Peter, 61, 63, 65, 67
Craftsmen, 17–18, 38–39, 57, 69, 94–100

D

Dahrendorf, Ralf, 157
Day laborers, 94, 97–98, 100
Demerath, N. J., 183
Diesing, Paul, 2
Distilling (of alcohol), 44
Dölle, Hans, 82, 92
Dovring, Folke, 73
Dowry, 76, 84

E

Eggan, Fred, 2
Endogamy, 57–59, 92, 97
Envy, 123, 145–146

F

Face-to-face interaction, 133–142, 182, 183
Factions, 146–147, 168
Family farms, 8, 36–38, 101–131, 134
Farming
  part-time, 38, 109–113, 178
  and women, 67, 74, 113–120
Fél, Edit, 164
Fertility, 53, 60–68, 125
Festivities (local), 45, 49
Frank, Walter, 178
Franklin, S. H., 101, 121
Franks, 9
Franz, Gunther, 12
Friedl, John, 30, 171

G

Ganshof, F. L., 11
Gemeinde (commune)
  administration, 26–27, 35–36, 151
  and citizenship, 28–30
  and corporate rights, 28–32
  origin of, 27
  physical composition, 27–29
  services and resources, 32–33, 36, 109–
    111, 151
Giddens, Anthony, 2
Glock, Charles Y., 2, 174
Gönner, Eberhard, 14, 27, 67
Greeley, Andrew M., 174, 176

H

Haag, Karl, 9–10
Hackenberg, Robert A., 52
Hammel, Eugene A., 52
Hammond, Phillip E., 183
Hardy, Kenneth R., 2
Health, 9, 63, 66, 67, 116
Hermelink, Heinrich, 67, 160
Hofer, Tamas, 164
Höffner, Joseph, 175

Hohenlohe-Franken
  farming and settlement, 8–10, 14–19
  industrialization, 16–19, 69
  location and population, 5–7
Hohenlohe, House of, 9–13
Households, 51–55
House names, 54–55
Hoyt, Robert S., 5
Hunting, 43–44
Hutchinson, David, 52

I

Income
  from farming, 106–108
  from non-farming sources, 109–113, 148
Inheritance, 17, 52, 56, 75–86, 97
  and choice of daughters over sons, 81–82
  and transfer contracts, 76–77
  and transfer price, 83–84
Inns, 39, 114, 134–135, 137–140

J

Jankuhn, Herbert, 28

K

Kappe, Dieter, 61, 66, 67, 68
Kayfitz, Nathan, 67
Kimball, Solon T., 1
Kinship, 57, 148–149
Klausen, Arne Martin, 2
Knapp, Theodor, 28
Köster, Reinhard, 163
Kramer, Karl-Sigismund, 46, 171

L

Land tenure, 73–75, 99, 178
Lenski, Gerhard, 2, 174, 184
Lison-Tolosana, 174
Livestock, 15–16, 93, 102–104, 106–108,
    112–113, 123–125, 140–141
Longevity, 116–117
Lueker, Erwin L., 160
Lütge, Friedrich, 5, 28

M

Mackenroth, Gerhard, 61, 68
Marriage, 55–60, 92, 151–152
Mayor, 34, 36, 151, 182
Mechanization, 126–131, 151
Meerwarth, Rudolf, 61
Milk pickup, 40, 136–137
Miller, Max, 9
Müller, Johannes, 61
Müller, Josef, 61, 64, 115, 165

N

Nazis (National Socialists), 146–147,
    149–150, 165
Neidhardt, Friedhelm, 61, 65
New Apostolics, 160, 166–167
Newby, Howard, 1

O

O'Dea, Thomas F., 2
Offenbacher, Martin, 2

P

Pastor (Protestant), 39, 149, 160–166
Peasants
    and liberation from patrimonial bonds,
        13, 16
    and patrimonial obligations, 15, 73
    and private property, 73–74
Pelto, Partti J. and Gretel H., 3
Pitt-Rivers, J. A., 57
Planck, Ulrich, 2, 64, 71, 74, 81, 118–119,
    173, 174
Political preferences, 134–135, 152–157
Population
    and inheritance practices, 16–17, 52
    and migration, 60, 67, 68–71, 178
Priest (Catholic), 39, 149, 161, 167–169,
    175, 180
Processions, 46, 169–171

R

Refugees, 68, 150, 168
Religion
    and cooperation, 141–142

and church membership, 159–160
and economic behavior, 1–2, 109–113,
    118–120, 121–131, 141–142, 179–184
and education, 118–120, 150, 180, 181
and fertility, 61–68, 125, 179–180, 182
and funerals, 166
and marriage, 56, 57, 118–120, 151–152,
    159, 160, 179
and the Peace of Augsburg, 12
and politics, 152–157, 182
and ritual, 175–176
and social integration, 182–183
and social interaction, 133–142, 179
and ties between God and the farmer, 161,
    162, 165
and the weather, 46, 170–171
Renner, Heinrich, 171
Riedenauer, Erwin, 12
Robertson, Roland, 176
Röhm, Helmut, 5, 82
Rössler, Hellmuth, 12
Roth, Guenther, 2

S

Saenger, Wolfgang, 5, 9
Samuelsson, Kurt, 2
Schaab, Meinard, 56
Schlauch, Rudolf, 5
Schöck, Gustav, 104
Schremmer, Eckart, 5, 27, 74–75, 77, 83
Schwarzweller, Harry K., 121
Sermons, 161–162, 169
Servants (farm labor), 51, 57, 67, 97–98,
    122–123
Setting (methodology), 2–4, 25, 179
Siblings (unmarried), 52–53, 77, 84
Slaughter, 41–43
Smallholder, 92–100
Social stratification, 29–32, 56, 92–100,
    122–125, 167
Spindler, George D., 55
Sprandel, Rolf, 5
Stark, Rodney, 2, 174
Stark, Werner, 176
Stycos, J. Myone, 67
Swabians, 9

T

Taxes, 16, 34, 107

Thaiss, Gustav, 1
Theiss, Konrad, 5
Tractorization, 121–126, 180, 183
Turner, Victor W., 182

V

Vassalage, 10–11
Village, see *Gemeinde*
Vogt, Evon Z., 2
Voting patterns, 152–157, 182

W

Wankmüller, Manfred, 9
Warriner, Doreen, 93, 101
Weber, Max, 1–2, 67, 165
Weinreuter, Erich, 28

Wetterläuten, 46, 170
Willems, Emilio, 2
Wirth, Hermann, 102
Wissler, Dieter H., 166
Wolf, Eric R., 52
Wunderlich, Frieda, 123
Württemberg, 13–14
Wurzbacher, Gerhard, 2, 166
Wylie, Laurence, 175

Y

Youths, 71, 139

Z

Ziche, Joachim, 165
Zorn, Wolfgang, 5